LOTUS

HAYNES CLASSIC MAKES SERIES

LOTUS

THE CREATIVE EDGE

RUSSELL HAYES

First published in February 2007

A catalogue record for this book is available from the British Library

ISBN 978 1 84425 249 7

Library of Congress control no: 2006924147

Published by Haynes Publishing,
Sparkford, Yeovil, Somerset BA22 7JJ, UK.
Tel: 01963 442030 Fax: 01963 440001
Int.tel: +44 1963 442030 Int.fax: +44 1963 440001
E-mail: sales@haynes.co.uk
Website: www.haynes.co.uk

Haynes North America Inc.,
861 Lawrence Drive, Newbury Park, California 91320, USA.

Edited by Jon Pressnell
Designed by Christopher Fayers
Printed and bound in Britain by
J. H. Haynes & Co. Ltd, Sparkford

ACKNOWLEDGEMENTS

I am especially grateful to the following people for the time they have spent talking Lotus with me: Tony Bates, Sir Terence Beckett, Bobby Bell, Peter Cambridge, Ron Hickman, Ray Hutton, Rob Ford of Club Lotus Avon, Roger Fowler (formerly GS Cars), John Hopkins, Mike Kimberley, Jamie Lister, Steve Morland (www.lotusservice.com), Patrick Peal, Roger Putnam, Malcolm Ricketts, Sir John Whitmore, and Oliver Winterbottom. Thanks for their help also go to Sue Cugley of Kia UK, Sylvia Davis, Alastair Florance of Group Lotus, Vincent Haydon, Anthony Kimberley, Michael Marsh (Lotus Elite & Eclat Register), Don McLaughlan, and Jon Moulton.

The buying hints sections feature input from Pat Thomas of Kelvedon Motors (www.racecar.co.uk/kelvedonlotus), James Waddington (www.lotus-carlton.co.uk), and Richard Winter of Banks Europa (www.banks-europa.co.uk). Cars for driving impressions were generously supplied by UK Sports Cars of Wingham, Kent (tel 01227 728190 or www.uksportscars.com), and Paul Matty Sports Cars of Bromsgrove (tel 01527 835656 or www.paulmattysportscars.co.uk). Finally, thanks to Dad, for moving me from comics to car mags.

Russell Hayes
London, 2007

ILLUSTRATIONS

Unless otherwise indicated, illustrations are from the LAT Photographic archive, and are mainly drawn from the files of *Motor*, *Autocar*, *Autosport* and *Classic & Sports Car* magazines. For details of the archive's services, write to LAT Photographic, Teddington Studios, Broom Road, Teddington, Middlesex TW11 9BE, visit website www.latphoto.co.uk, or phone 0208 251 3000.

contents

Colin
Chapman

There is no reason why, over twenty years after his death, the buyer of a new Lotus Elise should have heard of Anthony Colin Bruce Chapman. But chances are that they will have. "What I find incredible is how little it changes in terms of the attitude of the people and the spirit of the company," says long-serving Lotus dealer Bobby Bell. "Colin's been dead for so long, yet there is such a spirit in that company that whoever owns it doesn't seem to be able to break it."

This book concentrates on the Lotus road cars, but to Chapman they largely represented the cash to fund his racing. The racing story has been covered by many other writers, as has

Chapman's life – both by people close to him, such as the late Gérard 'Jabby' Crombac, and by those able to take more distance, such as Mike Lawrence, in his *Colin Chapman: Wayward Genius*. Even when Chapman's flaws are acknowledged – and some were serious – all biographies are written with great respect.

Why does he still hold this fascination? It is not just because thousands of devoted owners indulge the eccentricities of their Sevens, Elans and Elites because of the purity of design they represent: it is equally because Chapman's effect on the world of motor racing and sports cars was such that he has been credited with inventing the British Formula 1 industry. Against this backcloth, writers have taken to referring to certain car characteristics as 'Chapmanesque', without further explanation.

The man behind Lotus suffered a fatal heart attack at the age of 54. And like all lives cut short, his legacy is a series of 'what if?' questions. In the wake of the DeLorean scandal he certainly would have gone to jail, but would the passage of time and the stature of his cars have wiped the slate clean by now? Would he have gone on to the successful manufacture of aeroplanes, furniture or boats?

Fate played a hand in the start of Lotus. The time and place could not have been better for Colin Chapman's rise. Just young enough to have escaped active service, he started his working life in the grim days of post-war shortages, where anyone

Opposite: Colin Chapman – pictured in a MkIX in 1955 – ensured he became the public face of Lotus, and today the two names remain inseparable.

Right: By 1964, when this photo was taken at Goodwood, Lotus was enjoying worldwide fame with Jim Clark (right) as principal driver. Chapman was a changed man after Clark's death in 1968 driving a Lotus.

And about that name. . .

In the book of Lotus legends, there is none more puzzling than the origins of the name – about which Chapman was happy to leave people guessing. Depending on what you read or whom you ask, Lotus was the pet name for his wife Hazel, a genuine reference to Eastern mysticism, or a hangover from the post-war car trade where windscreens could be marked 'Lot U/S', for 'Lot Unsold'. Of course, if you want to annoy an owner, it stands for 'Loads of Trouble Usually Serious'. What is certain is that the name was only applied to the second car Chapman built, so the first Lotus only became thus named in retrospect.

Enthusiasts enjoy debating the origins of the Lotus name, but the founder's ACBC initials are a sacrosanct part of the badge. A 1980s redesign was a cause of bitter controversy and had to be reversed.

One of Colin Chapman's talents was to see the possibilities in components from other manufacturers. He is pictured here, in 1967, looking at the new Vauxhall Victor engine, which was to provide the test-bed for the first all-Lotus engine, the 900-series.

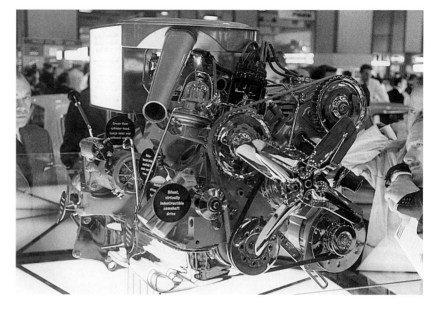

Seen here with the Cosworth DFV racing engine, Chapman was the epitome of the self-made millionaire and was awarded a CBE for his contribution to British exports.

with an entrepreneurial gift could thrive, where there was an urgent need for engineering skills, and where a breakdown in established social hierarchies was finally making itself felt.

The aftermath of World War Two brought hardship for many. But great shifts had taken place at all levels of society, including car-making and motor racing: crucially, there had been a 'democratisation' of skills among a whole generation of men and women who had learnt to build and service planes, tanks and ships. Many had driven for the first time in their lives, when car ownership would normally have been beyond their reach, and the conflict produced mechanics and engineers with a spirit of innovation, and a willingness to take risk and seize life's opportunities. Colin Chapman rode the wave of this post-war restlessness.

Gifted though he undoubtedly was, his rise and that of Lotus would not have been possible without the likes of the 'boys from De Havilland', caught up with his enthusiasm and willing to work for nothing. As Britain entered the jet age, the aero industry continued to have a huge influence: De Havilland in Hatfield, North of London, Hawkers in Kingston, to the South – and Avro in Manchester and Southampton and Handley-Page in Radlett and

Hazel Chapman

It can be argued that without Hazel Chapman there would have been no Lotus, for it was her loan of £25 that enabled the Lotus Engineering Company Ltd to be formed in 1952. But of course her input was far more than the provision of cash at a key moment.

Hazel Williams married Colin Chapman in 1954 after a nine-year courtship. Like many other couples on the post-war club circuit, the husband and wife combination was a true team, with Hazel driving as often as Colin did, when she was not providing support – and she was known on occasion to better him on the track. When Lotus became a full-time job, she provided admin support for the fledgling company and accompanied

the team in their first ventures to Le Mans. But progressively she became less of a public figure, although always present with Chapman on the racing social scene.

"We never used to think about the danger," she recalled when interviewed in *Classic & Sports Car* magazine in 2005. "I remember washing Colin's lucky Clydella tartan shirt in a special solution which supposedly made it fireproof. Colin was quick but never very good at finishing. Everyone in the factory used to say 'You should stick to designing them'. It was always thrilling to race the cars but we eventually decided it was best left to others, particularly with a young family."

As the Lotus legend grew, Hazel's

time was occupied with their children Jane, Sarah and Clive, but her influence, though subtle, was still felt. "She would appear in the factory but she wouldn't rush around issuing instructions," says former son-in-law Patrick Peal. "She was very much supporting Colin and looking after the family, and she shared his sense of fun. You got the sense that she was essentially a calming influence, sometimes offering the commonsense view of an outsider."

Seen here in 1951 in a MkIII, Hazel Williams, the future Mrs Chapman, was a skilled driver and she also helped found the company. Although her racing days gave way to raising a family, her behind-the-scenes influence was always considerable.

The 'Number Two' men

To Lotus employees, working with Colin Chapman could be both awe-inspiring and terrifying: he was apt to sack people, only to ask next day why they were not at their desks. There are numerous stories about his demands, such as no tea-breaks as he hated seeing mugs left lying around. Whatever he lacked in management style, though, he gained by inspiring others to think as he did.

His almost lifelong ally was not a racing driver but accountant Fred Bushell, from the days at the stables in Hornsey to going to jail for his part in the DeLorean fraud. He met Chapman in 1954 by chance when coming out of a public toilet near the Hornsey premises, and was invited to have a visit of the workshops. Never a motor racing enthusiast, Bushell began to build the Lotus empire of myriad companies and helped Chapman avoid unnecessary tax. A shy but astute man, always in the background, he was briefly chairman after Chapman's death but has been regarded as the fall guy. "He took all the pain," says former *Autocar* editor Ray Hutton. "He knew where all the bodies were buried – it was very complicated."

Another key early-days figure was merchant banker and amateur racer Peter Kirwan-Taylor. Although his input into the 1957 Elite's styling is undisputed, Kirwan-Taylor's financial skills were also much appreciated. He and Chapman got on

Peter Kirwan-Taylor was the inspiration behind the Elite's shape but his continued worth to Lotus was in his financial skills, and he became one of the few non-family directors.

well and he later became a director and negotiated the finance which enabled the purchase of Lotus's new Cheshunt factory in 1959.

If an equally strong character opposed Chapman they would be out, sooner or later. This was the case with Ron Hickman. Although Hickman was frozen out of the Europa project by the boss and opted not to move to

Norfolk, the ten-year Chapman/Hickman combination worked because it twinned Hickman's quiet patience with Chapman's mercurial spirit. Robin Read, sales manager at the time of the first Elite, summed it up in his book: 'Chapman undoubtedly inspired Hickman to develop his talents at an earlier age than would otherwise have been possible. Hickman's ability to extend plastic body moulding technology well beyond current practice was appreciated, absorbed and built upon by Chapman.'

Lotus has seen many talented engineers come and go but Tony Rudd and Mike Kimberley stand out. Rudd was the man from BRM who gave Lotus its own engines, had a deep understanding of what a Lotus car should be and latterly ran Team Lotus. Kimberley was another Lotus veteran, combining engineering skill with real business acumen and a talent for deals which kept the whole company in business. He rose from sorting out the problems of the early Europa to create Lotus Engineering and to broker the General Motors takeover, before leaving in 1992 to head GM's Malaysian operations. Between 1994 and 1996 Kimberley was instrumental in returning Lamborghini to health but always remained close to Lotus. He returned to the board of directors in 2005 and took the role of Chief Executive Officer the following September.

Cricklewood. Steel was in short supply but there was plenty of aluminium, the perfect raw material for the new breed of lightweight racing cars.

There can be no doubting Colin Chapman's skills as an engineer, but those around him were often equally skilled in their own fields; his talent was to take elements of the best practice, and either combine them into something new or else come up with his own unique solution. So was

Colin Chapman an innovative genius? Yes. Could he claim sole credit for everything he did? No. He created his own mythology and if people wanted to think he had knocked up the idea of a backbone chassis on his own, or built the early racers largely single-handed, he was not always quick to correct such an impression.

The use of the Ford-based split swing-axle front suspension is a classic example. Long before its

application to early Lotus racers, Leslie Ballamy had developing the conversion in the 1930s and it had been applied to a number of cars, notably the Allard. The same applies to the 'de-siamised' engine of the Lotus MkIII that made such an impact in 750 Motor Club racing: this was the idea of Australian Derek Jolly, with Michael Allen doing the work to modify the engine. On the other hand, Chapman's

Boats and planes

As the road and racing business continued to expand and finally seemed to be on a secure footing, Chapman started to apply his skills to other enterprises. He and Ron Hickman dabbled in glassfibre furniture to no great effect, but – to the surprise of many – his first major non-car venture was into boats, despite his having shown no prior interest in them. He bought Norfolk-based Moonraker Marine in 1971 from former Lotus dealer David Buxton, then acquired JCL Marine Ltd and installed Lotus marketing manager Roger Putnam as director. "He saw it as a cottage industry that could really benefit from his kind of vision in terms of dynamics," Putnam recalls. "A lot of the stuff he did was really crazy. He applied the same sort of thinking as to his cars, where he'd have components which did more than one job."

Mixing boat design at Hethel alongside the cars, Chapman re-designed the 1972 Marauder's hull in lighter glassfibre instead of wood, using the Vacuum Resin Injection process that was subsequently applied to the car shells. This caused problems coping with the stresses of the open seas. "The Marauder was an absolute disaster," Putnam remembers. "Instead of having a normal propeller shaft with bearings, he hung it off the bottom of the rudder. The stresses you were putting through the rudder were just amazing,

Tony Rudd and his team developed two microlight engines, both horizontally-opposed and air-cooled, but the project foundered after Chapman's death.

and shafts would sheer. And the VARI process – which is fine for cars – when applied to the huge hulls made them delaminate. Huge strips would come off." Hit by a fall in demand, JCL went into liquidation in 1980. Despite this misadventure, Chapman and his son Clive took up powerboat racing and design with some success.

A more obvious project was microlight planes. With its bare frame and engine, the traditional microlight fascinated Chapman and he brought some very early examples to England in the late '70s to show the family, giving them all Christmas presents of flying lessons. As with the boat designs, Chapman saw the first microlights as little better than World War One flying machines. He had long dreamed of a true commuter plane and he commissioned US aviator Burt

Rutan – who in later years built recordbreakers for Virgin boss Richard Branson – to build a prototype ultra-lightweight Lotus plane that could be used for business or pleasure and qualify as a microlight, thus escaping the certification costs of a traditional plane. Tony Rudd and his team set to work on designing a pair of microlight engines, a 480cc 'twin' of 25bhp and a 960cc four-cylinder of 50bhp, both horizontally-opposed and air-cooled. A striking-looking prototype was completed and flown after Chapman's death in 1983, but although then chairman Mike Kimberley had hoped to find a way into defence work, the microlight project was dropped in face of engine development problems and of the difficulty in getting product-liability cover for flying in America.

ambition in pursuing the glassfibre-monocoque Elite, and the racing monocoque hull with the engine bolted directly to it, are beyond question. He was an engineer through to the end. Interviewed by *The Sunday Telegraph* in 1974, the writer observed that 'the great Chapman passion, the dominating theme of his business life, is engineering. Even today, with a £10 million business under his control, Chapman regards

himself as an engineer first, not a financier, nor a marketer. He admits frankly that "I'm disappointed when I have to get involved in the management side.". . .'

If Chapman appeared a dedicated self-publicist, it was first for the glory of his racing team. Through connections such as the 750 Motor Club presidency, he quickly became a well-known motor racing personality and from the early 1950s was present

in Lotus advertising material, often appearing in a suit with his new cars, giving the impression Lotus was a fully-fledged motor-racing manufacturer rather than a bunch of gifted amateurs operating in a set of draughty sheds behind a pub. Lotus's openness to the racing press was in contrast to outfits such as Cooper which would allow writers to see them at work only if they were very lucky.

Search news-agency archives and

The peaked cap was a Chapman trademark, frequently thrown in the air when Team Lotus won. He is pictured here at the 1977 German Grand Prix, complete with a JPS Team Lotus belt. Colleagues knew not to call him from the factory while a race was on, and if it went badly, to steer clear the next day.

By the 1980s constant confrontation with the governing bodies of motor racing was adding to the stresses on Chapman (here at the 1981 Brazillian Grand Prix), while the road car business had its own troubles.

Colin Chapman is an ever-present figure with his racing cars and drivers, but even though it is well-chronicled that he progressively tired of the logistics of road-car manufacture in the 1970s, he was still a very visible figurehead, often seen flying into the factory and taking journalists for a spin himself at press launches. Although there were fewer demands from the media than bosses face today, Colin Chapman was happy to inspire public confidence through occasional documentaries and magazine features.

Lotus became a publicly-owned company in 1968, and Chapman became a millionaire several times over. In 1970 he was voted *Guardian* 'Young Businessman of the Year' and a string of awards for business achievement followed, including the honour of Commander of the British Empire (CBE). But there is a sense that he was a skilled but reluctant big boss.

"The pressure was on him all the time," wife Hazel Chapman told

Friends, colleagues and observers on Chapman

Roger Putnam, former Lotus sales director: "Chapman was unique, a man of great brilliance. Racing drivers who have turned businessman are strange characters. They only know one thing and that's to win, and it depends on their personality as to whether they can temper that. Some see a situation only in black and white.

"He had a very short tolerance. If somebody screwed up once he could live with that. Twice was borderline, and three times that was it. It was quite brutal too. He would push them off the ladder and if they tried to hang on he'd stamp on their fingers."

Ray Hutton, former editor of *Autocar:* "I always had the impression he wasn't terribly keen on the idea of having a manufacturing business with everything that entailed – health and safety, personnel managers, all that kind of stuff."

Sir John Whitmore, Lotus-Cortina racing driver: "He was one of those people who always sailed close to the wind. He was an idiot driver on the road. He drove far too fast. He flew aeroplanes well, but let's just say he had his ups and downs there too."

"Jimmy Clark's death was a total tragedy for Colin. I don't think he ever recovered from that. It would have shown up in a little less humour. He was always laughing and joking – it didn't stop, but it had an impact on it."

Peter Cambridge, Lotus Elite interior designer: "I just thought he was – how can I put it? – the hardest-working most dynamic person I've ever come across."

Patrick Peal, former Lotus engineer and son-in-law: "If he had ten ideas to everybody else's one and eight of them were rotten but two of them were brilliant, it was still twice as many good ideas as anybody else had just come up with.

"He wasn't the architect and the inventor and creator of everything good that came out of Lotus but he was the person that created the

Mike Kimberley (left) joined Lotus from Jaguar in 1968. His combination of engineering background and business acumen helped Group Lotus survive in the 1970s and 1980s.

environment and the atmosphere that allowed other people to flourish."

Mike Kimberley, former Lotus chairman: "He was a fabulous showman. He had such tremendous charisma he could keep people spellbound. He would always be talking cars. You were either dedicated or good, or you didn't work there. Maybe some people were unlucky."

Jabby Crombac. "You are manipulated by the Stock Exchange and there is so much going on which you know nothing about. Colin couldn't stand that side of it. He kept the maximum number of shares for himself and his family that he was allowed, because he wanted to remain the boss, but as far as he was concerned he was only a puppet."

Nonetheless, Chapman was assiduous in securing money to fund his racing activities by whatever means possible and with the help of others not averse to illegal methods, as the DeLorean affair testified. There were a number of theories that his sudden death was too convenient – most of them put about by the master fraudster John DeLorean

himself – but there can be no doubt that it was real and he remains keenly missed by many. Look at a Lotus badge and you can pick out his initials. Meddle with Anthony Colin Bruce Chapman's memory at your peril: a 1980s attempt at a badge redesign minus the 'ACBC' brought loud protest and was soon withdrawn. Colin Chapman was, and is, Lotus.

From Track to Road

Colin Chapman's third design, the Lotus MkIII, was the second car to bear the Lotus name. Thanks to an imaginative interpretation of the 750 Motor Club rules, in the right hands 'LMU 3' could cut a swathe through the British club-racing scene, because of the vastly increased performance wrung from its Austin Seven engine. The car and its famous cylinder head still survives.

The first Lotus – although not named as such – was a solution to a problem for the young Colin Chapman. He began his university career in 1945 aged 17, at University College London, studying civil engineering. This was to mark the start of his love of flying, as he was able to train as a pilot with the University Air Squadron – although he eventually declined a long-term career in the Royal Air Force.

In the immediate post-war period, production of new cars was almost exclusively for export, in order to build up currency reserves, and steel was in short supply. This created a thriving market for used cars (no matter how poor) and Chapman entered the motor trade as a sideline to studying. With a fellow student he penetrated the murky world of secondhand cars in London's Warren Street, then the centre of the city's kerbside motor trade, and by 1947 he had amassed a stock of cars worth around £900 – a great deal in those days. But at the end of that year the petrol ration for all but restricted professions was withdrawn, leading to a collapse in the used-car market.

After Chapman had applied his skills as a salesman, the only car left unsold on the lot was a tatty Austin Seven with a fabric body, and he opted to put his engineering skills into practice to improve on it and have some fun.

The Austin Seven was Britain's first mass-market small car. Between 1922 and 1939 around 290,000 Sevens were built in England alone, with more under licence in other countries – indeed, it formed the basis of the first BMWs. There was still an abundant post-war supply and it was known that there was ample scope for improving both the chassis and the tiny sidevalve engine. The standard Seven was hardly the fastest of cars but several sporting versions were developed by Austin

Lotus Six
1952–55

ENGINE:
Four cylinders in line (Ford), cast-iron block and aluminium cylinder head (non-standard), water-cooled

Capacity	1172cc
Bore x stroke	63.5mm x 92.5mm
Valve actuation	Sidevalve
Compression ratio	8.25:1
Carburettors	2 x SU
Power	40bhp at 6000rpm (approx)

TRANSMISSION:
Rear-wheel drive; three-speed gearbox

SUSPENSION:
Front: Independent front suspension by swing axles and coil springs, located by radius arms; telescopic dampers
Rear: Live rear axle with coil springs, located by radius arms and Panhard rod; telescopic dampers

STEERING:
Burman box

BRAKES:
Front/rear: Cable-operated drum

WHEELS/TYRES:
15in steel wheels
Tyres front/rear 4.5in x 15in/5.25in x 15in

BODYWORK:
Tubular spaceframe with stressed alloy panels
Two-seat sports-racer

DIMENSIONS:
Wheelbase	7ft 3in
Track, front	4ft 1in
Track, rear	3ft 9in

KERB WEIGHT:
8.5cwt

PERFORMANCE:
(Source: *Autosport*)
Max speed	88mph
0–60mph	12.6sec
0–70mph	16.6sec

PRICE (SELF-ASSEMBLY) WHEN NEW:
£425 approx (Ford-based, 1953)

NUMBER BUILT:
110 approx

and raced with success before the outbreak of war. With a bit of application and a few new parts, amateurs could pull a Seven into shape as a cheap sports car. The cheap and cheerful sport of trials driving – where you attempted to drive up a muddy hill with your passenger leaning over the rear wheels to help traction – was already popular, and Chapman opted to redesign his Seven for trials use, he and his girlfriend Hazel Williams competing together in the car. The growth of circuit racing on former airfields had yet to happen.

During 1946 or 1947, in common with many budget trials enthusiasts, Chapman went through the Seven, improving on each aspect as far as he could and according to what was considered standard practice: the springs were modified to give better ground clearance, the brakes were rebuilt and improved, the engine was given better carburation, and the fabric body replaced with one in sheet aluminium with plywood bulkheads. Colin Chapman's Austin Seven special owed nothing to aerodynamics but it was a thorough job. He subsequently

Colin Chapman's first design, an Austin Seven special, has long since disappeared, but a replica has been built, and is shown here in 1992 at a Lotus gathering, next to an M100 Elan.

Club racing in the 1950s

Pre-war British racing was largely the preserve of the rich or of the aristocracy. Racing cars were, on the whole, large, truck-like and expensive. World War Two created a new climate for a more democratic type of motor sport.

Young people went into the services, drove cars for the first time and it tore down the curtain of technical magic. After the war there was a lot of employment in the aircraft industry and the ideas from all these mechanically-enabled young people soon fed through to civilian life, cheap motor sport providing an exciting hobby in a time of grim shortages.

Many cars were still built on the Austin Seven and the Ford Eight/Ten chassis and as these became cheaper a whole structure arose to help the gifted amateur – the prototypical 'impecunious enthusiast' – to build his own racing car. Even those who couldn't afford to race could be involved on the fringes, servicing cars or making up parts. The Seven engine wasn't especially good – the crankshaft was notoriously fragile – but used Sevens were readily available, and £25 or £50 would buy a tired Austin Chummy. In Britain, too, there was a healthy tradition of young men building one-off specials, although many got no further than the garden shed, when marriage and children came along. However, husband-and-wife teams were common for those who finished their cars and raced.

The 750 Motor Club's idea was simple: take the engine and running gear from the Austin and clothe this in aluminium with the aim of achieving as low a weight as possible. Fortunately hundreds of small airfields had been built across Britain and post-1945 these were now empty, providing the perfect venue for circuit-racing. The land had often reverted to farm use but free access was usually no problem if the farmers were on your side. With a few sand-filled oil drums it was easy to arrange autotests and modest races. Safety was of little concern but there was a different attitude to personal safety for those who had lived through the war – a willingness to accept risk that faded in later generations.

By 1952 Britain had three official racing circuits: former bomber-training base Silverstone, Brands Hatch, and Goodwood. But if you counted the old airfields there was a race venue within 20 miles of most major towns. Later Lotus would make its home at Hethel, a former airfield among many dotted across Norfolk. The days of airfield racing were limited, however, as surfaces would gradually break up and become overgrown, while the land was more profitably used for industry and housing.

In the 1950s Britain experienced a boom in racing on disused wartime airfields. By the latter half of the decade an all-Lotus grid could be made up of the Six, Seven and aerodynamic sports-racers such as the Eleven.

split the front axle, with a pivot in the middle, to provide independent front suspension, and this was to be a notable feature of Lotus models well into the 1950s.

By 1948 petrol rationing had been relaxed and Chapman competed in two trials, and brought back some awards. He also finished his time at university although he had failed to graduate, having failed the maths part of the course. However, after a re-sit in 1949 he was awarded his degree.

He was soon set on the next road/trials car, again Seven-based, but the next logical step was to abandon the Austin engine for a more powerful Ford unit. He had accepted a short-term paid commission in the RAF and he built the next car in the lock-up garage belonging to Hazel's family, in Muswell Hill, North London. Expanding gradually into workshops, former stable blocks then factory units, North London was set to be the hub of Lotus for the next decade.

What is now known as the MkII retained the Austin Seven chassis and gearbox. At first a 933cc Ford Eight sidevalve engine was fitted, then a 10hp 1172cc unit originally developing 30bhp. These Ford engines were plentiful, having been introduced in 1932, and the 1172cc version continued in production, latterly redesigned, into the 1960s. This second car was entered for trials towards the end of 1949, under the name Lotus. As more money became available, the design was honed, with a nose cowling that incorporated twin headlamps behind the grille, the lights turning with the steering. Visually it was already set apart from the first special, as Chapman was now gaining more experience in fashioning aluminium. He was also starting to build his cars with the help of others, in this case RAF colleague John Hall. In retrospect it seems clear that Chapman was destined to build cars according to aircraft principles.

During 1950 his interest turned away from trials to circuit racing, which was now starting to boom on disused airfields around the country. Chapman did a full season of trials and races at club level and his success as a driver was noted by the motoring press. At the end of the season, both the first Austin Seven special and 'Lotus' were sold through display advertisements in T*he Motor* magazine

Bodied in aluminium, the MkIII set the parameters for Lotus racers for the bulk of the 1950s: minimal weight, structural rigidity and the most basic of driver comforts.

which included a picture, specifications and mention of wins with the cars.

Lotus was not yet a business – car building and racing remained time-consuming hobbies – but the determination was building year on year. The second car named Lotus was purpose-built for circuit racing and specifically to enter the 750 Motor Club's 750cc Formula. The 750 Motor Club was formed in 1939 as a club for Austin Seven enthusiasts and was thriving by the 1950s, as it offered a cheap entry into motor racing for the keen amateur – as it still does today. The Formula dictated the use of Austin Seven parts as the basis for the whole car, so the Ford engine had to go.

This was the modest start for the Lotus company proper. Although he initially set about building his car alone, Chapman became friends with Michael and Nigel Allen and the Lotus MkIII – as it became in retrospect (it was called the Lotus-Austin when

In an effort to improve the rigidity of the whippy Austin Seven chassis, Nigel Allen (one of Chapman's unpaid racing partners) built a tubular cage around and over the engine, foreshadowing the full spaceframe chassis of later Lotus cars.

The workmanlike cockpit of 'LMU 3': clearly visible is the simple remote change for the four-speed Austin gearbox, a modification typical of so many Austin Seven specials of the era.

sold) – prompted the idea of a team of three racers. Nigel Allen observed later that Chapman quickly spotted that they had a better equipped workshop than the Williams lock-up and suggested that they help him build a team of three identical cars, one for each of them. In the event only two of the chassis were used, to build a car for Chapman and a replica. Although the Allens didn't get their cars, nobody appeared to feel aggrieved that it ended that way.

The Lotus MkIII had an Austin Seven gearbox and steering, and as on the MkII a Ford Eight front axle was used, only this time split to give independent front suspension. This marked the debut of Chapman's innovative combination of relatively soft springs for a race car in conjunction with a rigid chassis: over a decade later this would be one of the Elan's notable features. The standard Austin Seven top-hat-section chassis – shaped like an 'A' – was very flexible and this fault was compounded by hard racing suspension, so Nigel Allen braced the chassis with a tubular cage around and over the engine, foreshadowing the full spaceframe chassis of later Lotus cars.

But it was the car's engine that really made the difference. For ease of manufacture, Austin had designed the Seven's four-cylinder engine so each pair of cylinders shared the same inlet port, rather than having a port for

each cylinder. This was an inherently inefficient design, but members of the 750 Motor Club put up with up with it, trying instead to improve the rest of the car. 750 racing was meant to be cheap, basic fun but Chapman didn't quite see it that way. With the help of the Allens, and still working entirely within the 750 Formula rules, he designed a steel strip extending into the cylinder block and making a 'wall'. This has been termed 'de-siamising', as it created four ports from two. To hide the fact that this had been done, the four-branch inlet manifold was filled and painted to look like a two-branch. It has been accepted that this revised porting was a stroke of Chapman genius but the trick had in fact been first used by an Australian friend of his, Derek Jolly.

There was a huge performance leap, with a top speed of about 80mph when a standard Austin Seven was all-out at 50mph. Chapman believed, in fact, that it was possible to produce a 100mph Seven and this was to be the unbuilt MkV.

Meanwhile the results of his labours and those of the Allens were devastating. Only Chapman's car was ready to race in 1951, and with the Allen brothers providing support, both he and Hazel drove it during 1951. Registered LMU 3, Chapman's third car won race after race and 750MC members became so disheartened that the following year de-siamising was banned.

After a successful season and the subsequent publicity, there was now a demand for 'Lotus replicas' from other enthusiasts and Chapman and the Allens had expended so much time on car-building – while still holding down day jobs – that the idea of turning the enterprise into something more formal began to take seed. The first firm order of 1951 was from Mike Lawson, who had bought the first Lotus, the MkII, and on 1 January 1952 the Lotus Engineering Company came into existence with just Chapman and Michael Allen as partners, Nigel Allen having declined to join in, while staying involved, all the same, in racing. Michael Allen worked full-time at the new company while Chapman decided to stay in his job at British Aluminium for a short spell. In fact he stayed another three years, his job being to encourage the use of aluminum in the construction industry.

Needing more space, the Lotus Engineering Company set up in a collection of buildings in Tottenham Lane, Hornsey, thanks to Chapman's father Stan, who leased him the former stables behind a hotel and pub he owned. The company offered to build replicas of the MkIII and carry out a range of performance modifications for enthusiasts on a small budget. Chapman strove to give the impression of a slick business and made the most of his growing reputation. When work couldn't be done by his small outfit, it was subcontracted out. The next Lotus car, known subsequently as the MkIIIb, was a replica of the MkIII, with small improvements, and was sold to customer Adam Currie. The MkIV was another trials car, built for Mike Lawson, but was not completed until 1954.

A word about numbers. It is around this point that Lotus numerology goes awry and different models either were not built or were not named in sequence: the 100mph Austin-engined MkV was planned but never built and the Lotus MkVII name was first allocated to the commission from Clive Clairmonte (see panel) that was under development in 1952 at the same time as the Six. However, the Lotus MkVII tag was subsequently dropped when Chapman pulled out of the venture, and was only reused in 1957 for the Seven. To illustrate how rapidly the business took off, the MkVIII aerodynamic racer appeared in 1954, three years before the Seven – now written as a word rather than using Roman numerals.

The MkVI – or Six – was the first Lotus to be built in serious quantity. For 1953, the 750 Motor Club announced a new Formula based around the Ford 1172cc unit and which no longer stipulated the use of an Austin Seven chassis. Still having

many of the features of the earlier cars, the Six was to be the first Lotus with a chassis made entirely of metal tubing arranged to give a spaceframe form of construction. The technique was used in the rarified atmosphere of grand prix racing but not in club circles, although it was standard practice in the aircraft industry.

Chapman was still working at British Aluminium but his social network included fellow enthusiasts at aircraft manufacturer De Havilland. It was from this company that three of the growing band of Lotus helpers came in their spare hours: Mike Costin, Peter Ross and Gilbert 'Mac' Macintosh. The latter was responsible for the spaceframe being fully engineered for light weight and torsional (twisting)

Chapman had planned to build three examples of the Lotus MkIII but only one was completed. An unused chassis formed the basis of a second car, with a Ford Ten engine, later known as the MkIIIB, and built in 1952 to a customer order.

The Clairmonte

The car carrying Roman numeral MkVII is the car that fell out of Lotus history – and the 1957 Seven is no relation.

Around the time the Six was taking shape, Chapman's childhood friend John Teychenne interested businessman-enthusiast Clive Clairmonte in a car to his own specification, to be built by Lotus. Intended to show what Chapman could do with a big budget, the Clairmonte car had a specification far ahead of the bread-and-butter Six, with its spaceframe chassis having de Dion rear suspension with inboard rear brakes, and wishbone front suspension. Lotus would build the chassis and Clive Clairmonte would provide a six-cylinder Riley or ERA engine and a Halibrand final drive unit.

Work started on the car at Hornsey in mid-1952 but the stretched little company started to run out of cash and Clairmonte, tired of waiting, reclaimed the chassis and had the car finished by his own mechanic. Bodied

by Williams & Pritchard, it first raced in 1953, with a Lea-Francis engine. The car's original designation was to have been the Lotus MkVII Formula 2 but as it finished so far from the Chapman design Clive Clairmonte ended up using his own name – perhaps because Chapman was unhappy with the project when it started to change, and was unhappy about the car using the Lotus designation. That's one

The Lotus MkVII designation was first given to a project funded by wealthy enthusiast Clive Clairmonte in 1952–53. It had a specification way ahead of the Six but the slow build led Clairmonte to finish the car himself and give it his own name. (Ferret Fotographic)

story, anyway. Another is that Clairmonte dropped the Lotus name because he was trying to obtain compensation from Chapman …

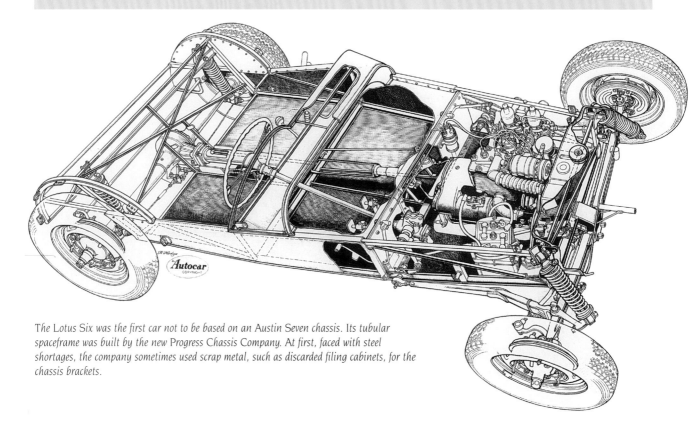

The Lotus Six was the first car not to be based on an Austin Seven chassis. Its tubular spaceframe was built by the new Progress Chassis Company. At first, faced with steel shortages, the company sometimes used scrap metal, such as discarded filing cabinets, for the chassis brackets.

stiffness. It was a design that formed the basis for Lotus cars through much of the 1950s and the bare frame was very light, at 55lb (25kg). In later advertising a photograph was used of well-known *Autosport* journalist John Bolster picking up a part-panelled spaceframe with both hands. Body panels were alloy and the undertray and cockpit sides were riveted to the chassis tubes.

The swing axle was once more used as a method of independent front suspension, with a Ford axle cut in half and bushes fitted to each cut end and springing by combined coil/damper units. The centre of gravity was low but the steering geometry gave rise to some interesting wheel angles when cornering. Braking was by cable-operated drums. The rear wheels were enclosed and a hood and screen were just about enough to keep the weather off. On production cars a hinged boot

Above: The 1953 Lotus Six was the company's first attempt at series production (in kit form) and it proved a great hit with amateur racers such as Peter Gammon, whose MG-engined car, shown here, enjoyed great success in 1954.

Below: The chassis was designed to accommodate a variety of engines, and this Six, photographed at Snetterton in April 1956, has a Climax unit. Spats were generally fitted to the rear wings, aiding aerodynamics – and looks.

Williams & Pritchard

It is said that many owners of 1950s Lotus cars opted not to paint them because the quality of the Williams & Pritchard bodywork was so good.

This was another small British company that was part and parcel of the growth of Lotus. Len Pritchard and Charlie Williams learnt their skills in the pre-war coachbuilding trade and set up their own business for accident-repair panelbeating in Edmonton, North London. They first ventured into body panelling when John Teychenne asked them to rebody a trials car he was building and this led to an introduction to Colin Chapman, at the time when he was designing the Six. "Colin brought us a frame, told us roughly what he wanted, and left us to get on with it," recalled Pritchard when interviewed by Mike Lawrence in 1989. "We took a great deal of care over it, not only in the way it was put together but the way it looked, because we virtually styled it. We felt that the body was important, it was part of the car, its look established the car, and we weren't prepared just to 'skin' a frame."

The company's skill in styling as well as shaping was sometimes overlooked. Frank Costin was wrongly credited with the styling of the Lotus

The Lotus 16 – also known as the 'mini Vanwall' – was bodied and styled by Williams & Pritchard. The company's skills in fashioning aluminium were vital to the early success of Lotus and the finish was such that owners would leave their cars unpainted.

16 – the 'mini Vanwall': it was down to Charlie Williams. The tools they used remained simple: the bodywork of an Eleven was made up of about 20 pieces shaped from cardboard patterns. Williams & Pritchard would roll them out in aluminium and then weld them together. "When Frank came up with the MkVIII, it was a step forward and a challenge, but it was the Eleven which excited me more than any other car," said Pritchard. "The sketches were exciting and it was exciting as it took shape in the metal and came alive before our eyes."

As with so many Lotus suppliers, the relationship was not always benign, with gripes over late payment of invoices and Chapman often in conflict with the duo over his drive for lightness. This went so far as to question the number of

rivets used or to request that an Eleven be built of lighter magnesium alloy – which Williams & Pritchard refused to do, on safety grounds, as in an accident magnesium would flare up dangerously.

Although they continued to build the prototype bodies for glassfibre moulds, the move to grp spelt the end of the firm's long-term relationship with Lotus. By then it had a growing roster of racing clients for one-off cars such as the Ian Walker racing Elan, and many other racing names would beat a path to the door in years to come. The 1970s saw a number of bizarre prototype commissions and more work in historic racing. By the late 1980s, however, work had tailed off and Len Pritchard – then beyond retirement age – brought the business to a close.

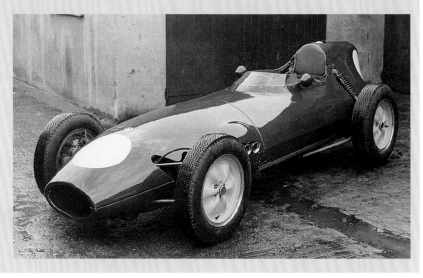

was offered and advertising suggested that this could serve to house a seat for a small child to have the ride of their life.

The Six was designed to take a variety of engines, but was primarily intended to use the 1172cc Ford sidevalve. Setting a trend of prototype Lotus cars having the best engines, the first car, however, used the latest 1508cc Ford Consul unit,

reduced in size to 1499cc so it could compete in the under-1500cc class. This new overhead-valve engine with its short stroke was far more advanced than the aged sidevalve but in 1952 Lotus was still a risky business to back, so Ford refused to sell Chapman a unit directly. Undeterred, he toured Ford dealers for new parts until he could assemble an engine himself.

Opposite: With over 100 built, the Lotus Six was the first significant move by Colin Chapman towards establishing himself as a motor-racing manufacturer rather than someone merely building cars for himself and his friends.

The first Six was raced twice before being written off in an accident. Its replacement competed several times in the latter half of 1952 and this generated enough interest in replicas for Colin Chapman finally to form Lotus into a limited company, although he still continued his day job. He started to advertise the 'Lotus chassis frame' for sale. Exactly one year on, in January 1953, the Lotus Engineering Company Limited was duly formed, thanks in no small part to a £25 loan from Hazel Williams. She and Chapman were sole directors, Michael Allen deciding to follow his brother and take a step back. He remained a shareholder and of course there were plenty of talented newcomers to help – especially the De Havilland trio. Chapman planned an initial run of eight production Sixes, which he largely built himself.

Two outside companies were the key to the success of the Six as a production car. The first chassis frames had been built by Chapman's friend John Teychenne and Dave Kelsey, and Teychenne formed a new business, the Progress Chassis Company, when orders started to arrive. Progress was located near the

The Six was both a road car and a track car and owners could specify extra instruments and even windscreen wipers if their budgets would allow.

buildings behind the Railway Hotel in Hornsey used by Lotus and at first, faced with steel shortages, the company sometimes used scrap metal, such as discarded filing cabinets, for chassis brackets and the like. Through John Teychenne an introduction was made to panelbeaters Williams & Pritchard of Edmonton, North London, and they made the first aluminium panels and mudguards for the Six. Chapman was so impressed by the quality of the work that Charlie Williams and Len Pritchard were eventually found space in the Lotus buildings for continued Lotus production. The combination of Williams & Pritchard and Lotus was to become an important component in the marque's success.

Chapman intended the Six to be used for both road and track and to be able to be built from a kit of parts, thereby avoiding purchase tax. Owners still had to find the mechanical components, but there were plenty of secondhand parts readily available. Although the Six – and later the Seven – started off as standard cars, they rarely stayed that way. Early buyers gave their cars a variety of engines, but most were Ford-powered. Other than the 1172cc sidevalve – perhaps with an Elva inlet-over-exhaust conversion – and the Consul unit, MG T-type or Bristol engines could be fitted, or else the desirable Coventry Climax FWA.

While the production Six's racing debut wasn't as dramatic as that of some Lotus models, Chapman and Michael Allen both took second places at Silverstone's July 1953 meeting, in a car with Ford Ten power. The point was less the good result than the lack of drama with which it was achieved. Nothing fell off or wore out: the foundations for the Six's long racing career were being laid down. It was enough, too, to merit the first Lotus road test by a car magazine.

'I feel that the Lotus is the best attempt yet to provide the enthusiast with a competition car at a price he can afford to pay,' wrote John Bolster in an October 1953 issue of *Autosport* weekly. 'In essentials it is just as sound an engineering job as the most expensive sports car, and the economy is only brought about by the clever adaptation of mass-produced components.' He estimated the car was producing around 40bhp and measured a 0–60mph time – usually on the optimistic side with Bolster – of 12.6 seconds.

This endorsement was used to good effect while the car was in production. Chapman at this stage wrote his own advertising, placing small advertisements with press testimonials and telling customers how they too could build a Lotus 'replica'. The chassis, panels, brackets and engine mountings were available for £110 and for a further £75 'approx' the panels could be fitted to the chassis. For those with deeper pockets, Lotus at Hornsey offered more specialised racing options such as a hydraulic brake conversion in place of the standard Ford cable set-up.

The demand created for the Six was such that more than 100 had been made by the end of 1955 when it gave way to the work needed to make the Eleven a reality. By comparison, production of contemporary Lotus race cars was in the tens and twenties. The Lotus Six was the first significant move towards Chapman establishing himself as a motor-racing manufacturer rather than merely building cars for himself and his friends.

Build your own

As it pushed its way into the luxury car market, Lotus had a great deal of trouble shaking off its 'kit car' image. But self-assembly sales were one of the main ways it prospered in the early days and they enabled a small but dedicated band of followers to own a car of far better design than a mass-produced item at a similar price. At the time Lotus sprang into being, few of its customers could have afforded, or indeed wanted, an off-the-peg racing car, while Lotus could not have coped with the regulations required of a traditional manufacturer. Apart from lowering the purchase price, farming out construction also helped ease space pressure in the early days of operating from Hornsey.

With its multiple engine combinations, the Six was the first Lotus to be produced in significant numbers and to be designed for a degree of self-assembly. Unfortunately, lucky owners would find components arrived days or weeks apart and then a lot of further work needed to be done hacking things about to make them fit.

Even if you bought all-new parts for the Lotus Six chassis frame, the whole car would only cost £425, when in 1954 a Triumph TR2 cost £844 including Purchase Tax. The tax concession was so key to the survival of fledgling racing specialists that journalist John Bolster formed a committee with Colin Chapman and others to oppose one government move to clamp down. For Bolster it was a real cat-and-mouse game against the 'little men at Customs & Excise'. In his book on the Elan, he wrote that 'although the amount of money that was involved was comparatively small, the Customs and Excise thought it worthwhile to employ snoopers, who would stop at nothing to trip up an amateur constructor on some triviality.'

Initially, if a kit were supplied with

everything you needed you would have to pay tax on the completed vehicle. So you had to source some components yourself, and have a go at assembling the car in your own garage – although most enthusiasts found a friend who could help for cash. Thanks to Fred Bushell, by the end of the 1950s Lotus at Cheshunt had split into several companies to supply self-builders, but all operating on the same site. The chassis came from Lotus Components and other parts from Racing Engines Ltd. If a sale went through, the Lotus staff would then help the buyer fill in the necessary forms and steer them through the process. The fully-built Elite was made by Lotus Cars Ltd, while pure racing cars did not attract Purchase Tax.

By the 1960s home assembly of an Elan or Europa was a well-established ritual, with the car and engine arriving from the dealer on a trailer on Saturday morning to be built ready for opening time at the pub on Sunday – or so the adverts said.

"If they could have been fully-built they would have been," says Lotus dealer Bobby Bell. "Lotus did the very least dis-assembly to get by the law,

The Six began the organised practice of allowing customers to build a Lotus from a kit and thereby escape purchase tax. The chassis, panels, brackets and engine mountings were available for £110 and for a further £75 or thereabouts the panels could be fitted to the chassis.

so cars were fully-trimmed and wired. The engines were fully-dressed with the carburettors and the distributor all timed-up. The buyer had to bolt the suspension corners on and put the engine and gearbox in. Everything was there. They weren't allowed to have instructions because that would have been contrary to the regulations, so they gave them pages from the workshop manual which explained how to dismantle the car, and you reversed them."

Then the dealer had to give the finished article a post-build check. "You'd get cars coming in with the most peculiar problems. People would cut things off if they thought they couldn't fit them in otherwise. On some cars the windows and wipers would work the wrong way because they'd put the battery in the wrong way round. There was quite a bit of trouble."

The *Sports-Racers*

Based on the Six but looking nothing like it, the 1954 Lotus MkVIII marked the first application of aerodynamic principles to a Chapman design, thanks to the expertise of Frank Costin.

Within a few short years, the Lotus company was operating in two parallel worlds. From the ramshackle collection of outbuildings behind Stanley Chapman's pub, flimsy-looking club cars were soon fighting for space with Atomic Age racers destined for Le Mans.

With his aircraft background, Frank Costin – the man from De Havilland – was instrumental in pushing Lotus into genuine aerodynamics. Other racing companies were producing bodywork that appeared sleek but owed little to science. In 1953 Chapman determined that his next race car, the MkVIII, should be a showpiece for Lotus and

Frank Costin

Frank Costin used to profess little interest in cars but when he turned his mind to Lotus aerodynamics in the 1950s the results were spectacular. His engineering career had been firmly rooted in the aircraft industry and his pre-Lotus portfolio already included work on variants of the Spitfire and on gliders, Costin being a particular devotee of wood structures – as used, of course, to such good effect on the De Havilland Mosquito. His younger brother Mike was initially drawn into the Lotus circle in 1952 to become a driver, and through him Chapman approached Frank, then heading De Havilland's Aerodynamic Rectification Department, to give his opinion on the initial design of the MkVIII.

After the success of the MkVIII, Costin's influence pervaded most subsequent designs, although he was most heavily involved with the Eleven and Elite and he also worked closely with Chapman on the Vanwall grand prix car. Nonetheless, he did most of his Lotus work for no payment (he belatedly got a Ford Anglia in recognition of his work on the Eleven streamliner), and he stayed with De Havilland until 1958 when he went freelance.

Frank Costin had a tremendous eye for detail and would make small adjustments to great effect. Wind tunnels were scarce in the 1950s and Costin would attach tufts of wool – and occasionally himself – to cars, and photograph the tufts in motion to see the direction of the airflow. In 1961 he was employed by a French competitor at Le Mans to improve the airflow on his Elite, with an eye to winning the Index of Thermal Efficiency. During the test day Costin attached wool to the car and used Plasticine to modify the shape of the nose. He then calculated that the front needed to be raised

fractionally, and he had the bumper removed and headlamp covers made so the join was flush. He claimed that this was equivalent to a power gain of 16–20bhp, and other Elite drivers weren't slow in attempting similar modifications.

The path of both Costins diverged from that of Chapman towards the end of the 1950s. Frank co-founded the Marcos company with Jem Marsh in 1959 (his is the 'cos' part of the name), and created the extraordinary plywood-monocoque Marcoses, and brother Mike went on to found Cosworth, in tandem with Keith Duckworth. Frank continued to consult for motor-racing teams and an efficiently engineered – if not especially pretty – sports car, the Costin Amigo, was produced in 1971; again built around a wooden monocoque, it was not a success. Costin's work diversified into boats and aircraft but he was still involved in car projects up to his death in 1995.

Although Frank Costin was said to profess little interest in cars compared to planes, when he turned his mind to Lotus aerodynamics in the '50s the results were spectacular. This photo shows Stirling Moss in the streamlined Eleven he piloted to a record-breaking 130mph at Italy's Monza circuit in 1956.

Costin in later life – and still the mischievous iconoclast.

be fully streamlined. He turned initial sketches over to Dave Kelsey of the Progress Chassis Company to build a model, but then called in Costin to give his opinion. Costin said that the car was overweight and needed a rethink on its aerodynamics. He extended and tapered the front wings, enveloping the headlamps under cowls, and introduced distinctive tail fins for added stability.

Costin would have preferred the car to have been a monocoque but as a spaceframe had worked well for the Six, and because the relationship with Progress Chassis was well-

The shorter MkIX followed in 1955, Costin having made the fins taller but more rounded. It was the first Lotus to be taken to the Le Mans 24-hour race.

established, the MkVIII was designed around a similar structure. Built to win races, and not necessarily be driven to them, it was a car of few compromises.

Unlike the Six, the bodywork was much more heavily stressed and mounted on steel bulkheads riveted in place – apart from the removable front section. The prototype had a major flaw in that the design of the spaceframe enclosed the engine so completely that most major components had to be taken off it before it could be removed; consequently the design was modified for customer cars. Streamlining extended to the underside of the car, where components were covered by an undertray and the body featured headlamps which popped up when the driver pulled a handle.

This was the true Lotus formula: a very rigid chassis (so rigid that it caused a number of failures) and the lightest possible weight, to make the most of a small-capacity engine. Even the seat cushion was a foam pad sprayed onto a pan shaped into the floor. Built for the 1500cc class, the MkVIII was fitted with a highly modified MG engine bored out to 1467cc and giving 85bhp, driving a four-speed MG gearbox. The swing-axle split Ford front axle was retained, albeit mounted lower, but Costin had real concerns about how this would cope above 120mph, hence the fins. At the rear was a more complex de Dion layout designed by Chapman.

The prototype, registered SAR 5, was ready to race for the 1954 season and Team Lotus (still assorted amateurs

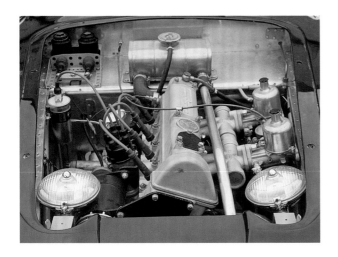

To keep a smooth profile for racing, the MkIX had spring-loaded headlamps which could be raised for night use once the bonnet had been opened. This brought Lotus into conflict with the Le Mans scrutineers and Mike Costin was forced to re-site the lamps in the air intake.

With better access to mechanical components, the Lotus MkIX had a degree more practicality than the MkVIII; it was sold in kit form, for Ford, MG or Climax engines. Visible here, in the passenger side, are the parallel tubes of the left-hand-side radius arms locating the rear axle.

The Vanwall project

As a sideline to the Lotus story, Colin Chapman also had a significant part in helping Vanwall become in 1957 the first British team ever to win a World Championship race – thereby launching Britain as the centre of Formula 1 expertise.

The Vanwall team was backed by Tony Vandervell, whose company made engine bearings and other components. In 1954, after racing Ferrari-derived cars for a number of years, the company came up with a car wholly its own design. Vandervell was determined to create a British car to end the grand prix dominance of Ferrari and Maserati, but while the engine, suspension and transmission of the Vanwall were sound, success was elusive.

In 1956 Vanwall started work to improve its 1955-season car and was tending towards spaceframe construction rather than the usual ladder chassis. As the team had little experience of this it was noted that Chapman was becoming an expert on spaceframes. Tony Vandervell had been thinking of Chapman when he invited designer Frank Costin to Oulton Park to watch the current car race and

then give his views on it. "I told Tony he'd got a good engine but the rest of the car was dire," Costin recalled when interviewed by Mike Lawrence in 1990. "I told him that the best thing would be if I did the body and Colin did the chassis. He looked thoughtful and soon afterwards he commissioned Colin and myself to go ahead."

So Chapman was invited to the Vanwall headquarters and methodically went through the plans, making suggestions and drawings which resulted in a redesign of the chassis and rear suspension. Costin's shape became a design classic and

Colin Chapman's input helped turn the Vanwall into a winner. This is Stirling Moss, in the 1957 German Grand Prix.

incorporated his usual level of detail such as recessing the exhaust pipe to sit flush with the body.

Chapman actually drove for the Vanwall team in 1956 – but only once, as he damaged his own car beyond repair and ran into Mike Hawthorn's in the process. This curtailed the possibility of any future F1 drives for Chapman, although by that point he had less and less time for such diversions.

Above: The 1956 Eleven marked another turning point in Lotus history: over 200 were destined to be built. It scored both at Le Mans and on the club racing scene.

Right: The third and last design derived from the MkVIII was the MkX with its domed bonnet concealing a tall 1971cc Bristol engine to enable it to compete in the 2-litre racing class. A handful were built – but were not well-liked by drivers. The wheel angle shows the split swing-axle front suspension in action.

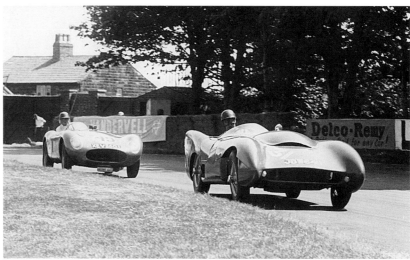

yet to become employees), had an exhausting summer gradually improving their results at English and European circuits such as Germany's Nürburgring, with Chapman driving much of the time. It seemed like David taking on Goliath when Lotus beat the two works 125bhp Porsche 550 Spyders

in the Silverstone 1500cc race of 17 July 1954. The MkVIII set lap records at many British circuits, and when tested by *Autosport* it achieved 121mph from 85bhp. As interest from private buyers built up, the chassis was changed to an adaptation of the MkVI frame to try to avoid some of the early failures.

The MkVIII was the last Lotus built by volunteers, and after nine examples had been built it evolved into the MkIX. Announced in March 1955, this marked the coming together of Lotus and Coventry Climax for the first time, being designed around the 75bhp FWA 1098cc engine. Lotus wasn't the only company to be using the FWA and now faced competition from Cooper, who used it in a rear-engined configuration. Team Lotus opted to run two 'works' cars, one with an MG engine and one with a Climax. With a shape derived from the MkVIII, the MkIX was slightly shorter, had higher and more rounded tail fins, and improved airflow and cooling for its bigger (drum) brakes. As with the MkVIII, the whole front came off – while a panel to the rear gave access to the inboard rear brakes and the axle.

Lotus's first trip to the Le Mans 24-hour race was not a success. The Climax-engined MkIX, XPE 6, was equipped with advanced disc brakes and started brilliantly, leading its class, but an oil leak onto the clutch was the first snag, then it was hit in the rear by a Porsche and had two 'offs' at bends in the circuit. Le Mans 1955 became famous for a horrific accident where a Mercedes ploughed into a group of spectators, killing over 100 people. The Lotus car was eventually disqualified after leaving a bend for the second time, as

Chapman had reversed back onto the track without waiting for a signal from the marshals, who in the hours after the accident had become very sensitive to even the smallest breach of regulations.

Interviewed in 2005, Hazel Chapman recalled how stressful Le Mans had become. "It was a horrible experience. We stayed in grotty places and always seemed to be arguing with the French officials over regulations," she told Mick Walsh of *Classic & Sports Car*. Typical of such disputes was one concerning the MkIX's headlamps. These could be pulled up on stalks through a panel in the bonnet, and the scrutineers were not happy with this arrangement, forcing chief mechanic Mike Costin (brother of Frank) to refit the lamps within the air intake.

Customer MkIXs went on sale after Le Mans in two versions: a Le Mans and a Club, the latter being a cheaper version without the Climax engine and supplied as a kit – with plenty of advice on hand from the factory about how to complete the car. 'XPE 6' was loaned out to magazines by Chapman,

to show that the cars could be driven on the road.

At the same time the MkX was announced, to cater for the 2-litre class. Although not a prime target for Team Lotus, this class was popular in the mid 1950s and so the MkIX was modified to take the heavier 142bhp 1971cc Bristol engine. The MkXs were easy to recognise as the taller six-cylinder engine necessitated a bonnet line raised by the use of a domed lid. Only six were built and the car was not well regarded: famous driver Cliff Davis hated his car, registered NOY 1. "In one race my co-driver told me it was bloody unmanageable," he recalled in a 1980s interview. "We spent a week when we got it rebuilding

Costin's painstaking body design made for the best possible aerodynamics and the Eleven is still considered beautiful. The partially enclosed front wheels gave a limited turning circle but that was not a great concern on a racetrack.

With front and rear sections that hinged to reveal all the mechanical components, access for maintenance posed no problem.

it and rectifying various faults. And with that swing front axle it was horrible, especially in the wet." In a strange footnote, film star James Dean was about to take delivery of a Lotus MkX when he was killed in his Porsche.

The first family of streamliners served Lotus well on the track and in terms of image. Within less than two years the company had moved from skinny-wheeled specials (although the Six was produced in far greater quantity than the Costin-influenced cars) to sleek Le Mans contenders. But then instead of building a range of different racers based on one design, Colin Chapman opted to discontinue them all and concentrate on just one model which could be built in a decent quantity. The number sequence was observed but he opted to do away with the near-unreadable Roman numerals and named the next car – built for road and track – the Eleven. Subsequent race cars reverted to numbers but the 'Marks' never returned except to denote an improved model for road cars.

As a sum of parts, the Eleven was not a radical change on the racers that preceded it, but the cumulative effect of the lessons learnt on the previous cars was clear. In the winter and spring of 1956 Chapman set aside time to concentrate solely on developing the Eleven and it was ready for press presentation – as biographer Mike Lawrence points out, cannily timed for a slack period in racing.

The Eleven was built around a MkVIII-type spaceframe modified to increase stiffness; the split-beam front axle was used again, with a lower pivot point to try to improve on its tendency to promote understeer, where the front wheels run wide into a corner. Frank Costin turned his hand to a painstaking body design to maximise aerodynamic efficiency and the result, unusually for a Costin design, was and still is considered beautiful. The car seemed to hunker down to the ground and wrap itself around the wheels, which were so enveloped that the top of the rear wheelarches became small fins. The semi-enclosed front wheels limited the turning circle but this was not a great concern on a racetrack. Taking the aerodynamics to their logical conclusion, a version with a completely faired-in canopy for the driver was subsequently taken record-breaking at Italy's Monza circuit in September 1956, achieving in excess of 130mph.

The passenger side of the Eleven cockpit could be covered with a metal tonneau to become a single-seat

The Ghia Eleven

Although for most people the Lotus Eleven was an attractive car in itself, the spaceframe chassis lent itself to being reclothed to order. In 1957 a Swiss enthusiast took an Eleven chassis to Swiss coachbuilder Ghia-Aigle. The result was known as the Ghia-Aigle Coupé, and was listed by Ghia as a Lotus 1100 Le Mans Coupé.

The car was said to have been prepared for the March 1957 Geneva Motor Show in such a rush that there was no time to modify the chassis tube that very obviously ran across the passenger footwell, although the car did at least have cabin trim and carpets.

When it reappeared the following year with a hardtop, the stray tube had been removed. The car became

Although most considered the Eleven pretty enough, the Swiss arm of Italian coachbuilder Ghia rebodied one for the 1957 Geneva Motor Show, where Colin and Hazel Chapman were able to inspect the conversion.

famous among Lotus enthusiasts and was used in what limited motorsport existed in Switzerland. Only the one was built, and the car has been variously said to have been the inspiration for the Elite and the Elan – although the Elite shape was in fact well advanced by spring 1957.

The Lotus Twelve – Chapman's first single-seater

The tiny and short-lived Lotus Twelve was not a great success on the track but it did constitute a number of Lotus firsts. It was built for a single racing purpose (Formula 1 and 2) and as such had no space for a passenger and hence could not be sold to road drivers. It also saw the debut of Chapman's ingenious twin-wishbone front suspension, in which a high-set

The short-lived Lotus Twelve of 1956–57 was small and complex and incorporated a number of advances, including the wishbone front suspension fitted to the Series 2 Eleven. This is the first car built, and has de Dion rear suspension.

anti-roll bar formed the forward element of the upper wishbones. Finally, it used for the first time his cleverly minimalist strut design for the rear.

As with all Lotus models up to that point, the Twelve stuck with a front-engined rear-driven layout – although competitor Cooper was forging ahead with mid-engined cars, using Coventry Climax power units. In 1956, however, the front-engined route was still seen as having some value.

With the Twelve lacking the width of a two-seater, a problem was how to run a propshaft through the cabin to the rear wheels in such a small car:

you risked either placing the driver too high or else having to use transfer gearing to offset the propshaft to one side. In the end a dedicated transaxle was designed, enabling the propshaft to pass low under the driver.

Lotus invested in its own design of gearbox to reduce weight and transmission size. Nicknamed the 'queerbox', this was a five-speed design not unlike some modern semi-automatic systems. The driver would push the lever forwards each time to step up a gear and backwards to go down (you could not skip a gear). Perhaps a case of too much too soon, it caused a great deal of trouble in service and it took a dedicated team to develop it for use on subsequent cars.

As launched in late 1956, the Twelve ran with a de Dion rear suspension but this was replaced by the first example of the 'Chapman Strut', where the halfshaft was an active part of the suspension system and the suspension strut was steeply angled away from the wheel and anchored to the bodywork. A steel radius arm ran forwards to locate the axle fore and aft. The cars were picked out by the new design of Lotus magnesium-alloy 'wobbly-web' wheels, which were inspired by aircraft design.

racer, and to ensure the driver's head didn't obstruct the airflow too much a headrest flowed into the rear bodywork. The grille was reduced to a small slot of an air intake, good ducting ensuring the Eleven didn't overheat. Gone were the gripes about access, finally, as the entire front and rear sections tipped open.

The Eleven was sold as a series of cars rather than offered with a collection of options. Buyers could initially opt for Club or Le Mans versions, and a Sports later appeared. The Le Mans was of course the costliest option, with two Climax engine choices (1100cc or 1500cc),

four-wheel disc brakes, and de Dion rear suspension. Next down came the live-axled Climax-engined Club. It was intended to be usable as a road car and as such could even be supplied with a full-width windscreen and a hood – although this looked somewhat odd, because the screen was so low and narrow. That was about it for practicality, as there was no luggage space, heater or sidescreens and just one windscreen wiper. The Sports, meanwhile, was the 'starter' option, with an 1172cc Ford 100E sidevalve engine, and was intended for '1172' club racing or for road use – for which it was generally

equipped with a full-width flat screen and a hood.

The 1956 Le Mans race ushered in many new regulations and these favoured efficient smaller-capacity cars. That year a Team Lotus Eleven won the 1100cc class, took seventh place overall and fourth in the Index of Performance. In 1957 an Eleven took the Index fitted with a Climax engine of just 744cc. On home ground Elevens were at every race and winning consistently. From 1956 until the end of the decade it was such a success in club racing that the 750 Motor Club had to ban it from the 1172cc Formula. Tested by *The Autocar*

Even in the roadgoing Eleven, interior fitments were kept to a minimum, with just the essential instruments. Part of the spaceframe chassis is visible in the passenger footwell; the black box on the left is for electrical fuses.

After its racing victories the Eleven was put on sale in both road and race versions. The Sports version came with a hood of sorts and a tiny windscreen wiper, while the Le Mans was for racing.

in 1956, the 1098cc Climax-engined Le Mans car recorded 0–60mph in 10.9 seconds and top speed of 111mph.

The Eleven was upgraded in 1957 to become the Eleven Series 2 – the Lotus Twelve had since appeared, and Chapman avoided unlucky 13 for obvious reasons. The Series 2 marked the transition from swing-axle front suspension to a coil-spring and wishbone set-up, based on that of the Twelve racer of 1956. This was fitted to the Le Mans model, cheaper variants generally sticking with the swing axle.

Again sold under the Le Mans, Club and Sports names, Series 2 cars were distinguished by their unpainted lower panels and were offered with a broader range of engine options. Most were now sold with two seats and a full-width low-cut Perspex racing windscreen.

Around 270 Elevens of both types were produced between 1956 and 1958, making it the most numerous Lotus to that point. It brought Le Mans and circuit success but the world of racing didn't stop for it and neither did Chapman, who was broadening out with the Elite, the Seven and single-seat racers. As Team Lotus headed towards Formula 1, the divide between the Lotus race and road cars was starting to widen and with each model change they owed less and less to each other.

For 1957, when this photograph was taken of Chapman, the Eleven had been developed into the Series 2 (there was no unlucky thirteen) which ushered in proper wishbone front suspension. In sales terms it was easily the most popular Lotus to that point.

The Westfield Eleven

Modern indicators and a numberplate from the donor vehicle identify this as a Westfield Eleven, a 1980s replica of the Eleven, using MG Midget parts, that was good enough to tempt owners of the Lotus original to buy them as everyday transport.

The Lotus Eleven was produced in a reasonable quantity and over 200 are thought to have survived, but buying one comes at a hefty premium. In the 1980s, as the classic car boom got underway, ex-racer

Chris Smith and business partner Mark Hancock built themselves a Lotus Eleven replica, patterned on a real Lotus body, and using a genuine chassis together with components from a 1275cc MG Midget.

After being tested by the motoring press, such was the clamour for replicas that Smith launched Westfield Cars in 1982 with the Eleven kit and in 1983 added a Lotus Seven replica. This ran into litigation because it was so similar to the Caterham, but was then modified to become the

Westfield SE and is sold to this day.

Such was the quality of the job that the Westfield Eleven became prized in its own right as far easier to live with than a Lotus Eleven on a day-to-day basis. 162 Elevens were produced between 1982 and 1986 and most were snapped up by Japanese collectors. In 2004, to the surprise of enthusiasts, Westfield announced the Eleven was going back into production, again based on an MG Midget donor car, and selling for the price of a new supermini.

The *Lotus* Seven

You can still buy a Lotus Seven, in all but name, half a century after Colin Chapman rushed the cheap and cheerful sports car onto the market to bankroll his racing activities and the ill-fated Elite.

1957 was a significant year in the Chapman Grand Plan, the year that Lotus would make its entry as a serious road-car manufacturer. The ambition was the Elite, the bread-and-butter earner the Seven: half road car, half club-racer, it was intended to fill lulls in production outside the racing season and be put to one side when racing restarted. The Six had done good business between 1953 and 1955 and there were plenty of customers who expressed an interest in buying an updated version.

Development of the Seven was rapid, thanks to the intercession of Edward Lewis, owner of racing footwear manufacturer Westover Shoes and a keen amateur competitior. He raced a Six in 1953, and progressed to a Lotus-supported MkIX in 1955 before he opted to build his own Lotus for hillclimbing in 1956.

What became know as the Edward Lewis Special was a Lotus in all but name, based on a Six chassis and the running gear from a MkIX complete with inboard rear brakes, a de Dion rear axle

Lotus Seven
1957–72

Note: figures only for Seven Series 1 (Ford sidevalve), Series 4 (Ford 1600 crossflow), Series 4 (Lotus-Holbay twin-cam 125bhp)

ENGINE:
Four cylinders in line, cast-iron block and cylinder head (aluminium head on twin-cam), water-cooled

Capacity	1172cc/1599cc/1558cc
Bore x stroke	63.5mm x 92.5mm/
	81mm x 77.6mm/
	82.5mm x 72.7mm
Valve actuation	sidevalve/pushrod/
	twin overhead cam
Compression ratio	8.5:1; 9.0:1 (S4 1600);
	9.5:1 (S4 twin-cam)
Carburettor	Solex; Weber; 2 x Weber
Power	40bhp at 4500rpm
	84bhp at 5400rpm
	125bhp at 6200rpm
Maximum torque	58lb ft at 2600rpm
	96.1lb ft at 3600rpm
	116lb ft at 4500rpm

TRANSMISSION:
Rear-wheel drive, three-speed gearbox (four-speed on S4)

SUSPENSION:
Front: Independent by coil springs and twin wishbones; telescopic dampers; anti-roll bar
Rear: Live axle (BMC/Ford), location by radius arms and transverse link; coil springs and telescopic dampers. S4 has location by two leading and two trailing links.

STEERING:
Rack-and-pinion

BRAKES:
Front: Drum (disc on S4)
Rear: Drum

WHEELS/TYRES:
15in steel/13in steel

BODYWORK:
Tubular spaceframe chassis with alloy/grp panels (Series 4 glassfibre-reinforced plastic panels) Two-seat sports-racer

DIMENSIONS:
(S1/S4)

Length	10ft 9in/12ft
Wheelbase	7ft 3in/7ft 5in
Track, front	3ft 11in/4ft 1in
Track, rear	3ft 10.5in/4ft 3.5in
Width	4ft 6in/5ft 0in
Height	3ft 7in/3ft 6in

KERB WEIGHT:
9cwt (S1)
11.4cwt (S4)

PERFORMANCE:
(Source: *The Autocar/Motor*)

Max speed	81mph/100mph*
0–60mph	17.8sec/8.8sec*
30–50mph in top	7.9sec/7.2sec*
50–70mph in top	16.5sec/7.9sec*

* 84bhp Ford 1600 crossflow

PRICE IN COMPONENT FORM WHEN NEW:
£690 (S1, 1957)
£950 (S4 1600 crossflow, July 1970)

NUMBER BUILT:
2477

The aluminium nose-cone and cycle wings of this Seven identify it as a Series 1; only the S1 had a chip-cutter grille, later cars having a simple wire grid. Clearly visible here are the substantial tubular lower wishbones of the front suspension and the cheese-paringly small S1 headlamps.

Opposite: An essay in continued development: Closest to camera is a Series 2 Seven, with a yellow S3 behind and a red S4 to its right. Behind is an S1 with the A-series engine, while to the rear is an R500 Superlight Caterham.

Above: Its squared-off tail is the quickest way to tell a Seven from a Six: this is an S1 Seven with a BMC A-series engine. Bodywork was once again by Williams & Pritchard, with panels riveted to the spaceframe to compensate for its simplified design. Many owners still opted to leave their cars unpainted.

Left: Red vinyl cushions drop into the floorpan and add a splash of colour to the bare-bones Seven. The dash panel is an integral part of the bodywork, forming the scuttle.

and an 1100cc Coventry Climax FWA engine. In Lewis's capable hands it soon built up a reputation in club racing circles, enough for Chapman to take notice. It was said that this encouraged him in his plans for a cheap club/road special and he proposed that Lewis swap his special for a Seven prototype when it was ready.

Lotus historians have speculated that the Lewis Special was the prototype of the Seven but Colin Chapman always denied this. Another theory is that Chapman might even have wanted the Lewis Special off the streets in case it showed Lotus up in the days when the company's

'FVV 877' was the test car supplied to The Autocar magazine in 1957. The first engine choices were two Ford sidevalves, of 40bhp or 48bhp, making the Seven eligible for the 750 Motor Club's 1172 Formula. In late 1958 a Coventry Climax unit was added – but this was an expensive option.

Club racers took the Seven to their hearts, and it excelled on small circuits and at hillclimbs.

reputation as a builder of road cars was vulnerable. The Special was sold on, out of the country, soon after Chapman bought it.

The prototype Seven took shape through the spring and summer of 1957. It retained similarities to the Lewis Special although the bodywork – panelled in aluminium by Williams & Pritchard – was markedly different around the rear. In so much as it could be described as having styling, the easiest way to tell a Seven from a Six was to look at either end. At the front the nose took a gradual downward slope, while the Six's rounded rear was replaced by a boxy tail. Front wings were separate and were fixed so they didn't turn with the wheels.

The chassis, based on the design of those for the Six and Eleven, was supplied once more by the Progress Chassis Company. The welded tubular frame was always labour intensive to manufacture, so the Seven chassis was systematically simplified, with extra panels such as the transmission tunnel, rear body and body sides being riveted to the structure to compensate for some loss of chassis-tube stiffness. The tubes were a mixture of round and square sections, the latter being used where rivets or bolts had to be inserted, and the flat dashboard served as the scuttle panel. This paring-down would happen again

Introduced in 1960, the S2 Seven was designed to increase profit and broaden sales. Distinguished by the sweeping glassfibre wings generally fitted, it took full advantage of Ford's ever-improving engine range. Always sold in component form, a kit could be yours for only £399 in 1961 if you could supply your own engine. The car pictured is wearing non-period wheels.

for the Series 2, with serious consequences.

Ian Jones was Lotus's first full-time draughtsman, joining in January 1957. Chapman had met Jones during his consultancy work for Vanwall, and Jones worked out the production version of the Seven, based on Chapman's designs. "There wasn't much to it really, it was all pretty well-

known stuff, the sort of thing you could dash off in a weekend," Chapman later claimed.

The prototype Seven took a bow in the hands of Edward Lewis at the Brighton Speed Trials of September 1957. It was a sophisticated little beast by comparison with the bulk of customer cars that were to follow but it showcased what could be done, given deep enough pockets: most Seven buyers would not be fitting the de Dion axle, Climax engine and all-round disc brakes of the Lewis car, although to do so was perfectly feasible. The production Lotus Seven had not yet been announced – that was planned for the following month's Motor Show at Earls Court. Meanwhile, though, after the Brighton

outing word began to spread and it filtered back to Hornsey Road that potential buyers were queuing up for replicas.

Lotus was soon swamped with orders both for Elites and Sevens. The initial choice of engines was between two versions of the trusty 1172cc Ford 100E sidevalve engine, of either 40bhp or 48bhp, both variants naturally enough being eligible for the 750 Motor Club's 1172 Formula. These were coupled to the Ford three-speed gearbox.

Front suspension was fully independent along the lines of the Elite and Twelve, with lower and upper wishbones. Early cars used a cheap Burman steering box but soon changed to a more precise rack-and-

A Seven for Number Six

Over the winter of 1967–68 the Lotus Seven had a guaranteed piece of primetime British TV exposure every week in the title sequence of *The Prisoner*.

Appreciation societies still ponder what on earth it was all about, but every week the hero, played by former *Dangerman* star Patrick McGoohan, ran out of his front door, jumped into 'KAR 120C' and blasted through sixties London to deliver a resignation letter. This was the prelude to his abduction to 'The Village' where he became 'Number 6' and where weekly attempts were made to prise some kind of information out of him. In one episode a character quizzes our man on his car. Like a true Seven devotee he recites the registration and the engine number. "I know every nut and bolt and cog. I built it with my own hands." But did he call Cheshunt for any missing bits? Who can say?

The tale of how this promotional plug fell into Lotus's lap was that McGoohan called Graham Arnold and initially requested an Elan, this by 1965 getting a good airing in *The Avengers*. Arnold showed him an

Elan and 'KAR 120C', the works demonstrator Seven which was sitting around neglected in the parking lot. Although Graham Nearn maintains Arnold would rather have pushed the Elan, McGoohan fell for the Seven as the non-conformist symbol of freedom it is.

Filming took place over 1966 and 1967 in London and Wales, where the 'Village' of Portmeirion is still a major tourist attraction. Arnold was then taken by surprise by a subsequent request to have 'KAR 120C' back – as

it had been sold! Thus Caterham cars was called on to help out and to mock-up a second car. Graham Nearn is actually the driver who screeches up to the kerb in the opening titles.

The Prisoner returned to prominence with the 1984 launch of Channel 4 and its first British rerun. This provided enough momentum for Caterham to capitalise on the link, with a *Prisoner* special edition in authentic colours, after Nearn had tracked down McGoohan in the States and obtained his blessing.

The 1990 Motor Show saw the launch of a limited edition 'Prisoner' Caterham Seven in the appropriate green and yellow colour scheme; it is shown here at the celebrated Portmeirion village in Wales.

Pretty it isn't, but with a gullwing-doored hardtop from Fibrepair Ltd, a Seven became a coupé eligible for GT racing.

pinion design from the Morris Minor. The simple live rear axle came from the Austin/Nash Metropolitan. Brakes were now hydraulic rather than cable-operated as on the Six.

In basic tax-free kit form a 1957 Seven was £536, and basic meant basic. The Series 1 had no fuel gauge – you just took off the cap and used a dipstick in the tank, which was held in place with elastic straps. There were no doors and the rudimentary hood was optional; nor were there any indicators. Seats consisted of slabs of leathercloth-covered foam that were slotted directly into the untrimmed

Once Lotus had moved to its new factory at Hethel in 1966, the Seven would have been discarded but for the persistence of Graham Nearn of Caterham Cars, whose suggestions for the Series 3 shown here included the adoption of Ford Escort and Cortina engines.

floorpan, at least adding a dash of colour in their standard red. The windscreen was demountable and if you wanted wipers a motor could be fixed to the top of it. And of course the distinctive externally-mounted exhaust pipe was a trap for careless shins …

With a full racing programme occupying Team Lotus and with the troubled development of the Elite, the Seven did not have a roaring start, but all the same around 100 kits were sold during 1958, most of them for Ford engines. The range-topping 75bhp Climax-powered Seven was launched in 1958, at a considerably higher kit cost of £892. Called the Seven 'C' or Super Seven, it had wire wheels almost invariably and a leather-covered steering wheel. Deposits for the Seven were already paying the car's way as the development of the production Elite dragged on, and by the time of the 1960 Series 2, around 250 sales had been notched up – although Lotus

production figures should always be taken with a pinch of salt. So should specifications: kits may have been standard but few Sevens were the same, as owners could add or substitute parts while Lotus would of course oblige with tuning conversions.

Sales were soon subject to lulls. Robin Read, who joined as sales manager in 1959, recalled that sales of the Seven had slowed right down by that point, and he recommended that Lotus expand the way in which the car was sold, finding dedicated and enthusiastic dealers to handle the Seven and indeed the Elite. Production was made easier with the move to the first purpose-built Lotus premises at Cheshunt in 1959, but much of the Seven – such as the chassis – remained outsourced.

Read also says it was he who recommended that the engine choice be expanded beyond the antiquated Ford 100E sidevalve and costly Coventry Climax to include the 948cc BMC A-Series unit, a modern engine by then widely used in the Austin-Healey Sprite, Austin A35 and Morris Minor. It was also more familiar to American car enthusiasts, having proved its worth in the Sprite, and with the Elite

reducing Lotus to near-bankruptcy Chapman had to try harder to expand American sales. Thus the Seven America was rapidly conceived.

Self-assembly was irrelevant to an American buyer who having decided to go for a quirky foreign import in the first place would have no need to skimp on costs. To this end Lotus loaded the Seven America with a full range of options as standard: wire wheels, carpets, spare wheel, tonneau cover and even a chrome-plated silencer. It had proper windscreen wipers too, with a motor mounted under the scuttle.

The instant distinguishing feature of the Seven America was its front wings in glassfibre, created by Elite designers Peter Kirwan-Taylor and John Frayling. Sweeping further along the car to meet the door, these gave some measure of protection from rain and road debris. The design first became an option on the Super Seven, eventually becoming standard on the Series 2 and being carried through to the Caterham.

Meanwhile, work was in hand to re-design the Seven, more because sales were yielding so little profit than because of any major faults.

Throughout its Lotus career, the Seven was very price-sensitive and sales could always be encouraged with a spec change or price cut. The Series 2 was a thorough rethink of the formula to increase profit.

The spaceframe chassis was simplified to try to take some of the labour out of it: in particular the distinctive diagonal tubes that ran through the engine bay disappeared. This cheese-paring led to failures later, especially when cars were fitted with more powerful engines, but indulgent owners became used to having to make their own strengthening modifications.

Looking around to replace the BMC rear axle with something cheaper Lotus settled on an item from the Standard 10 Companion estate car. This went out of production in 1961 but the practice of buying in near-obsolete components was not a great problem as manufacturers were committed to making spares available for at least ten years after a given model went out of production. However, the poor little Standard axle was never built to have Climax engines attached to it and unsurprisingly caused trouble in service.

Similar attention was paid to the suspension system, with an eye to bringing costs down, and some ingenious Lotus doubling-up was employed, such as using the rear-axle drain plug as one of the suspension mounting points. This was soon abandoned, as the plug would work loose under repeated on-off application of the throttle. The rear

suspension was certainly better located, with a full 'A' frame being used, and the steering rack, now a Triumph Herald part, was moved ahead of the front axle as opposed to behind it, allowing the angle of the steering column to be changed and space around the pedals improved. It wasn't all ruthless cost-cutting. In Seven history small things count and the Series 2 was the first to see a pair of sidescreen 'doors' that kept most of the weather out. You also got a hood as standard and the petrol tank lost its elastic straps in favour of steel ones.

Instead of the hand-beaten Williams & Pritchard aluminium nose cone, a glassfibre one was used. The clamshell wings of the America soon became standard and were available in self-coloured red, yellow, blue or green, which combined with the nose cone made even an unpainted Seven a colourful sight.

The Series 2 was offered with a much broader range of engines. From 1961 the free-revving 105E Anglia unit became the base unit. This was joined by a choice of 948cc or latterly 1098cc A-Series engines. The Climax engine option was dropped, which was no great loss as it was such a costly choice and would also not fit the new engine mounting points. In 1961 the arrival of the Super Seven added a Cosworth-tuned Ford Classic 1340cc engine to the mix. With 83bhp in 1025lbs (465kgs) of car, the power-to-weight ratio was 200bhp per ton and the Super Seven would hurtle to 60mph in under nine seconds. In

component form the 1961 Super Seven cost £599 but if you supplied your own engine a Seven kit could be yours for only £399, a price which gave sales a healthy lift. As further Ford engines became available so the Seven came to adopt the Cortina's 1498cc unit, which in Cosworth form pushed power to 95bhp. Lotus stopped short, however, of offering the Elan's twin-cam in the Seven.

During 1959 and 1960 the first real Lotus dealers were set up in the UK, to sell the Seven and push the Elite. Called Lotus Centres, they were largely existing customers with a strong enthusiasm for the brand and some business acumen. One of these was Graham Nearn's Caterham Car Sales in Surrey, which was later to play a key role in rescuing the Seven from extinction before buying the design rights in May 1973.

However, factory sales of both cars continued, with a demonstrator Seven and Elite kept at the Lotus works for demonstrations on a particular combination of local roads. This undercutting became a source of friction between the Lotus Centres and their supplier. Many fell by the wayside but Graham Nearn bought the name of Caterham and developed a strong reputation as a Seven guru.

After saying it couldn't be done, Lotus squeezed in a twin-cam and created the SS for the 1969 London Motor Show – and thus for the final year of the Series 3. Only around 13 are thought to have been built.

The Lotus 51R

A Lotus with even fewer creature comforts than a Seven? A road-legal racing car? Try the Lotus 51R, a bizarre racer with mudguards, lights, and little else.

In 1967 a new British junior racing formula was created, called Formula Ford, and Lotus won the initial contract to build the first 25 cars. Ever with an eye to a publicity stunt, sales supremo Graham Arnold concocted the idea of a roadgoing version.

Thus this strange little beast appeared at the Racing Car Show, complete with a 'flower power' paint scheme. With a 1500cc Ford Cortina engine it had an ambitious £1085 price-tag in kit form and Lotus Components announced it would build replicas, although it was said not to be very keen to carry out this promise as the Type 51 was difficult to build.

Shorn of its flowers, 'NVF 1F' was eventually loaned to the press. In

December 1967 Autocar tested it at a frightening 103mph and observed that once over 90mph the front wings stopped flapping and trying to lift the front wheels. After being frozen, shaken and then stranded by the 51R when the battery gave up, the writer concluded that it probably was a joke. Nonetheless, a single order

The bizarre 51R appeared in 1967, complete with a 'flower power' paint scheme. A road-legal Formula Ford racer, most people thought it a joke, apart from the individual who dipped into his pocket to buy the car.

was received from the US, allegedly from a friend of Henry Ford, and the car still survives.

As the whirlwind development of the Elan, Lotus-Cortina, Elan Plus 2 and Europa occupied much of the 1960s, the Seven was left to its own devices, with no real development, but buoyed up all the same by the magic of Lotus racing successes and by unsolicited TV attention from its appearance in *The Prisoner*. Kits were built by Lotus Components on the upper floor of one of the buildings at the Cheshunt factory while downstairs concentrated on single-seat racing models.

Lotus Components was initially handed the Europa project with the idea that this would be the new Seven, but the design shifted direction into something more sophisticated and it became a production-line model. Meanwhile, Colin Chapman had long ceased to be interested in the Seven. "I never had one for personal transportation and I didn't have anything to do with the car after its production began other than to approve and test drive the newer versions," he later confessed. "I really enjoyed the Seven in the early days …

I'm surprised it's still going."

A seemingly final point came in late 1966 with the wholesale move of Lotus to the modern new facility at Hethel in Norfolk. Lotus Components went too, but sales manager Graham Arnold – who had joined in 1963 – told Graham Nearn of Caterham that this time the Seven wasn't coming with it, and for several months after the move to Hethel no Sevens were built. However, Nearn put in an order for 20 cars which was enough to justify restarting production. In 1967 he went further, and persuaded Chapman to allow him sole distributorship, as he had built up such a well of experience of the little car and its idiosyncracies. This was agreed without protest, as other dealers were happy to get on with the job of selling Elans.

There would have been no Series 3 Seven without Caterham. In 1968, mindful that the car and his livelihood hung by a thread, Graham Nearn suggested a specification update including the use of the current crossflow Ford Cortina engine and

the manufacture of a limited edition, and both these propositions were taken up. For his efforts, Nearn got to launch the car himself at a local pub, where he was besieged by excited enthusiasts.

Having lost the Europa, Lotus Components was relying on the new Type 51 Formula Ford to keep going, and the S3 was seen as a quick fix, a stop-gap car until the company could pick itself up and respond with a genuinely new Seven. Boss Mike Warner started by looking at an S2 to try to reduce its cost of manufacture as a self-assembly package. As might have been expected, the S2's highest cost was the chassis – its labour-intensive manufacture had been obvious a decade earlier. The Elan chassis was now much cheaper to manufacture but a new Seven with an Elan chassis was considered a blind alley because the Elan itself by then had a limited lifespan ahead of it.

The S2 chassis wasn't ideal but there was no time to redesign it, so the first Series 3 chassis was nearly

The Caterham

The classic Caterham shape is that of the Lotus Seven Series 3 but Caterham by no means rejected the S4 they inherited out of hand: industrial strife put paid to it in mid-1974 after 38 had been built. "When supplies for essential components from the Midlands became erratic, that was it," Graham Nearn recalls. "We decided to introduce our own updated S3 because of continued demand for S3s and the fact that the S4 was more of a production-line car. Here in Caterham, it was very much like the old Hornsey days so a return to the S3 style of Seven, which most people preferred to the S4 anyway, seemed the way to go."

So Caterham has continued, followed by a worldwide string of Seven look-alikes yet always being seen as closest to the Lotus ideal. It is a testament to the simple effectiveness of the design that it can still sell in hundreds every year with just detail changes. As the motor industry has changed its products, so Sevens have gained fuel injection, catalysts, six-speed gearboxes, and better brakes and tyres. Within the limitations of the design, safety has been improved by an aluminium honeycomb side-impact structure and a standard rollbar. Marketing has also capitalised on the cult following of the Seven, helped by celebrity owners such as musician Chris Rea, while motorsport support has remained a key part of business.

When the twin-cam faded away, Ford continued to be the mainstay for engines, followed by Vauxhall's 2-litre twin-cam and then the Rover K-Series (also found in the Elise) from 1990. In common with its rivals, Caterham has dabbled with the installation of motorbike engines, and conversions are possible. While the rebodied Caterham 21 proved to be a stalling point, Caterham has re-engineered the Seven to create the wide-bodied SV option. You can still opt to build

your own Seven, too, or add your parts to starter kits.

In 2005, and after 45 years of owning Caterham Cars, Graham Nearn sold the business to a private equity company headed by an ex-Lotus managing director, Ansar Ali. Although Rover's collapse put the K-Series engine in doubt, it still formed the bedrock of the four-model Caterham range up until late 2006 when cars reverted to Ford 1.6-litre engines of 125bhp or 140bhp, with the whole range topped by the £31,000 factory-build-only CSR200/240, available with a Ford/Cosworth engine of 200bhp or 240bhp and having a claimed 140mph top speed and 0–60mph time of 3.7 seconds.

Caterham Classic to the left, Lotus Seven S1 to the right. The Caterham Seven dates back to 1973 when the company bought the rights to produce and refine the Seven in Britain. It built the S4 until a lack of components brought a return of the S3 and the classic Seven shape.

While it looks the same from a distance, the CSR is claimed to be 85 per cent new and marks a decisive move away from the Chapman design. The suspension, developed by ex-Lotus race driver John Miles (the man who made the M100 Elan work), is now fully independent at the rear, using wishbones, and a new design of F1-inspired pushrod suspension at the front takes the struts within the nosecone, to help aerodynamics.

In 2005 Caterham changed owners for the first time but the car still looked essentially the same and was still an extraordinary performer by modern standards. This CSR model, however, has a wider body, as well as a new suspension system and a Cosworth engine.

Right: In its short three-year career, almost 600 S4s were sold. With its self-coloured bodyshell and bigger cabin, it was aimed at a new kind of market, away from the club racers and hoping to capitalise on the Californian beach-buggy craze that had by then reached the UK.

Below: Bodied entirely in glassfibre, the controversial Seven Series 4 was an attempt to attract buyers of Triumphs and MGs by offering improved weather protection and sliding windows.

Seven down under

Caterham did not get an exclusive deal from Lotus – but its competition was on the other side of the world. As the end of Seven production neared, Steel Brothers Ltd, based in Christchurch, in New Zealand, bought two sets of jigs and moulds with a view to having a go at their own Seven, under licence. As they were more used to making heavy earth-moving equipment it was a bizarre idea, but one conceived to get around import duties in New Zealand and Australia.

The company moved from assembling kits to building cars when Lotus production ended. The design was beefed up to cope with the tougher driving conditions, with a heavier strengthened chassis, reinforced suspension points and slight bodywork changes. After a slow production run for the first couple of years, supplies of the twin-cam became difficult so the company looked to the new 16-valve '907' 2-litre. A prototype was built to accept the new engine and five-speed gearbox but production was stopped by safety regulations. Around 100 Steel Brothers Sevens are thought to have been built.

The Caterham 21 – a smoother Seven

In 1995 the respective fortunes of Lotus and Caterham were such that it was even rumoured Caterham might have made a bid for Lotus. Instead, just ahead of the Elise, Caterham was bold enough to produce its very own lightweight sports car with just a few more creature comforts, the 21.

Although initial thoughts were for a mid-engined car, it was felt the safest route would be to re-work the Seven chassis and clothe it with as attractive a shape as possible. The cockpit sides of the spaceframe were modified to give better passenger space and the engine moved back far enough behind the front axle to provide almost the same balance as a mid-mounted engine, or so Caterham claimed. Side-impact protection was improved, and to brace the engine bay two extra tubes were added, running from under the scuttle to points above the front wheels. These tubes were removable for servicing.

The attractive shape was developed in-house by Iain Robertson who was on the Caterham sales team but who was also a graduate of the Royal College of Art's industrial design course. At the rear the decent-sized boot was shaped around tail lights from the Ford Mondeo and there were definite shades of the Elise about the twin bonnet scoops. Commentators observed that there was something of the feel of a Lotus Eleven, too. Leather seats were offered but apart from doors there were not many more creature comforts, and the door glass had to be removed rather than wound down.

In 1994, the 21st anniversary of the Caterham Seven, the 21 was unveiled – with the hope it would be ready for sale the following summer. However, development of the glassfibre bodyshell took longer than anticipated and production cars were not ready for sale until spring 1996. The production 21 mirrored the Seven in its engines, with the 113bhp 1.6 K-series at £19,495 and the 136bhp 1.8 K-series Supersport at £22,995; a K-series V6 was mooted as an option for a later date. However, even at those prices both 21s were still 'amateur build', requiring a claimed 50 hours of work, or factory-built for an extra £2500. At the time Caterham was selling around 600 Seven kits a year for the UK market and it geared up to produce 100 of the newcomer each year.

Caterham had aimed for a target weight of 600kg (11.7cwt) and in production the 21 Supersport weighed 648kg compared to the first Elise's 678kg, with a claimed 5.8sec to 60mph for the Supersport. But while it looked different, testers found

In an attempt to make a car that was truly its own, Caterham unveiled the 21 in 1994, to mark 21 years of Seven production. Although attractive, it found few takers, being outshone by the Elise by the time it reached the market.

that the 21 retained many of the Seven's habits, being just as twitchy and bumpy to drive on its largely unchanged suspension. This seemed at odds with trying to attract new customers.

More crucially, by 1996 the UK was awash with soft-top sports cars. The MGF, Alfa Spider and BMW Z3 might not have been direct rivals, but the Elise was a deadly competitor. By the time the 21 was production-ready the Elise had gathered unstoppable momentum. The 1996 Elise range started at under £20,000 ready-made and by the middle of the year Lotus had already sold the first year's production and set its sights on an annual run of 2500 thereafter. In the end, just 50 Caterham 21s were produced, perhaps proving yet again that if somebody wants a Seven, they want a Seven – all or nothing.

identical. The Seven had long since ceased to be competitive in racing but some parts were strengthened to take the extra stress of larger engines and occasional sporting use. Occupants' ankles gained a little more protection, thanks to a redesigned exhaust with a shroud, the system now curving round

under the axle to exit at the rear. The old Standard Ten axle was at last pensioned off in favour of that of the new Ford Escort. Front disc brakes became standard, too, as did seatbelt mounting points, and the dashboard gained a minor reorganisation of switches while there were carpets for

the first time on a UK Seven.

Engine choices were initially all Ford, starting with the Escort GT's 1298cc 68bhp unit and progressing to the 1599cc Cortina engine rated at 84bhp. Both were offered in standard Ford tune with Ford gearboxes. There was no Super Seven as such but

Driving a Lotus/Caterham Seven

Unless the rain is hurling down, putting the hood up on a Seven is not the done thing. Instead you just fold the sidescreens forward and up, grab a side panel and throw yourself in and down into the footwell. Then you reach forward, grab the sidescreen (if it's being used) and shut it with a pop fastener.

Then there's that view through the tiny windscreen, served by equally tiny wipers. A sweep of bonnet capped off by two shiny headlamps pointing towards fun. If you're in a later Caterham a fuel-injected engine will most likely start on the key and burble away but the horizontally-disposed handbrake on all but the most recent cars will remain tucked under the passenger side of the dash.

There's no cabin storage space at all, although the handbook may be strapped to the footwell.

All the controls seem miniaturised: a chunky wheel no bigger than a dinner plate, pedals which demand small feet or racing boots, and a gearchange that's more of a stump than a lever. Few of the switches on the dash are labelled and a number look the same: there are no steering-column stalks and the indicator toggle-switch flicks left or right without self-cancelling.

The car responds immediately to every input without being jumpy, steering where you point it; if the back end is going to swing out in a tight bend or roundabout, you'll know when, and a small correction will resettle the car on its course. The ride is firm on rigid-axle cars but surprisingly supple in de Dion models and there is no discernible body roll. A heavy right foot will waggle you away from a loose surface if you're feeling exuberant. Noisy? Sure, but in the best kind of way. For all that, it needn't be frenetic. For example the 2-litre Vauxhall unit is very flexible and most modern Caterhams have five-speed or even six-speed gearboxes.

The Seven is the nearest you'll get to a grown-up go-kart. Wrapped up warm, there's nothing like a quick blast in a Seven to put a smile on your face. It's small wonder that many owners can't bear to be parted from their car.

tuners Holbay (better known to British buyers for their H120 Hillman and Sunbeam engines) offered a range of options. More as a crowd-stopper than anything else, for the 1969 Racing Car Show a Seven S was displayed with a 120bhp Holbay-tuned engine under its bonnet. The car was luxuriously trimmed, with chromed suspension parts, wool carpets, ivory-coloured leather seats, and even a radio. Dubbed the 'ultimate Seven' by the press, several would-be buyers were not put off by its alarming £1600 fully-assembled-only price tag, but in the end the 'S' remained a one-off.

Although it was to be short-lived as a Lotus, the Series 3 left with a rousing finale later the same year. After saying it couldn't be done, Lotus squeezed in a twin-cam and created the SS. With a great dollop of extra power and with customer Sevens suffering chassis failures, some effort was at last expended to beef up the chassis tubes of the SS, and the side panels were made in steel despite the resultant extra weight. Only around 13 of the SS are thought to have been built.

The Series 4 is the plastic one. The one Seven people throw their hands up in the air about, the horrid square one, the car that Caterham opted to side-step in favour of making its predecessor instead. Well, so the story goes. But in its short career almost 600 S4s were sold: over twice as many as in the first two years of the Series 1. The S4 was aimed at a new kind of market, away from the club-racing scene. The Californian beach-buggy craze had hit the UK by the end of 1960s, sufficiently so for establishment magazine *Motor* to put together a test of eight different Kings Road cruisers in 1970. Plastic-bodied cars with minimal weather protection were suddenly the 'in' thing. Against this background, the idea was that the new Seven would be just user-friendly enough to pull in people new to the brand, who would then graduate to more expensive cars.

The S4, or Lotus Type 60, was designed by Peter Lucas and styled in-house by Alan Barrett in under a year, once given the green light in March 1969. One of the many Lotus legends is that the whole project was carried out behind Chapman's back. But Barrett, interviewed in 1983, said that Chapman would always keep an eye on Lotus Components and had seen quarter-scale models.

The body was glassfibre, produced on site, and dropped onto the chassis. Once bolted down, the shell contributed to the overall stiffness of the car. It was self-coloured and only consisted of two major parts – the outer shell with the rear wings and an inner one comprising the passenger compartment and scuttle. Sweeping flared wings (with built in indicators on later cars) were then bolted on and the bonnet was a massive one-piece structure that tipped forward to offer unprecedented engine access. The seat recesses were moulded in, as was the transmission tunnel. Given that that Triumph and MG owners might just be tempted into an S4, weather protection received a thorough rethink with a top designed by Weathershields and sidescreens with sliding Perspex windows.

The chassis was a much simplified spaceframe, using square and round tubing but more as a conventional ladder chassis. The job went to Arch Motors, with another company standing by in case they were overloaded with the higher volumes expected of the S4. There was no stressed undertray and the sides were panelled in sheet steel instead of alloy, following the example of the SS.

Mechanically, the S4 raided the Lotus parts bin. The front suspension was based on that of the Europa, with pressed steel wishbones but no anti-roll bar. The rear end was substantially different from an S3 in its method of location, being designed to put less strain on the axle. The Escort axle was retained and each end was secured by both a leading and trailing arm (otherwise known as a Watt linkage), with lateral movement controlled by a triangulated arm on one side.

Engines, carried over from the S3, were the 1300 or 1600 Fords with optional Holbay tuning and at the top of the tree the Lotus twin-cam, optionally Holbay-tuned. Launched in spring 1970, the Seven S4 received a favourable press and initial output was 15 kits a week, well above the average

1960s rate of Seven production, when fewer than ten cars were being put together weekly. Six additional dealers were signed up because of this additional volume, and Caterham Cars lost its sole distributorship.

In 1970 a Seven S4 kit cost £945 when an Elan was £1498. Perhaps, with hindsight, the S4 landed in the middle of two markets. It was far more sophisticated than any beach buggy, but a fully-built buggy came in at around £500. On the other hand, a Triumph Spitfire cost £875 tax-paid and although slower and lacking Lotus handling, was more refined and easier to run. Nonetheless all went well for a time. "Contrary to what many people think, the S4 sold very well. It came along at the close of the 'You've Never Had it so Good' sixties boom and as an everyday car it was a great deal more practical than the S3," Graham Nearn recalled in the 1980s.

However, as early as 1971 the writing

was on the wall for the Lotus Seven, with the prospect of Value Added Tax (VAT) replacing purchase tax. VAT was one requirement of the UK joining the EEC in 1973. The principle of VAT is that tax is paid on all goods (with certain exemptions) at the point of purchase. So the collection of parts that made up a Lotus kit would be taxed in the same way. There would thus be scant saving to be made by carrying out your own assembly. Also, the kit-car image really didn't fit, with the new Elite waiting in the wings. When Mike Warner left Lotus Components in 1971, Chapman wound down Seven production. However, he gave Graham Nearn ample warning and after S4 manufacture had ended in October 1972, the Caterham deal was struck and the Seven moved on to a more secure future than it had ever enjoyed with a Lotus badge on its nose.

Buying Hints

1. Lotus Sevens are now rarely on the market and original Series 1 or Series 2 cars are highly prized by collectors. The S4 is still relatively cheap, even fully restored, but is an acquired taste. Caterhams are plentiful and offer an improved driving/ownership experience.

2. A lot of Sevens were customised during the '70s but now an original spec is desirable. That means the original engine or a correct replacement, and the appropriate wheels, dashboard covering and seating. Steel wheels and hubcaps are required wear on early Sevens.

3. Most Lotus and certainly at least some early Caterham Sevens will be running with a replacement chassis by now, as a result of accident damage or corrosion. Check for rust on the chassis tubes towards the rear, although

this may only be on the surface, where the powder-coating has cracked. Chassis failure around the differential is also possible.

4. If badly neglected, the front suspension can fail through lack of lubrication, but this is rare. Look for evidence of poor welding, such as messy joints, as a clue to possible accident damage.

5. Plastic windows on hoods can discolour with time but new hoods are easily available. Panelling is aluminium and so doesn't rot, but side-panel replacement is not straightforward. Nosecones are glassfibre and readily replaceable: a parking-space bump can lead to unsightly cracks.

6. Nearly all Caterhams have rollbars, so that doesn't necessarily mean they've ever been near the track. If you want a road car avoid

Sevens which have been raced. With track use back axles can get starved of oil and wear prematurely. A noisy axle can be a clue to an ex-racer, as can extra stickers, holes drilled into the bodywork and even gravel in the footwells from an excursion into a circuit gravel-trap!

7. Most later Caterham Sevens have the superior de Dion back axle but don't assume this is the case. A good car should brake and run in a straight line, regardless of what axle is fitted.

8. The Vauxhall and Rover engines in later Caterham Sevens are considered modern and smooth units, and will start easily after being left for long periods. However, the 1.6 and 1.8 K-Series have a reputation for head-gasket failure, even at low mileages. Caterhams are simple cars and can be serviced by any competent garage. Club membership is strongly advised.

The *Elite*

It proved to be over-ambitious for the early days of Lotus, but the Elite's beauty was never in dispute. Parts such as the front bumper were custom made – a practice which was not to be followed on subsequent models.

In 1956 the Fédération Internationale de l'Automobile (FIA) created a new international racing class for Grand Touring cars of up to 1300cc engine capacity. Colin Chapman saw an opportunity for a race and road car to finance the long-term future of the company, the racing team and his own fortune. It was a decision that spawned one of the world's most beautiful cars and nearly brought the runaway success of Lotus to a premature end.

The Elite's specification was exotic from the start, when Chapman determined that its entire structure would be made of the relatively new material of glassfibre, more accurately referred to as glassfibre-reinforced plastic (grp). What we're talking of here is a matting made of fine strands of glass that is laid up layer after layer into plastic resin, in a mould. In 1956 most manufacturers had only just started making steel-bodied monocoques and it was thought that a grp car without a chassis would just break up under stress. However, Chapman was said to have seen the tiny 322cc Berkeley sports car at the 1956 Motor Show, noted its all-plastic construction, and wondered how it could be applied to a more powerful car.

In making a glassfibre monocoque, Chapman set himself a huge

Peter Kirwan-Taylor's initial sketches for what was to become the Elite included modest tailfins, but input by Peter Cambridge and Frank Costin's adoption of a more aerodynamically efficient Kamm tail meant a simpler design entered production.

challenge. But it was the only material which met his engineering and manufacturing needs. The spaceframe construction of previous Lotus racers was too labour-intensive and couldn't accommodate the correct door, bonnet and boot openings of a conventional sports car. As Chapman wanted his own design of suspension, building on top of an existing chassis was also out. He thus gave himself a thorough education in engineering with glassfibre, taking college courses and doing his own stress calculations in order to work out how to build an all-in monocoque plastic shell.

These first thoughts coincided with Chapman's friendship with London-based accountant/financier Peter Kirwan-Taylor. A keen racing enthusiast with a penchant for styling his own sports cars, Kirwan-Taylor had a Lotus Six chassis bodied to his own design, and later approached Lotus with the idea of a car on an Eleven chassis. Chapman admired the lines of Kirwan-Taylor's Six and asked him to work on the new project in his spare time. To arrive at the first clear concept, months of sketches and trips to motor shows followed: like so many at that time, Kirwan-Taylor was prepared to work for Lotus for the love of it while maintaining his day job. It is also believed that as a fluent French speaker he suggested the name Elite, starting the long tradition of Lotus 'E'

The glassfibre shell of the 1957 Motor Show Elite (seen here at the workshop in Edmonton) was made up of over 50 separate panels and it was a gruelling task to simplify the process of building the production cars.

Lotus Elite
1957–64

ENGINE:
Four cylinders in line (Coventry Climax), aluminium block and cylinder head, water-cooled

Capacity	1216cc
Bore x stroke	76.2mm x 66.7mm
Valve actuation	Single overhead cam
Compression ratio	10.0:1
Carburettor	Single SU
Power	75bhp at 6100rpm
Maximum torque	77lb ft at 3750rpm

TRANSMISSION:
Rear-wheel drive, four-speed gearbox (MG or ZF)

SUSPENSION:
Front: Independent by coil springs and twin wishbones; telescopic dampers; anti-roll bar
Rear: Independent by Chapman struts, location by radius arms (lower wishbones on S2); fixed-length driveshafts; telescopic dampers

STEERING:
Rack-and-pinion

BRAKES:
Front: Disc
Rear: Disc, inboard

WHEELS/TYRES:
15in wire wheels
Tyres 4.80 x 15in crossply

BODYWORK:
Glassfibre-reinforced plastic monocoque with partial steel strengthening
Two-door coupé

DIMENSIONS:

Length	12ft 4in
Wheelbase	7ft 4.5in
Track, front	3ft 11in
Track, rear	4ft 0.25in
Width	4ft 11in
Height	3ft 10in

KERB WEIGHT:
13.25cwt

PERFORMANCE:
(Source: *The Motor*)

Max speed	113mph
0–60mph	11.4sec
30–50mph in top	10.1sec
50–70mph in top	10.8sec

PRICE INCLUDING TAX WHEN NEW:
£1966 (1960)

NUMBER BUILT:
1078

Viewed from the rear three-quarter position the smooth lines – with only the thinnest of guttering around the side windows – are clearly apparent. The neat door handles come from the Hillman Husky.

names – the Lotus Type 14, as the Elite was numbered in Lotus's model sequence, having at first been given the name 'Electra'.

Chapman's requirements for an advanced, lightweight engine ruled out mass-produced items from the mainstream manufacturers and he turned to racing-engine makers Coventry Climax, whose units Lotus had been using since 1955. He persuaded Climax chairman Leonard Lee that the company should design a unit specifically for the Elite. Derived from the 1098cc FWA and 1460cc FWB racing units, the single-overhead-cam FWE – for 'Feather Weight Elite' – had its capacity reduced to 1216cc and was adapted to make it more tractable for road use; canted over slightly to one side, the engine's modest height had a major influence on the Elite's final profile. Both cylinder block and head were cast in aluminium, as was the case with the Porsches at which the Elite was aimed, and this became one of the main factors contributing to

the high price tag. Climax was contracted to supply 1000 FWEs.

If the output of 75bhp at 6100rpm looked small on paper, that was discounting the low weight of both engine and bodyshell. In any case, with its racing pedigree, those who wanted knew they could easily tune the FWE; Lotus later coaxed it up to 105bhp. These factors also gave the Elite fuel economy of up to 40mpg, which is still impressive by modern standards. Initially, the Climax engine was coupled to a sturdy but unsophisticated four-speed gearbox from the MGA.

Suspension specifications were similarly exacting, drawing on years of racing expertise. Based on that of the Lotus Twelve and the Eleven Series 2, each wheel was independently sprung with its own coil-spring-and-damper unit. The front used twin wishbones based on the Type 12 design and the rear suspension had a distinctly Lotus configuration, soon known as the 'Chapman strut'. In this the rear driveshafts terminated in aluminium hub carriers supporting the coil spring and its concentric telescopic damper, lateral location being by two kinked radius arms. The struts were tall enough to protrude into the cabin behind the seats, thereby becoming a

feature of the Elite interior – and one that was responsible for some of the in-cabin noise that became the car's trademark. As per racing practice, both front and rear brakes were discs, at the rear mounted inboard next to the final drive.

Chapman was keen that the Elite make its debut at the June 1957 Le Mans race in order to garner enough publicity to start orders flowing. Engineering the Elite prototype in such a short timescale was a major undertaking for the small company. Consequently the whole project was managed independently of the racing cars, in a measure of secrecy, work being confided to a dedicated group of newcomers.

In November 1956, with Kirwan-Taylor already a major influence, the team that was to make the Elite a reality first met Chapman under the guise of a casual Saturday-morning trip to the works. South African Ron Hickman was employed at Dagenham by Ford subsidiary Briggs Motor Bodies, but had reported on the Earls Court motor shows for a newspaper back home. At the show he met Alfred Woolf, a PR contact with Lotus who suggested he give his opinion on the sports car project. Hickman then enlisted fellow

Ford designers Peter Cambridge and John Frayling for the visit.

Hickman subsequently had to return to South Africa for some time, leaving Frayling and Cambridge to work on the initial clay model at evenings and weekends while they continued to work for Ford – Cambridge having obtained his bosses' blessing soon after the first meeting. Of the trio, Frayling was first to join Lotus full-time in early 1957, followed by Hickman.

But although Chapman offered Cambridge more work, he opted to go into aircraft interior design – only to return the next decade on a freelance contract to assist with the Elan +2 and Europa.

Frayling worked largely on his own, by eye, with tremendous accuracy, turning the sketches into a fifth-scale model, and soon the final Elite shape began to emerge. Peter Cambridge worked through a number of designs

for the dashboard and interior until he arrived at a dashboard shape which echoed the side view of the Elite.

Then came aerodynamisist Frank Costin's input, most recently used to great effect on the Eleven. Often advising on modifications to early scale models by having photographs sent to him, Costin made minor adjustments which Frayling then interpreted on the model. Much of the detail incorporated racing practice,

Coventry Climax – the racing fire-pump

Lotus and Coventry Climax became inextricably linked in the 1950s and 1960s. Climax seemed to come from nowhere to become one of the world's largest racing-engine manufacturers, and then faded away, all within barely ten years.

Coventry Climax had built some racing car engines pre-WW2, but in the 1939–45 conflict it won a substantial government contract to build fire-pump engines. This saw it through to the end of hostilities and it then expanded into forklift trucks. The 1951 FWP 'Feather Weight Pump' light-alloy engine was built for a British government arming for hostilities in Korea. The brief was for a 1020cc petrol-engined pump light enough to be carried by two men and able to deliver 350 gallons of water a minute and give 35bhp – while being able to rev to flat-out from cold with no damage. All these attributes made the little all-alloy units very attractive to motor-racers, as they were far more sophisticated than contemporary engines, and Climax started to attract interest from people who didn't want fire-pumps.

A return to racing engines was boosted by the 1950 arrival of Walter 'Wally' Hassan, who joined as chief engineer, having worked for Bentley at Le Mans and having later developed the Jaguar XK engine. Hassan recruited Harry Mundy from BRM, as chief designer – Mundy subsequently becoming a key

figure in the development of the Lotus-Ford twin-cam.

In 1953 Climax launched two engines for racing, a 2.5-litre 'big four' and a 1098cc unit based on the FWP pump, the 'Feather Weight Automobile' or FWA. Racers took eagerly to the lightweight and zippy FWA, which was first used by Lotus in the 1955 MkIX. The racing-engine business thrived and various versions of the FW were created for motor sport, the engine being used in Lotus racers up to and including the 19, and as a high-cost option for the Seven.

Yet as quickly as Climax had entered motor racing, it was gone. At the 1962 Motor Show Lee announced that his company was withdrawing from racing because although

demand for the engines was high it was not profitable to keep up to 40 engineers working on the engines, at the prices Coventry Climax was charging. Alarmed, racing constructors banded together and agreed to pay more for their engines – a new V8 engine for the 1963 season cost £5000 – but the writing was on the wall. Jaguar took over Climax in 1963 and pulled it out of racing in 1965.

The 1216cc Coventry Climax FWE was tailor-made for the Elite, and if the output of 75bhp at 6100rpm looked small on paper, that was discounting the low weight of both engine and bodyshell. Readily tuned, Lotus later coaxed it up to 105bhp. Its downfall was excessive oil consumption.

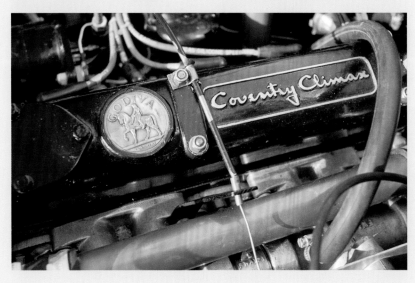

such as a near-smooth underside with recesses for the exhaust system, propshaft and final drive and with the engine virtually enclosed from below, save for an aperture for the sump. Costin insisted that the side windows be flush with the bodywork and the shape of the doors ruled out winding windows, so they were made in detachable Plexiglas. There were many adjustments, small or otherwise, made to arrive at the final dimensions. For example, Frayling was impressed by the roofline of the Volkswagen Karmann-Ghia and asked for the roof to be moved forward several inches, which allowed a boot lid to be

Below: In no way more than a two-seater, the Elite's design allows room for luggage behind the seats as well as in the boot. Note the prominent cones for the 'Chapman strut' rear suspension and the moulding to cover the spare wheel.

incorporated in the design.

Around the time of the Elite's development the Kamm tail, where the bodywork flows back and is then cut off square for ultimate air flow, was gaining favour in the racing world. Costin initially proposed that the Elite should fully follow the Kamm principle. But in the end there was a compromise, with a degree of cut-off giving a flat tail panel at the same time as the luggage capacity required of a grand tourer. All this was done by calculation. The sheer talent of the team in shaping the body was stunning: the Elite was not subject to a wind-tunnel test until 1962, when it was revealed to have a drag coefficient of 0.37, and when *Autocar* tested an Elite in 1982 it arrived at a 0.29 figure.

The full-sized model for the first set of moulds was made in spare premises owned by Lotus bodybuilders Williams

& Pritchard, where Frayling and a small team struggled to apply Plaster of Paris over a plywood former. They missed the target of June 1957, so Chapman aimed for a debut at October's Motor Show. He worked on the structure and box sections that were to be the other half of the first Elite moulding. To save the weight of a steel tank and for optimum weight distribution, the Elite's fuel tank was originally planned to be housed in one front wing, behind the wheelarch, but it proved impossible to seal the join and in the end a metal tank was fitted in the boot. The interior behind the seats was moulded to take the spare wheel, covered by a second moulding with a tray on top. Where needed, some parts were borrowed from other cars, Peter Cambridge leafing expertly through the Wilmot Breeden parts catalogue. But although the exterior door handles came from the Hillman Husky, the bumpers were bespoke stainless-steel items made to aero-industry standards by Miles Aircraft, a mistake not to be repeated.

By late August 1957 the first set of four moulds was ready. These made up the shell, and 56 to 60 further panels constituted the interior bulkheads. The frantic run-up to the Earls Court show that October has become the stuff of legend. Paint was still drying on the car the night before opening when Chapman broke the only windscreen and a replacement had to be sourced from the glazier; then the correct Coventry Climax engine arrived too late so an Eleven engine was used. The show Elite was no more a runner than today's concept cars, but

Far left: The Elite's cabin was as carefully considered as its exterior. Chapman was determined that it should have an Italian-style wood-rimmed steering wheel, while the layout of the instrument binnacle reflects Peter Cambridge's desire for good ergonomics.

Left: Winding windows were not possible due to the shape of the glasshouse, with its pronounced tumblehome, so owners had to unclip the Plexiglas windows and store them either in the boot or, on Series 2 cars, in pockets on the seat backs.

The Elite in competition

It may have looked like a continental tourer but the Elite was really a dressed-up racer and it excelled on the track right from that first win in the hands of Ian Walker in 1958, whether in the hands of private drivers or professional teams.

Two cars with unforgettable registration numbers spent 1961 sparring with each other. Graham Warner, owner of the Chequered Flag garage in West London and one of the early Lotus dealers, ran 'LOV 1' while accessory king Les Leston raced 'DAD 10', or 'daddy-o'. From 1959 future World Champion Jim Clark cut his teeth on Elites, as GT racing grew more popular in the UK, while in America the Lotus consistently out-classed cars with much larger engines.

A number of assaults were made on the Le Mans 24-hour race. The first Elite victory came in 1959, with a first-in-class and this was repeated every year until 1964, with other cars scoring high in the Index of Thermal Efficiency. Sir John Whitmore, later renowned as a Lotus-Cortina driver was in the 1959 team. "The Elite was a wonderful car, and I love it to this day," he recalls. "It really felt good to

drive, it was straightforward, and it did everything right."

With mechanics on hand, the Coventry Climax engine thrived, but going to a capacity of 2 litres proved to be a stretch too far; in 1960 a private commission for Le Mans saw an Elite fitted with a 180bhp 2-litre FPF Climax engine, but despite as wide a set of tyres as tyre technology would allow, even famous racing driver Innes Ireland refused to drive the car and it was eventually re-engined.

Two cars with unforgettable registration numbers spent 1961 sparring with each other: 'LOV 1' and 'DAD 10', or 'daddy-o', as pictured here.

When sales of the road-going car had ceased, and the Elan was beginning to be raced, Elites were still notching up significant victories and it was still competitive in the 1965 American Sebring 12-hour race, by which time Lotus had long given up actively supporting it.

finished in two-tone silver and gunmetal it looked sensational. This was only two years after Lotus had first appeared at Earls Court as an accessory manufacturer. The '57 show stand should also have seen the debut of the Seven, but in the haste to complete the Elite this was left unfinished at the works.

The Elite created massive interest on account of its looks and specification alone. Now Lotus had to make good on its promise, with rapid development of real cars. Chapman only allowed the ten pre-production cars to be used for racing, these having thinner panels to give them a performance advantage and to test how much stress the shells could be put through. Also, by enlisting trusted

drivers the cars could be hauled back to the factory and modified as they went. Its job done, the motor show car, meanwhile, was broken up.

The first Elite was delivered to garage-owner and racer Ian Walker in May 1958 and on the same day he took it to Silverstone and won the 1600cc class of the *Autosport* production-car race. The second went to John Lawry who also ran his car on the road. Interviewed later, he recalled it as being pretty shoddy, with the wheelbase shorter on one side than on the other.

Racing success meant orders were building at an embarrassing rate before the company had the means to move to the Cheshunt factory and expand as planned. The development

was frantic, with Ron Hickman joining full time in September 1958. "It was explained to me that Colin had been making promises for about a year," he recalls. "Everybody was placing orders, without dealers, or salesmen, or brochures."

With no space and no experience of glassfibre, Lotus entrusted bodyshell manufacture to Maximar, a firm of boatbuilders in Sussex. John Frayling was dispatched to work on-site developing the Elite moulds and production processes, and Maximar was contracted to provide what seemed like a modest 250 bodies. According to former sales manager Robin Read, the boatbuilders were, like many who worked with Lotus, pleased to have the glamorous association, but the Elite's woes started before the cars even reached their first customers.

Frayling had been inspired by the construction of Maximar's 505 racing yacht and decided that the internal structure of the Elite had to be double-skinned to conceal the evidence of glassfibre construction in the interior: this was a pleasing notion, but it added to weight and to construction costs. Chapman was reportedly furious, as he had intended the Elite to be single-skinned and to have the rough surfaces concealed by trim panels; subsequent Lotus cars reverted to single-skin construction. More fundamentally, metal reinforcement was added in a number of places, with a bonded-in hoop for the windscreen and a front suspension subframe.

Hickman worked hard to cut down the number of moulds for series production. But even when simplified, the build process was still time-consuming, with panels bonded together and held in a jig until they had cured. Fitting had to be done first as a dry-run and it was difficult to tell when sections were curing at different rates. Production began in October 1958 and bodyshells were delivered to Lotus painted and trimmed, to meet the mechanical components. The pace was painfully slow and production would yo-yo from month to month.

When the first production Elite was delivered in December 1958, the relationship between Maximar and Lotus was already deteriorating. The Sussex company had been knocked sideways by the stress of manufacturing the shells, and wanted to end its contract as soon as possible. It didn't help that Chapman had made it agree to a contract related to the weight of each shell: if they got too heavy, Maximar lost out, yet there was little it could do, as the shell thicknesses were so difficult to control.

Ron Hickman was instructed to find a new body-builder and approached a number of companies with marine, plastics or coachbuilding expertise, including the Bristol Aeroplane Company's plastics division. He spent a great deal of time assembling a sample car to a gruelling standard for Bristol to match. Part of the plastics division's winning pitch was that if there were problems they could draw on the expertise of the Bristol car company – and the link-up would be a good publicity coup for Chapman too.

Duly contracted in September 1959, Bristol was to supply 1000 shells at £200 each. It built new jigs, ironed out some of the problems, and 'Bristol' Elites began to supersede Maximar cars at the new Cheshunt factory from July 1960. This was an opportunity to re-launch the Elite as a Series 2, while at the same time trying to tackle some of the many faults experienced in service, and to enliven sales. However,

The Bates fastback

With no separate chassis, the Elite didn't appeal to coachbuilders – and who could have improved on the shape anyway? The most famous modified Elite was thus a skilfully home-built coupé, created in 1965 by RAF squadron leader Tony Bates.

After having rescued a tired 1963 car from a London dealer, Bates discovered it had suffered badly-repaired rear crash damage and when Lotus could not quickly supply replacement mouldings he embarked on an imaginative conversion.

Needing space to carry his young daughter in the back and having completed a course in the use of glassfibre, Bates designed a handsome fastback tail over several months, inspired by the Aston Martin DB5. Cutting the shell from the top of the rear screen, he fashioned a new shape on a plywood former. This had its own tailgate on rose-jointed struts made from helicopter parts, while inside a

custom-built fuel tank allowed the spare wheel to move rearwards so the child seat could be bolted to the top of the differential mounting.

Bates sold his unique Elite to make way for a Lotus-Cortina and it fell into neglect before being taken off the road in 1972. Discovered by UK Lotus enthusiast Malcolm Ricketts in

Tony Bates's unique fastback conversion of his Elite expertly blends a custom-made tailgate to a crash-damaged rear section.

1999, it has now been fully restored. Tony Bates went on to become a leading expert in the restoration of Elites, including designing a replacement shell.

The twin-cam Elite

The last Elite kits had been sold by January 1964 but there were still 40 leftover bodyshells and 'new' Elites continued to emerge for several years. The Climax contract exhausted, the obvious thing for Lotus to do – if it wanted to wring something more out of the Elite project – was to fit a twin-cam.

Chapman had the idea before the Elan went on sale and ordered Team Lotus to fit a twin-cam in an Elite shell to see how it worked. It didn't work very well, as the project was done in a rush and the engine fitted too far back in the chassis to give good handling.

However, in 1965 David Lazenby became manager of Lotus Components and persuaded Chapman to let him build his own company car: an Elite with a twin-cam. He also needed something to occupy his new workers. The Lazenby car was better conceived than the earlier effort, having specially-made engine and gearbox mountings, a dual-circuit braking system, a thicker front anti-roll bar, and uprated springs, while it sat lower than the original on its wire wheels. The interior was retrimmed

with Elan-style seats because the Elite items had run out.

Lazenby was confident enough to entrust the Elite Twin-Cam to *Car* magazine for a week in late 1967, and it ended up cover star of the January 1968 edition – although even for a prototype it was pretty rough-and-ready, initially missing its bumpers, having a non-functional handbrake, and suffering from an exhaust leaking into the cabin so badly that Lazenby was forced to drive with one window out. All the same, *Car* loved the way the prototype '1968 Elite' handled, but found it didn't feel even as fast as an Elan, while it was very noisy, and had a poor clutch. With a bit more

Apart from its period wing mirrors and a late-'60s registration plate, there is nothing to identify 'MPW 804E' as the twin-cam Elite loaned to Car *magazine in late 1967.*

sorting, though, the magazine confessed that the idea of a run of 'new' Elites was quite appealing.

A possible price was said to have been estimated as about £1500 fully-built, which would have made it little more than an Elan kit, and this with a six-month parts and labour guarantee. But the project – pie in the sky? – never went any further: the Elan and Europa were the future, and the Elite had long had its day.

changes could only be minimal as the big development money had been spent. It was already clear that the Elite was a dead end, and that effort should be concentrated on the Elan – or M2 – project. All the same, improving knowledge in plastics saw new moulded door panels complete with armrests, and new textures for the seats and the transmission-tunnel trim. Changing the rear radius arms for wishbones helped tackle an alarming tendency for rear-wheel steering if the suspension became worn, and spring rates were revised to give a more compliant ride, in conjunction with different tyre options. The handbrake was moved under the dashboard and the seat backs gained pockets for the windows, but as Chapman had

decreed that the bonnet stay open under its own balance (which it didn't), there were still no bonnet or boot struts and every Elite owner continued to carry their own piece of wood for that purpose!

Chapman had resisted letting the motoring press loose in Elites until he was confident of good results, so writers only got their hands on Bristol-built cars. *The Motor* tested one and observed that while at £1966 saving money wasn't an issue, fuel consumption of 29.5mpg at 100mph was astonishing. The design also drew praise for its detailing and style and the engine was found to be very potent for its modest 75bhp, giving a recorded maximum speed of 111mph. The magazine was fairly kind about

the noise, too, as although the engine bay had received sound-deadening material the interior still had 'various resonances' from engine, transmission and road. It concluded that the Elite was 'immensely desirable'.

With the Series 2, Lotus started to make the most of the tuning potential of the Climax engine. The Special Equipment or SE Elite of autumn 1960 boasted twin SU carburettors and a four-branch exhaust to give up to 85bhp. Stage 2 tuning boosted this to 90bhp and a German ZF four-speed gearbox replaced the BMC unit which had no synchromesh on bottom gear and had been regarded as a bit agricultural. All SE models had silver-painted roofs and a heater as standard. An Elite SE cost £2118,

Although it had been designed to be sold as a fully-built car, the Lotus Elite was offered in partial component form in late 1961. The saving was such that its flagging sales underwent a minor revival.

against the regular Elite's £2006.

But by now Elite owners' tales of woe were legendary and word had spread. Fit and finish problems persisted: differentials detached themselves from the shell, gearboxes whined, doors sagged, windscreens leaked, and trim fell off. But it was that fire-pump ancestry which gave the FWE engine its real reputation for unreliability. Because its fire-pump predecessor had been designed to go to maximum revs from cold, it had been produced with wide clearances so the whole engine would be flooded with a good supply of oil from start-up. Most engines of the 1950s needed topping up, but the Elite's thirst was excessive all the same, owners being advised to top up every 500 miles.

Coventry Climax's haughty response was that the engine needed very careful running-in and it gave the somewhat absurd instruction that owners continually speed up and slow down, even when driving on motorways. It made no difference. Sales manager Robin Read recalled that engine matters became even

worse as the relationship between Chapman and Coventry Climax chairman Leonard Lee deteriorated, with Lotus being slow to pay for engines and Chapman resentful of the deals other racing teams were being offered. Cheshunt suspected that the forklift division of Climax was assembling the Elite engines to lower standards, and consequently the majority had to be rebuilt before going out, adding to the numerous reasons why the Climax engine was not an option for the Elan.

Meantime a whole other drama was unfolding across the Atlantic. America, especially California, has always been a tempting market for Lotus. But the handling of Elite distribution nearly caused the company's financial ruin. Chapman gave exclusive distribution to racing driver Jay Chamberlain, who then created a demand for Elites that Lotus couldn't handle. When cars did arrive there were a host of sometimes bizarre problems such as body panels changing to a completely different colour if the cars had been left sitting in the sun before being sold. By the end of 1960 Lotus had managed to ship 300 Elites, but the car's US reputation was ruined and Chamberlain bankrupted.

As a last resort, from October 1961 the Elite was made available in Britain as a kit, even though it had

never been designed for self-build. Having said that, Lotus made sure just enough parts were left off to give the DIY builder something to do while still escaping purchase tax. Sales literature cheekily warned buyers not to resist 'the automobile bargain of all time' and promised all it would take would be a weekend to assemble the components. A kit Elite was listed at £1299 when a Super Seven was £599: the saving was considerable and UK sales staged a minor revival, the first five months of 1962 seeing 158 Elites sold on the home market compared to 94 cars for the whole of 1961.

Overlapping the Elan, the discredited Elite was kept on, struggling, while the company's new baby found its feet. Thus 1962 saw 'The latest expression of the Lotus theme' in the form of Super 95, Super 100 and Super 105 versions, with engines in a higher state of tune and more equipment. The Super 95 had, naturally enough, 95bhp, along with servo-assisted disc brakes and the all-synchromesh close-ratio ZF gearbox. When purchased in component form it cost £1595, still dearer than the Elan at £1299, and it was no surprise when all Elite production ceased in September 1963. The remaining shells languished in a field for several further years.

Driving an Elite

Driving a perfectly-restored Elite is not quite the assault on the ears that you might expect. Certainly the Climax engine chugs away at idle, and has a kind of vintage mechanical thrash to it, but the legendary resonances from other components don't manifest themselves unless something is working loose – and there are plenty of known fixes for the old design faults. You need to raise your voice as the speed rises, all the same, but conversation is still possible at 60mph. Coming to a halt, the differential can be heard whining on the engine overrun but that's all part of the car's character. Additionally, the ZF gearbox of the Series 2 is known to be less vocal than the BMC unit initially used.

Despite being a little 1216cc 'four' of only 75bhp, the Coventry Climax FWE combines with the lightweight bodyshell to pull an Elite forward with gusto, and the car keeps up easily with modern traffic. The engine doesn't feel lively at first, but neither is it intractable at low speeds, pulling away cleanly in fourth from 2500rpm. Starts have to be well-judged, juggling the short clutch action with the longer movement of the accelerator, but such niggles are soon forgotten once the engine has hit 4000rpm in top and is nicely on song at 70mph or so, pulling strongly and with more to come. Thankfully, the all-disc brakes provide reassuring stopping power, especially with modern pad material.

With your hands at a quarter-to-three on the steering wheel, the left is close enough to rest on the tip of the gearlever – or perhaps 'stick' is more accurate as it's the height of a Biro and little thicker. The gear positions are easily found but need a decisive short movement which becomes slicker as the 'box warms through. Both driver and passenger are treated to generous shoulder support from the high-backed seats and the pedals are well spaced.

The Elite's wood-rimmed steering wheel is large and thin by modern standards but a smaller version would negate Peter Cambridge's attention to ergonomics, as the whole range of instruments remain visible through it and all switches can be reached without stretching. Its movements are true and accurate although amplified by its large diameter. There's some body roll but the suspension sets the scene for the future: well controlled but supple, with strong reserves of adhesion.

Buying Hints

1. Fifty years old in 2007, the Lotus Elite has been through adulation, neglect, restoration and speculation. It is now settled as a revered classic car whose foibles are known, accepted and accommodated. Surprisingly, there are around 690 known survivors of a run of only 1078 cars, and one or two cars re-emerge from hiding each year. Totally unrestored cars are like gold dust.

2. Remove the bodyshell and there is very little else to an Elite, so if the monocoque is sound all will be well. To restorer Tony Bates, the ideal situation is to strip a shell of all paint and trim so you can assess its condition and after any repairs then repaint it using modern materials. Sunroofs are to be avoided, as cutting the aperture weakens the structure, as do poor accident repairs. Be warned that the plastics on a car left outside can start to break up.

3. The crucial check area for the shell is the front subframe, which is embedded in the moulding and cannot be seen. If moisture has penetrated and rust started, corrosion can be detected as a bubbling of the surface around the front suspension mounts. There is also a metal hoop running across the windscreen and down to the door posts, ending in jacking points where corrosion can start.

4. Although twin-cam production far surpassed it, the Coventry Climax engine is well served by specialists and some can even build you a new one for an appropriate sum. The actual Korean-issue fire-pumps occasionally turn up as army surplus items in their original carrying cages and can be rebuilt to car specification by experts.

5. Being all-aluminium, the Climax engine is sensitive to having the correct anti-freeze mixture and as many Elites get very little use, internal corrosion can also set in if coolant is left sitting in the block. High oil consumption is a fact of life but engines should not rattle at tickover.

6. The Elite was famed for the differential coming away, as there was no reinforcement where it was fixed to the body, but owners have devised ways of ensuring it stays put. Cars with a ZF gearbox command more than those with the earlier MG (BMC) unit.

The Elan

Pop-up headlamps and foam-filled bumpers instantly identify the little Elan; the car was to become synonymous with Lotus. Although even in kit form it was far more expensive than either the Triumph Spitfire or larger MGB, the Elan was the ideal for the sports car enthusiast.

While the Elite was Chapman's idealised vision of a conventional road car, the Elan benefited from his willingness to compromise: here was a small sports car that could run rings around the competition in its handling and performance, yet still make money. It remained in production, little changed, for over ten years, and is still synonymous with Lotus.

The British motor industry took notice of the 1958 Austin-Healey Sprite, especially its subsequent success in the American market. Here was a tiny two-seat convertible based on mass-produced components from the British Motor Corporation, with crude suspension by Lotus standards and clothed in a distinctive but not especially pretty steel bodyshell. So in 1959 the first Lotus thoughts on what was to become the Elan were as a car to replace the Seven, slotting in under the Elite and competing with the Sprite. Glassfibre was again the chosen material, low-volume car-makers such as Berkeley, Elva and Turner having shown the way with small grp-bodied two-seat open cars. Chapman also envisaged a larger 2+2 Ford-powered car to supplement the Elite, thoughts which later materialised as the +2.

Further use of the Elite's Climax engine was out of the question. For cost and reliability the new car would have to have a unit available from an established manufacturer at a competitive price. Ford soon became the obvious starting point. The 1959 Anglia 105E with its mini-Thunderbird fins and reverse-sloped rear window was Ford of Britain's response to the Mini but it was its short-stroke 'oversquare' 997cc engine, known as the 'Kent' engine, that made racers including Chapman take notice. It lent itself to capacity increases, was capable of sustaining high revs, and responded well to tuning. Worked on by ex-Lotus man Keith Duckworth, who co-founded Cosworth, it became the anchor engine for the Seven S2 and was soon the cornerstone of cheap UK motorsport.

Until very late in the day the new small Lotus sports car was to be a glassfibre monocoque convertible without a chassis. The new production method – following advice from Maximar – was dubbed the 'Unimould', and was to use a one-piece body moulding which started out by laying the outer shell in a mould and then building the inner shell with wheelarches on top (the exact opposite of Elite construction where a number of assemblies were moulded then bonded together). Hickman had a long and difficult task on his hands, as being a convertible made the design task much harder

Lotus Elan
1962–73

Models quoted: S1/S3/SE/Sprint

ENGINE:
Four cylinders in line, cast-iron block and aluminium cylinder head, water-cooled

Capacity	1558cc
Bore x stroke	82.6mm x 72.8mm
Valve actuation	Twin overhead cam
Compression ratio	9.5:1
	10.3:1 (Sprint)
Carburettors	2 x twin-choke Weber
	2 x twin-choke Weber/Dellorto
Power	105bhp at 5500rpm
	115bhp at 6000rpm (SE)
	126bhp at 6500rpm (Sprint)
Maximum torque	108lb ft at 4000rpm
	113lb ft at 5500rpm (Sprint)

TRANSMISSION:
Rear-wheel drive; four-speed gearbox (five-speed optional on final Elans)

SUSPENSION:
Front: Independent by coil springs and twin wishbones; telescopic dampers; anti-roll bar
Rear: Independent by Chapman struts and lower wishbones

STEERING:
Rack-and-pinion

BRAKES:
Front: Disc
Rear: Disc
Servo assistance on SE and Sprint

WHEELS/TYRES:
13in steel
Tyres 4.5 x 13in cross-ply then radial

BODYWORK:
Glassfibre-reinforced plastic; steel backbone chassis
Two-door convertible/coupé

DIMENSIONS:

Length	12ft 1in
Wheelbase	7ft 0in
Track, front	3ft 11in
Track, rear	4ft 0in
Width	4ft 8in
Height	3ft 9in

KERB WEIGHT:
11.5cwt (Series 1)
13.7cwt (Sprint)

PERFORMANCE:
(Source: *Autocar*)
Models quoted:
Elan 1600 and Sprint

Max speed	115mph/118mph
0-60mph	8.7sec/7.0sec
30-50mph in top	6sec/7.7sec
50-70mph in top	6.7sec/7.2sec

PRICE IN COMPONENT FORM WHEN NEW:
£1436 (Series 1, 1964)
£1663 (Sprint, 1973)

NUMBER BUILT:
12,224

Elan +2
1967–74

As Elan SE/Sprint except:

TRANSMISSION:
Five-speed gearbox (Lotus) on +2S 130/5

DIMENSIONS:

Length	14ft 0in
Wheelbase	8ft 0in
Track, front	4ft 6in
Track, rear	4ft 7in
Width	5ft 3.5in
Height	3ft 11in

KERB WEIGHT:
17.5cwt (+2S 130/5)

PERFORMANCE:
(Source: *Autocar*)
Models quoted: +2 and +2S 130/5

Max speed	118mph/121mph
0-60mph	8.9sec/7.5sec
30-50mph in top	8.7sec/15.1sec
50-70mph in top	8.4sec/13.9sec

PRICE INCLUDING TAX WHEN NEW:
£1923 (+2, 1967)
£2974 (+2 S130/5, 1973)

NUMBER BUILT:
5168

than the Elite which had a fixed roof to give it rigidity. A convertible shell would have to be strengthened in a great many places, and especially around the screen and door openings, just not to fold in half.

By 1960 mechanical development was running way ahead of the

bodywork, so something to provide a rolling testbed was becoming essential. A simple steel backbone chassis was drawn up, branching out at the front and back to take the engine and rear suspension and with holes cut into it for lightness, ease of assembly and access to components.

Shown as a detail in this Autocar *cutaway, the backbone chassis accelerated the Elan's development and became a design feature of Lotus models right through to the last Esprit. Built in steel, with no corrosion protection and several rust traps, the chassis would always need replacing long before the glassfibre bodyshell required serious attention.*

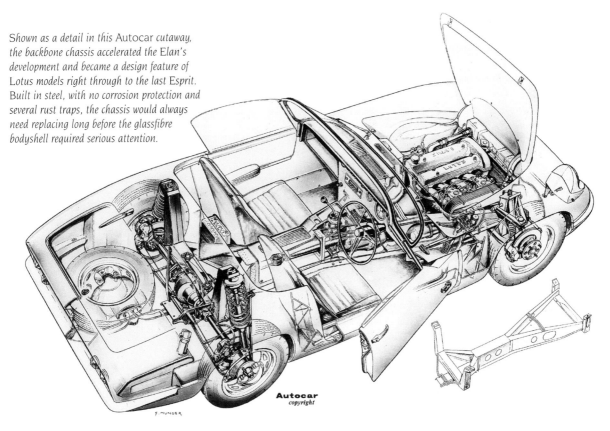

Autocar
copyright

Below: The dashboard of the original S1 Elan was bitty and somewhat sparse, albeit very much of-the-moment in its style.

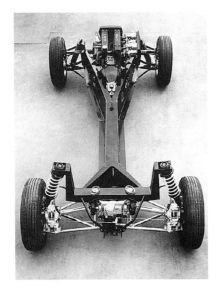

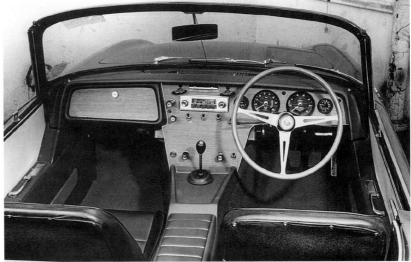

As the driveshafts were an active part of the suspension system, Rotoflex rubber 'doughnut' couplings were fitted either side of the differential and at the wheel hubs (partially hidden by the rear disc brakes). The Elan defied contemporary sports suspension thinking by being softly sprung yet well controlled.

Chapman is said to have drawn up the backbone chassis concept within a weekend, although this may be a bit of misleading self-publicity on his part. The prototype running gear was then tested by hiding the chassis under a Falcon Caribbean glassfibre

body, this being a British kit-car shell of the time.

After 50,000 miles of testing it was realised that the make-do backbone chassis was an extremely rigid unit and would cost only £10 to make – when Lotus was paying Bristol £250

per Elite shell. Hickman suggested to Chapman that every car could have an open-topped glassfibre monocoque bolted to a backbone chassis and that his agreement would speed up the design process by a year – which with the Elite in such trouble would be a big boost. Chapman readily concurred, preoccupied as he was with Team Lotus's move to rear-engined racers.

By spring 1961 Hickman's shape was near to that of the production Elan. It was now clear that the Elite did not have a future and the small sports car project diverged from being a cheap Seven replacement – the Seven had been given a price cut which had boosted sales, in any case – and became instead the Elite's successor. As the concept changed, Hickman dubbed it the M2, which was to set the trend for future Lotus project names. Chapman wanted to call it the Elite again but Hickman's choice of Elan prevailed when Lotus employees were asked to vote for their favourite.

With the twin-cam engine project on line it became more likely that the Elan would receive this rather than a humble 105E one-litre pushrod unit and so the Elan began its push up-market and up in price. However, Lotus did not make the mistake of using as many bespoke components

Above: The decision to launch the Elan first as a convertible was down to the initial plan to produce a cheaper car to compete in the US against the Austin-Healey Sprite; this is a rare Series 1 model, wearing the unique Lotus presssed-steel wheels.

Below: Mass-produced British sports cars used tuned versions of ohv family-car engines. The Elan twin-cam unit, however, may have been Ford-based but its special Lotus cylinder head produced a much higher power output for its 1558cc than that of competitor cars.

The twin-cam engine

In the club-racer days of the 1950s it was normal practice to use other people's engines and accept their limitations. But as Lotus became a fully-fledged motor manufacturer Chapman believed it needed to build its own power unit. The twin-cam was the first step towards that goal.

After experimenting with a tuned Ford Consul engine in an Elite, Chapman initially opted to design a bespoke twin-overhead-camshaft cylinder head for the 997cc Ford 105E block, for series-manufacture. He contracted Harry Mundy, a former Coventry Climax engine designer working as a journalist for *The Autocar* magazine, to direct the design of the new light alloy cylinder head. Mundy had already part-designed a twin-cam for the ill-fated Facel-Véga Facellia sports car and the Lotus unit was developed by Mundy, ex-BRM man Richard Ansdale and Steve Sanville, later to work on the Lotus 907 engine.

Before much work could be done, Ford's rapid engine development dangled the possibility of more power and an engine big enough for a larger car. Chapman's connections with Ford gave him access to prototype engines so rather than a one-litre 105E unit in 1961 the twin-cam work moved

instead to an early 1340cc Ford Classic 109E block. Then once more Ford of Britain's expansion played a role, and the new 116E unit planned for the 1962 Cortina became available, presenting Lotus with a stronger five-main-bearing 1498cc bottom end and the prospect of at least 100bhp. By this stage, too, Ford was looking at selling a Cortina powered by the twin-cam.

Lotus retained the iron Ford block, crankshaft and pistons but added its own alloy head, (chain) timing gear and water pump. Cosworth carried out the final stages of development and the engine was then manufactured for Lotus by JA Prestwich of Tottenham, North London, better known for its JAP motorcycle engines.

The Ford-Lotus or Lotus-Ford 1498cc twin-cam engine made its debut in a Lotus 23 in May 1962, at Germany's Nürburgring circuit. Driven by Jim Clark, the car didn't last the full race but established the fastest lap time in the 2-litre class. By summer of 1962 production had been signed off and a twin-cam had been fitted to a humble Ford Anglia, making it capable of some phenomenal journey times. At the same time the 1500cc

Elan's days were looking numbered as the racing change to a 1600cc cut-off was announced. The capacity settled at 1558cc for the Elan, +2 and Europa, but further race development enlarged it to 1593cc.

JA Prestwich was taken over by Villiers and production of cylinder heads finally moved to Lotus after the company relocated to Hethel in Norfolk in 1966. Production of the 25,000th twin-cam was marked in 1970 and it ended its time with Lotus on the demise of the Europa in 1975. Lotus then subcontracted all manufacturing and refurbishment to Essex-based performance engine builder Vegantune who continued to supply Caterham, eventually designing its own engine using the Ford 'Kent' engine block.

Vegantune also produced its own take on the Elan in the 1980s, based on an updated Elan shell over a tubular backbone chassis and cheekily called the Evante. Always presented as a new car, the Evante was wider than an Elan, had no bumpers, and incorporated front and rear spoilers. It could be specified with deep-pile carpet and leather seats and with power outputs ranging from 140bhp to 200bhp. Legal difficulties with Lotus arose, over it being too Elan-like, and curtailed production, but today the company – alongside fellow specialist Quorn Engine Developments (QED) – continues to support the Lotus twin-cam.

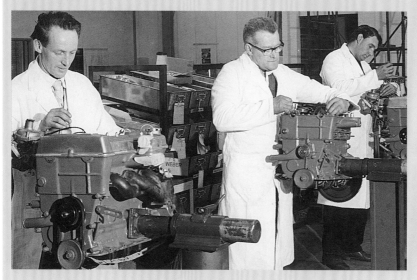

The Lotus twin-cam engine was a combination of a Ford cylinder block and an aluminium head with chain-driven twin overhead camshafts, following in the footsteps of more exotic foreign sports cars. Its design was contracted to Harry Mundy, and because it was based on a stillborn project he had undertaken for Facel-Véga, much of the initial work was already done, helping its rapid development. Production and assembly was contracted out until Lotus moved to Hethel (shown here) in 1966. (Lotus/author's collection)

*Light weight, small size, aerodynamic
efficiency and a potent engine combine to give
the Elan a strong performance even by modern
standards; this Series 2 has a non-standard
roll-bar. Visible are the sliding windows
retained on the S2 cars.*

*Right: Snug and perfectly laid-out for the
sporting driver, the Elan's cabin became
progressively more luxurious, with a full-width
wood-veneer dashboard from the Series 2 and
electric windows from the Series 3 (as here),
controlled by switches on the door; almost
unheard of in a small sports car, these replaced
the awkward sliding windows of the early cars.*

as on the Elite. The double-wishbone
front suspension and the steering
rack were derived from those of the
1959 Triumph Herald (and shared with
its later Spitfire derivative), while the
rear suspension was a simplified
version of the Elite's strut set-up,
using Ford Consul Classic front coil
springs and with the driveshafts again
forming an active part of the
suspension – but this time with
broad-based lower wishbones to give

lateral location. One of the Elan's
trademarks was the use of circular
rubber couplings at both the
inboard and outboard ends of the
driveshafts. Called Rotoflex, and
also to be used on the Hillman Imp,
these rubber 'doughnuts' were meant
to cushion driveline movements. It
was planned to have inboard-
mounted rear disc brakes but these
were moved outward to behind the
wheel hubs to tackle a 'wind-up'

problem with the couplings which
allowed the car to roll away even
when the handbrake was applied. The
Elan's suspension formula was pure
Lotus, giving a very supple yet well-
controlled ride for a sports car.

While using more mass-produced
parts than the Elite, the Elan gained
features which set it well apart from
the competition. In an example of his
far-sighted thinking, Ron Hickman
produced a written paper for

Right: Elan styling changed very little during its lifetime, the main identifiers being the tail lights borrowed from various contemporary cars. The 1964 Series 2 used Vauxhall Victor units which combined stop, tail and indicator lights. An optional hardtop is fitted to this car, giving an appearance little different from that of the Elan coupé that was to follow.

Below: This S3 Special Equipment model again has a non-standard roll bar; note too the centre-lock steel wheels. As a S3 it will still have the Vauxhall tail lights.

Chapman on how difficult the Elite's nose was to repair if it was hit, how hard it was to conceal joins between two glassfibre sections, and how as cars were starting to be designed without headlamp peaks or fins at either end this made low-speed parking knocks more common.

Elite bumpers were little more than an expensive way to hide a join, and after a study of varying bumper types on contemporary cars, Hickman advocated the use of glassfibre bumpers to hide the join between the upper and lower panels. He observed that styling choices would be limited if Lotus were obliged to use steel bumpers from other manufacturers – although it did however revert to these for the Europa and +2. He reasoned that a plastic-foam and glassfibre sandwich might be capable of absorbing minor knocks and actually be a selling point: 'this car could have the nose of a Vanwall or a Ferrari (or a Lotus),' he said, asking to be allowed one of the development Elites to use as a test bed.

Pop-up headlamps were to become another Elan trademark and bugbear. Hickman wanted a smooth line to the front, but US regulations demanded that headlamps be set at a fixed height. Hickman experimented with a lever in the cockpit pulling a cable but then adapted a principle from old Fords where a vacuum created by the inlet manifold was used to power the windscreen wipers, albeit feebly. Hickman fully enclosed the space inside the front chassis crossmember and used it as a reservoir of air to

Talk of takeovers

Although in the 1980s Lotus would be desperate for a buyer, in the 1960s and 1970s Colin Chapman explored a number of more Lotus-led alliances with British manufacturers.

Jaguar was fit enough at the start of the 1960s to start empire-building and founder Sir William Lyons bought truck-maker Guy and ailing car manufacturer Daimler – one of whose few assets was the V8 engine from the controversial SP250 sports car, a power unit which Lotus found tempting for the +2 then under development.

"I think Lyons saw Chapman as a surrogate son for a long time," says Roger Putnam, who joined Lotus in 1965. "There was a very strong possibility Jaguar was going to buy Lotus, with Chapman running the combined company – a lot of work was done. Lyons saw in Chapman somebody who had the same flair as he did. He'd lost a son whom I'm sure he had hoped would inherit the business. I think it was the Lotus-Cortina deal that killed the Jaguar opportunity."

In his book on Chapman, Mike Lawrence ponders a different motive: 'All Colin wanted to do was go motor racing, but Lyons was interested in Lotus because he wanted Chapman to inject his talent into Guy Motors and make it a modern company.'

While Jaguar might have seemed a

One of Ron Hickman's early sketches of the Metier prototype, destined to become the +2. Talks with Jaguar over a takeover were encouraged by thoughts that the upmarket Lotus coupé could use the much-admired Daimler V8 engine, which was in the hands of Jaguar following its takeover of Daimler.

good fit, Reliant looks like a bizarre one with its staple trade in three-wheelers. Nonetheless there were some similarities: in the early '60s Reliant was also building the glassfibre-bodied Sabre sports car and had designed grp-bodied saloon cars for Israeli and Turkish manufacturers. A marriage was a prospect intriguing enough for Ron Hickman to organise a visit to Reliant in 1963, but nothing came of it.

In the early 1970s Colin Chapman considered buying Aston Martin – in a shaky state at the time. He is said to have worried that the M50 Elite was such a leap upmarket that the Lotus name alone might not be enough to

carry it: the prestige of the Aston name could help justify the higher price. The Aston works were at Newport Pagnell, North of London on the M1, and could have become a Lotus and Aston Martin maintenance centre, but after a visit Chapman decided the methods of hand construction were too disorganised and archaic.

power the headlamp-opening, retraction being looked after by a spring catch. Chapman obliged by allowing a test rig to be fitted to the front his Jaguar.

Getting the headlamps to work reliably went right up to the Elan's debut at the 1962 London Motor Show but on the day they were wired to flash as they popped up (in less than a second), which was a real crowd pleaser. The show over, the Elan was largely developed and ready-to-go, so there was no comparison with the

Elite's slow progress to sales start-up. The 1498cc Elan 1500 cost £1499 fully-built and £1095 as a kit. If they opted for a component car – and most did – buyers had to fit the engine, gearbox, exhaust, some parts of the front suspension, the battery and the wheels. The factory or dealer would then check it and correct any mistakes. With the sizeable saving to be made, kit-building was to become part of the Lotus Elan experience and the process could allegedly be completed in a weekend. Bodyshell-

building was initially sub-contracted but soon came in-house at Cheshunt to meet the required volumes.

The Elan 1500 was short-lived. Group 2 saloon-car racing regulations were changed in the latter half of 1962 to allow a maximum 1.6-litre limit. Ford's Lotus-Cortina had been developed in tandem with the last stages of the Elan and launched early in 1963 with a 1558cc twin-cam, and in May 1963 the Elan followed. Only 22 Elans had been built with the 1498cc engine and these were recalled

Rebodied Elans

The Elan Frua SS was entirely rebodied in steel by the Italian coachbuilder for the 1964 Geneva Motor Show; a limited production run was talked of at the time, but the car remained a one-off.

North London's Ian Walker Racing had Williams & Pritchard fashion an aerodynamic aluminium-shelled Elan for 1964's Le Mans. Although the car crashed before it reached the famous race, it was rebuilt, and survives to this day.

The Shapecraft Elan was not inelegant. Here it is on display at the Racing Car Show, derscribed as the 'Lotus Elan GT'.

A number of attempts were made to change the shape of the Elan – some for racing, some for practicality. In 1963 well-known Lotus racer Ian Walker set out to build a special-bodied Elan specifically to carry off the Index of Thermal Efficiency at 1964's Le Mans. The slippery shape – which looked nothing like an Elan – was crafted in

aluminium by Williams & Pritchard, the North London firm who shaped the bulk of '50s Lotus racers, and incorporated a Kamm tail with cooling ducts and a small lip spoiler, finished off with Ford Cortina rear lights. Sadly the IWR Elan was crashed before it could make it to Le Mans; it was subsequently rebuilt and sold on.

Walker built a further special-bodied Elan for road use, inspired by the Le Mans racer, at the request of a Swiss customer. Also bodied in alumimium, it had many of the Le Mans car's design features but was far more luxuriously trimmed, in best-quality cloth and leather. With distinctive double slanted headlamps the second Ian Walker Elan was often compared with the Gordon Keeble of 1964 and Colin Chapman is said to have taken quite a liking to it, asking for it to be brought to the factory to show to him.

Racers often tried to improve the Elan's aerodynamics by fitting revised rear ends and car dealer Barry Wood's 1963 fastback Elan led to the Shapecraft Elan conversion for private customers. An aluminium fastback was bonded to the top of the windscreen and blended into a Perspex rear window with two rear side windows (deleted on roadgoing cars) and a new bootlid. The top was neatly joined to the rear wings and shaped with filler. The conversion cost £170 and around 20 were built between 1963 and 1964.

At the 1964 Geneva show, meanwhile, Italian coachbuilder Frua unveiled a very pretty Elan coupé complete with a tailgate. The Elan Frua SS was finished in red with an ivory leather interior and the lines were similar to those of two other Frua creations, the Maserati Mistral and the AC 428. Commissioned by a Swiss Lotus importer, ambitious plans for the car were announced, with bodyshells to be made by Frua and assembly in Italy, Switzerland and the UK, but nothing more came of this.

Above: The roadgoing IWR Elan coupé had a retrimmed interior and a frontal treatment seemingly borrowed from the Gordon-Keeble. Below: Mockingly known as the 'Elambulance' because of its looks, the Hexagon Elan Sprint estate conversion was well executed – but only two examples were built.

In 1972, for owners who wanted a bit more space but didn't want to be parted from their Elan when a baby, dog or golf club came along, North London Lotus dealer Hexagon of Highgate announced an estate car or 'shooting brake' conversion of the Elan. The conversion entailed cutting away the rear of the body and then bonding the estate car portion on, with the aid of a jig. This new superstructure was double-skinned, insulated, and reinforced to take the tailgate. New internal mouldings formed the luggage area behind the seats and trim and bespoke side window glasses were then fitted, before adding the Reliant Scimitar tailgate glass and wash-wipe. This was a thorough conversion and cost £595; only two were built.

to be fitted with the new unit. Power was up slightly, from 100bhp to 105bhp, but the Elan was already well ahead of the 56bhp Austin-Healey Sprite, and the larger but of course heavier 95bhp MGB.

Long having fretted over whether to have its own two-seater, Ford was to take an active interest in the Elan – even considering adopting it as its own and letting Lotus use its dealer network, before it backed off due to nervousness about potential reliability problems. Nonetheless the first Elan had its press showing at Ford's Regent Street showroom. Reaction to the new Lotus was swift and favourable, the press observing that the sharpness of the Elite had been retained, yet combined with a whole lot more comfort and refinement. In 1964 American magazine *Car & Driver* said 'it fits like a Sprite, goes like a Corvette and handles like a Formula Junior'.

The concept was so essentially right that Lotus settled into a series of regular but small updates and running improvements for a number of years. Although production of the chassis and cylinder head was at first handled by outside companies, Lotus gradually brought this in-house. Many of the detail changes made each Elan more upmarket than the previous one, foreshadowing the direction in which Lotus Cars was

A styling model for the Metier, which was to become the +2 after Colin Chapman had toyed for a time with using the name 'Elite 2'. The styling concept fluctuated through the early '60s, with interchangeable roof panels being one possibility, before the conservative GT shape of the production car was finally settled upon by Hickman and his team.

The Elan 26R

Unlike the Elite, Lotus designed the Elan as a road car. But with the Lotus name riding high in motor sport, almost as soon as it was on sale customers rushed to the track in their Elans – then complained they were too softly sprung, as the rubber 'doughnuts' in the driveline tore themselves apart under suspension movement. Chapman gave in to the inevitable. "The fact that customers bought them and then tried to race them was originally no concern of ours," he said. "But in the second year we thought, well, if these people insist on racing them then we'd better get down to some proper development."

Graham Warner, owner of the Chequered Flag Lotus dealership, first raced a prototype Elan in May 1963 and found it just as awkward as everybody else. With the blessing of Lotus he embarked on a development programme and most of these changes were fed into Lotus's official Elan racer, the 26R.

This was launched in 1964 and built

for two years by Lotus Components. Very much more expensive than the road-going Elan at £2450 for a kit, it had a thinner and lighter bodyshell, lower and stiffer adjustable suspension and a Cosworth or BRM-tuned twin-cam good for up to 145bhp. This huge dose of extra power was controlled by a limited-slip differential and dual-circuit brakes. The rear suspension revisions allowed wider wheels and larger tyres and the pop-up headlamps were replaced by smaller fixed headlamps behind

Although the Elan was not designed as a racing car, Lotus offered the Elan 26R from 1964 to 1966. As racers usually discarded the pop-up headlamp mechanism to save weight, the 26R featured fixed units behind Perspex covers. This Elan is being pursued by a Lotus 23 at Brands Hatch in 1965.

Perspex shields. The 26R took the British motor racing scene by storm, improving as it went along, and with even more power (up to 158bhp), until it was replaced by the Europa-based 47.

Top: This later +2S wears Lotus alloy wheels, as do most cars.

Above: From the rear the extra width of the +2 body is readily apparent. The rear lights are shared with the Alfa GTV and the Series II Jaguar E-type.

heading, but by staying in kit form the price was kept within reasonable limits. Fortunately the bodyshell could be gently adapted, such as changing the profile of the doors or bootlid, without major investment.

The 1964 Series 2 had tail lamps from the Vauxhall Victor FB and moved towards a more up-market interior by gaining a full-width wood-veneer dashboard with a lockable glovebox lid. The Elan had been designed with sliding side windows lowered by a spring-loaded mechanism, but by the time of the Series 2 Hickman had devised a way of building in an electric window lift using cables and a small motor. This became an option on the S2 instead of the slightly awkward sliders. The S2 also benefited from larger front brake callipers.

The next Elan development was significant enough to warrant a new Lotus type number, the 36. While in no sense a 2+2, the Elan Coupé offered a taste of luxury, with its fully-closed body. Styled by John Frayling, it was an elegant shape with slimmer windscreen pillars and longer side windows. Some observed that since a hardtop had been available for the Elan for some time this was a pointless exercise. But for Lotus, while not as radical as the 1964 Frua Elan SS, it offered a useful economy of scale: both coupé and convertible Elans could be produced in the same mould, with the starting point for the convertible being simply to saw off the roof of the coupé shell.

Coupé buyers could specify an alternative axle ratio for more relaxed cruising: testers often complained that a high-speed Elan was somewhat frenetic. Chrome-plated bumpers briefly became optional, too, although they never looked quite right and the chrome eventually fell off. Another detail was that coupé side windows gained frames to improve sealing, and from mid-1966 these found their way onto the convertible Series 3 Elan – which also had a much improved hood. At this stage electric windows were made standard on all Elans.

By 1966 the Elan had proved a fantastic success and this enabled Lotus to bring manufacture of the twin-cam engine in-house at the new factory in Hethel, Norfolk. New moulds were also made at the same time. That year also saw the first boost in power, from 105bhp to 115bhp, with the arrival of the SE models. As well as the increased power, these 'Special Equipment' cars had servo-assisted brakes and knock-on wheels as standard, fitted carpet in the cockpit and boot, and a leather-rimmed steering wheel. Top speed for the Coupé was a heady 123mph. An SE Elan cost £1566 complete or £1295 as a kit – about £40 more than a standard car.

When the Europa was announced in 1966, plans for an upward expansion of the Elan concept were well in hand. Chapman had not abandoned the idea of a 2+2 fixed-head Lotus and in his choice of personal transport was tending towards something that could accommodate his growing family. He reasoned correctly that there would be a market among other enthusiasts with the same considerations and with enough money to buy a more luxurious Lotus.

The idea had been around since 1962 and the shape of the +2 was largely set by 1963. Ron Hickman had toyed with the idea of three cars in one, using different detachable roofs: a convertible, a Porsche-style Targa and an estate car. But the need for different rear spring rates and doubts that such a car could be properly built put paid to such thoughts. Lotus opted instead to play safe with a fixed-head coupé, with a convertible to come later. Initially, the car was to be called the Elite +2, but that name had to wait until the next decade for revival.

A lot of design difficulty centred around the decision to give the car up-market metal bumpers rather than the Elan's grp items. In the end Lotus used the front bumper of the soon-to-be-obsolete Ford Anglia and the rear was adapted from the blade used on the Wolseley Hornet and Riley Elf. The glasshouse was designed around the short-lived Ford Consul Capri coupé windscreen, although by production time the tooling had been scrapped –

Above: Extra instrumentation such as a clock, and a rear demister, came as standard on the +2, and more equipment, such as a fitted radio, was added during the production run. London coachbuilder Harold Radford (famous for customised Minis) offered an even plusher version of the +2S.

Below: Although initially offered as a kit, the +2 became solely factory-built from 1968 onwards. Concerned by its reputation for poorly-built cars, Lotus started to make more efforts to control quality in the late '60s – although problems were often caused by components bought in from other manufacturers.

Right: This Sprint has the upper part of the two-tone in British Racing Green, an unusual but effective choice. Note the framed sideglass that came in with the S3, and the Alfa/Jaguar lights.

Below: In redeveloping the Lotus twin-cam to produce 126bhp, Tony Rudd followed what many tuners had done during the Elan's career. The best road tests attained a top speed of over 120mph. Under the bonnet there's no mistaking the extra urge, thanks to the 'Big Valve' cam covers.

without anybody noticing – and Lotus had to commission its own.

The first full-scale prototype, the Metier 2, was shown to the Lotus board in December 1965. It went down well but Chapman felt the looks were too narrow for its length, and so the track of subsequent versions was widened by seven inches. The final +2 was nearly two feet longer than an Elan to accommodate two very small rear seats and the wider track brought about wider tyres and accompanying suspension adjustments.

Early brochures featured a couple of schoolboys happily installed in the rear seats. 'To be certain on this point we did the obvious thing, we covered many hundreds of miles with children in the car,' said the brochure. 'One tester made the sensible report that

"of course children don't sit in seats, they stand on them, kneel on them and fight on them." So we have made certain that the whole rear area is right for the antics of children as our design requirement specifically stated that "children should be comfortable".'

Weight was up by about 3cwt but this was offset by better aerodynamics than on the Elan, as a consequence of the +2 having been windtunnel-tested. The headlamps were once more pop-up items using stored air pressure but they were operated by an electrical solenoid. For the later +2S 130, the headlamp failsafe was set so they stayed up rather than flopping down, in the event of a problem, and thus a Lotus with leaky vacuum pipes could sometimes be seen parked with one headlamp winking at passers-by ...

Launched in June 1967, the +2 initially used the 115bhp SE version of the 1558cc twin-cam, which was good enough for a claimed maximum speed of 118mph and 0–60mph in around eight seconds. This was linked to a four-speed gearbox. Although it was aiming at a new breed of Lotus owner, the 1967 +2 was still offered as a kit for £1672 as well as fully-built at £1923. The original +2 was relatively short-lived, as dealers felt the car was not quite plush enough for the asking price, which was in Jaguar E-Type territory. Accordingly in March 1969 the +2S was introduced, with more soundproofing, better instrumentation and standard items such as foglights and a radio. Priced at £2600, it was only available as a fully-assembled car, which would remain the case for the rest of the +2's life.

Further developments on the Elan were driven by the dictates of the American market. Safety laws meant more padding on the dashboard, flush-fitting switches, hazard warning lights and a low-brake-fluid light, while dual-circuit brakes became standard. These changes were incorporated into the 1968 Elan S4, recognisable by its slightly flared wheelarches to accommodate wider tyres and by its Jaguar E-Type tail lights. A bonnet bulge was added to accommodate another change, a short-lived move to Stromberg carburettors.

Chapman hated having to bolt things onto engines to meet

legislative requirements and although the 907 engine, which was designed to run 'clean' from the start, was well on track by 1968, it was never designed to fit the Elan. More needed to be done to the twin-cam, therefore, to keep the Elan competitive. When Tony Rudd left BRM to join Lotus in 1969 as engineering director, one of his first tasks was to extract more power reliably, similar to the way that BRM had done so for the Lotus-Cortina and had offered in conversion form on the Elan some years previously. Rudd duly re-designed the cylinder head to accept bigger valves and opened out the inlet ports. The 'Big Valve' engine had a higher compression ratio and delivered 126bhp, revving to 6800rpm

in the process. This resulted in extraordinary performance in such a small car and to cope with the increased power the Rotoflex couplings were stiffened.

The new engines were fitted to the Elan and +2S, which were relaunched in 1971 as the Elan Sprint and the +2S 130. So nobody missed it, the new engine was treated to 'Big Valve' labelling on its cam covers. The Europa had to wait its turn, making do with a tamer version of the twin-cam because of the limitations of its Renault four-speed gearbox. From October 1972 the Elan Sprint and the Elan +2S 130 were given the option of a Lotus five-speed gearbox derived from that of the Austin Maxi, in advance of its fitment to the new Elite,

and this was a significant step on the road to Lotus becoming a self-contained manufacturer.

The Elan Sprint was offered in an optional two-tone Team Lotus finish reflecting the colour scheme of racing sponsor Gold Leaf cigarettes, while the +2S 130 received a restrained two-tone with the roof finished in silver. At this point the Elan Sprint became available only in component form while the +2S 130 remained on offer only as a fully-built car.

In summer 1973 the motoring world bid a genuinely sad farewell to the Elan. The introduction of VAT mean that even a car in component form was liable for the new tax, but equally the design was not going to meet 1974 US safety regulations.

Re-engineered +2s

Although it had been mooted during the car's development, Lotus never made a convertible +2 and this became even less likely as the '70s dawned and potential US safety legislation looked set to spell the end for soft-tops. However, a number of specialists were willing to have a go at conversions for private customers and the car's lines took to it well.

One of the first to try was Hexagon, in 1972, the same year it announced its Elan estate. For £295 it would slice the top off, reinforce the windscreen and modify the rear deck, although the hood had to sit on top, rather than in a well. Only one Hexagon soft-top is said to have been completed.

The classic car boom of the 1980s gave new impetus to the idea and converting what was considered the

Finishing what Lotus had intended for the +2, a number of specialists offered soft-top conversions in the 1980s, such as this Cabriolet from Christopher Neil Sports Cars. As the bodyshell sits on a separate chassis, removing the roof does not cause a major loss in rigidity, and can be countered by appropriate reinforcement.

less desirable +2 then seemed acceptable. In 1986 Christopher Neil Sports Cars of Staffordshire claimed that such was the quality of their conversion that a £3500 +2 would rise in value to £6750 given the chop; possibly influenced by this sales pitch, around 100 conversions were carried out.

Classic Transport in Staffordshire

also offered the Classic DHC, with a steel-strengthened bonded windscreen and mohair-lined hood, while for those who wanted a +2 to use every day, the Spyder Cars +2 Zetec conversion was launched in 2001. Based on a restored +2 shell, this combined the Spyder replacement chassis with a fuel-injected 16-valve Ford Mondeo 2.0-litre Zetec engine good for up to 200bhp.

Driving the Elan and +2

It's true what they say: there are few things more delightful than a well set-up Elan. It's a tiny car by modern standards and you may well find yourself peering over the top of the windscreen, but you feel connected to it straightaway, with the small steering wheel and that lovely gearchange which clacks back and forth like a well-engineered switch. The rasp of the twin-cam is music to the ears and these engines still thrive on being revved once warmed up – you can see immediately where the Mazda MX-5's inspiration came from. Modern tyres add to the roadholding and the suspension still does its work without sending crashes into the cabin.

The +2, although not a great leap in size over a classic Elan, feels like the businessman's express it was intended to be. The wooden dash seems more imposing, with its multitude of dials and switches, and the cockpit has definite shades of Jaguar, especially when trimmed in cream.

There's good and poor design in the +2, such as seatbelts neatly hidden in the door pillars on one hand but on the other an awkward umbrella-handle parking brake buried under the dash where you can't reach it once strapped in with a static seatbelt. This must have seemed anachronistic even in the early 1970s.

It's still a low Lotus, with the transmission tunnel just above hip level, and the bucket seats, which support all the way up to the shoulder, still feel good. The rear is entirely fitting for two children or in an emergency two very small and compliant adults. With its slim pillars and big rear window, the +2 has an airy cabin and with the wing tips just visible it is easily placed on the road.

The twin-cam engine is the same as on the Elan, as is the four-speed or five-speed gearbox. Although hidden by a hardtop, the exhaust note still has that characterful rasp and the gearchange is again short-throw and direct. But the +2 encourages you to think of it as a grand tourer and if you don't want to hustle along you can take advantage of the suppleness of the suspension and just relax.

In its final form available from 1972, the lengthily-named +2S 130/5 had the first Lotus-developed five-speed gearbox and the 126bhp Big Valve engine. Identified by a contrasting metal flake silver roof, it was a bridge to the far more expensive Elite of 1974, which used the same gearbox.

Exactly 12,224 Elans had been sold, making it the most popular Lotus up to that date, and its demise was thought to herald the end of the Lotus convertible. Early in the 907 engine's development an attempt was made at fitting a +2 with the new unit, but it proved to intrude on footwell space; in any case this venture was overtaken by the M50 Elite project. The +2S 130 hung on to the end of 1974, by which time 5168 of the Elan's big brother had been sold, marking it a success.

Buying Hints

1. Original Elans, some even retaining their first chassis, are occasionally found, but the cost of restoration can be excessive. Specialists recommend buying a car that has already been restored – with plenty of supporting bills – and going to a known Lotus expert. Series 1 cars are prized in any condition in the UK for their eligibility in historic racing rather than with a view to returning them to the road. Road cars restored to historic-racing specification are accordingly worth more.

2. In the 1960s, when no manufacturer paid much attention to rustproofing, Lotus opted not to galvanise the Elan's chassis, although it would have been possible. The key rot point is the front suspension turrets, where the drain holes can become blocked. Some cars may have had poorly welded repairs here. Replacement galvanised chassis are still sold by Lotus and can be ordered through dealers. Quite a few cars will now have a Spyder tubular chassis fitted. While less elegant than the Lotus item, it is a useful modification, as it makes suspension upgrades possible.

3. Bodywork is subject to some flexing and this results in stress cracks around the door handles, bonnet and boot catches and badges. Doors didn't fit perfectly even when new, by the way. New shells and repair sections are available. It is possible to make paintwork look good from a distance with a cheap respray but a proper paint restoration will involve many hours of stripping back layers of old paint, filler and accident repairs. A good restoration will be accompanied by photos of the work done. Shells should be painted in dry surroundings or trapped moisture will result in microblistering.

4. In general most Elan parts – such as screen trim – have now been re-manufactured, but there are some items which will only be found at autojumbles – in the UK, Club Lotus runs its own Lotus-jumbles. The +2's front bumper is from the Ford Anglia and the rear is made up of two Wolseley Hornet (or Riley Elf) bumpers. The foam-filled bumpers of the Elan, meanwhile, last well.

5. A lot of Elan interiors will have had bits substituted from later cars. Trim can be remade by specialists.

6. In the rear suspension the condition of the Rotoflex rubber 'doughnuts' is crucial: they can have a life of as little as 5000 to 10,000 miles and certainly by 20,000 miles are likely to have split. If these couplings fail, a driveshaft can come loose and wreck a car as it flails around; the +2 has a peg on the driveshaft to stop this happening. Have the Elan you are viewing jacked up safely so the rear wheels can drop and you can inspect the Rotoflexes for cracks and splits. The MoT test will also reveal if the rubber has perished and if a joint needs replacing; it is recommended both sides be done at the same time along with all the securing bolts. Rear wheel bearings wear more on the heavier +2.

7. Original wheels are important and very old steel wheels can collapse as rust can hide on the inner surface. The wrong-sized wheels will result in a miscalibrated speedometer – not that these are ever that accurate.

8. The Elan's vacuum-operated headlamps rely on a system of pipes connected to an air reservoir contained in the front chassis crossmember. If you are driving up a hill in the dark and the headlamps start to droop, this is a sign that the system has leaks or even that the

chassis is damaged or corroded. Another test is to start the engine, let it run for a while with the headlamps up, and then switch off. The pods should stay up for 5–10 minutes. New headlamp air reservoirs are available.

9. Check that all the electrical items work and do not have poor connections. If left unused for a long period, as with any classic car, the battery will benefit from being put on a trickle-charge when stored. The electric windows can stick if not used, or if the cables come off their pulleys.

10. Twin-cam engines leak a little oil but should not continually drip. A little smoke on starting is not a problem. The overhead cams are driven by a timing chain and these can be too tight or slack. It is worth replacing the chain every ten years. There is a tensioner screw on the front of the engine on the right-hand side. If this is showing half an inch of thread this is ideal: if there is none the chain will need replacing. Engine oil pressure on a twin-cam should be around 40psi at 3000rpm with a warm engine.

11. Over-tightening the fanbelt can damage the water pump and renewing the pump is one of the worst jobs on an Elan as the cylinder head has to come off for access. Radiators corrode, so look for seepage and ideally replace with a more modern unit. During production a Kenlowe electric fan replaced the two-blade fan and owners sometimes fitted one themselves. If there is an electric fan, check it cuts in correctly.

12. Back axles run on modern oils and are regarded as bulletproof. Gearboxes are generally trouble-free, especially the four-speed boxes. The rare Maxi-based five-speeder can be a little more fragile; rebuilds can be expensive.

The Lotus-Cortina

Closely following the Elan, the Lotus Type 28, or 'Cortina developed by Lotus', was an unusual departure for Ford of Britain. It had fought shy of building a dedicated sports car but the tiny production run of Lotus-Cortinas served equally well to enliven the company's image.

By the early 1960s the Ford empire had collectively decided it was too staid. In the States, company vice-president Lee Iacocca realised that the new generation of post-war baby-boomers was not going to buy a Ford just because their parents had done so. In the UK the success of the 1959 Anglia – and the adoption of its free-revving engine by racing specialists – had come as a welcome surprise to Ford of Great

Britain, which was all the same well aware that it was losing to BMC in sports car sales.

With a vast budget to play with, Iacocca initiated a worldwide drive for performance. In 1962 Ford-US approached Team Lotus for its input into a new state-of-the-art car to shake up the Indianapolis 500. The same year Walter Hayes arrived at Ford of Great Britain. As editor of the *Sunday Dispatch* newspaper, Hayes had employed Colin Chapman to write a motoring column and under Ford boss Sir Patrick Hennessy he set up an all-new public affairs department and pitched the idea of a fast version of the near-production-ready Cortina, using the twin-cam engine being developed for the Lotus Elan. Ford did consider improving the performance of the Anglia, but the Cortina was judged to offer a more up-market choice.

Using the latest American research methods, the Cortina was the most ruthlessly analysed car Ford of Great Britain had ever produced, and was a conventional car notable for a light but well-engineered body structure. It was to prove a great commercial success. But even while the Cortina was under development, Ford felt that BMC was already gaining a better reputation for engineering innovation with the Mini, and would surely consolidate this with the forthcoming 1100.

"Ford had no innovation: that was the cry of the time from the journalists and even from our own dealers," recalls Sir Terence Beckett, head of Product Planning in 1962. "We needed something to match all this innovation – a little bit of stardust. People were astonished with Lotus's success – we all were – so Sir Patrick Hennessy and I went to see Chapman. Sir Patrick was fascinated by his technical ability and he gave us a long talk about getting weight down. That did two things: a better power-to-weight ratio and a lower cost of materials."

Work on the Ford-derived Lotus twin-cam was well advanced and the engine was now based on the 116E Cortina block; it was thus an obvious fit, and it was production-ready for the Elan launch that autumn.

Ford factored in the Lotus-Cortina as one of the three stages of tune for the Cortina 1500: a Ford-developed 75bhp car, a 125bhp twin-cam competition version (developed and managed by Lotus) and a 100bhp twin-cam road car sold through Ford dealers. The Lotus-Cortina had to have a minimum run of 1000 cars to satisfy motorsport homologation rules which decreed that racing saloons based on a production car had to have a roadgoing equivalent. Ford asked Chapman if Lotus could assemble the homologation cars at Cheshunt so as not to disrupt the main production line at Dagenham. It was a dream deal for Lotus, with the Elite on its last legs and the Elan yet to go on sale.

True to Chapman's words, the Lotus-Cortina was an exercise in trimming down a car whose weight was already well under control. To the two-door bodyshell Lotus fitted aluminium door skins, bonnet and boot lid, and some castings such as the differential casing and gearbox bell housing were also in alloy. These were perhaps of dubious benefit for the road cars. 'The extra weight of the new cylinder head, two-choke Weber carburettors, rear end stiffening and suspension arms must more than make up for any saving,' *Autocar* magazine pondered in November 1963, comparing the Lotus-Cortina with the regular 1200 model.

The radiator grille on Ford's new hot-rod was painted black and flanked by quarter bumpers, while Lotus badging was applied to the rear wings and grille; the finishing touch, of

Lotus-Cortina MkI
1963-66

ENGINE:
Four cylinders in line, cast-iron block and aluminium cylinder head, water-cooled

Capacity	1558cc
Bore x stroke	82.6mm x 72.8mm
Valve actuation	Twin overhead cam
Compression ratio	9.5:1
Carburettors	2 x twin-choke Weber
Power	105bhp at 5500rpm
Maximum torque	108lb ft at 4000rpm

TRANSMISSION:
Rear-wheel drive; four-speed gearbox

SUSPENSION:
Front: Independent by MacPherson struts; telescopic dampers; anti-roll bar
Rear: Live rear axle, coil springs, location by radius arms and A frame; from 1965 semi-elliptic leaf springs located by radius arms; telescopic dampers

STEERING:
Recirculating ball

BRAKES:
Front: Disc
Rear: Drum
Servo assistance

WHEELS/TYRES:
13in steel
Tyres 6in x 13in

BODYWORK:
Steel monocoque
Two-door saloon

DIMENSIONS:
Length	14ft 0in
Wheelbase	8ft 2in
Track, front and rear	4ft 3in
Width	5ft 2in
Height	4ft 5in

KERB WEIGHT:
16.5cwt

PERFORMANCE:
(Source: *Autocar*)
Max speed	108mph
0-60mph	13.6sec
30-50mph in top	9sec
50-70mph in top	8.9sec

PRICE INCLUDING TAX WHEN NEW:
£1100 (November 1963)

NUMBER BUILT:
2894

Lotus-Cortina MkII
1967-70

As late Lotus-Cortina MkI except:

ENGINE:
Power	109bhp at 6000rpm
Maximum torque	106lb ft at 4500rpm

WHEELS/TYRES:
Tyres 5.5in x 13in

DIMENSIONS:
Track, front	4ft 5.5in
Track, rear	4ft 4in
Width	5ft 5in
Height	4ft 6in

KERB WEIGHT:
17.9cwt

PERFORMANCE:
(Source: *Autocar*)
Max speed	104mph
0-60mph	11.0sec
30-50mph in top	9.8sec
50-70mph in top	12.4sec

PRICE INCLUDING TAX WHEN NEW:
£1068 (August 1967)

NUMBER BUILT:
4032

The Cortina bodyshell was carefully designed to maximise space without adding weight. Lotus modifications substituted aluminium panels for steel for the bonnet, doors and bootlid, although this became optional later in the production run.

The Lotus-Cortina cabin was dressed with the sporty must-haves of the time, some of them unique, such as the front seats. On this first-generation MkI, round instruments replace the ribbon speedometer used on Cortinas until September 1963. A Lotus-badged wooden gearknob complements the steering wheel.

The twin-cam cylinder head was a tight squeeze in the engine bay despite the block being based on the Cortina unit. A brake servo (top right in the engine bay) was added to boost the stopping power of the specially-developed Girling front disc brakes.

course, was the green flash that is said to have been Chapman's idea. The Lotus-Cortina sat an inch lower on wider wheels and tyres, with new front springs, different damper settings and an anti-roll bar, but only at the front. This is why most period photos of racing MkI Lotus-Cortinas show the inner front wheel cocked in the air. New 9½in disc brakes, developed by Girling, rounded off the front end.

Chapman's influence was most apparent in the design of the rear suspension. The standard Cortina was pretty much horse-and-cart, with a sturdy live axle located by leaf springs. It had none of the sophistication of the Elan and Lotus radically altered the layout by discarding the leaf springs and attaching either end of the axle to links which trailed forward to pick up on the original forward

Sir John Whitmore on racing a Lotus-Cortina

Sir John Whitmore's racing career with Lotus was brief but dazzling. After driving for the Le Mans Elite team of 1959, he went on to race for BMC and won the British Saloon Car Championship (BSCC) in a Mini. In 1964 Ford invited him to join one of the Cortina teams: Team Lotus, Ford dealer John Willment's outfit, or the European team fielded by Alan Mann Racing. "My first take was to go with Lotus – it was obvious – and be in the team with Jimmy Clark, but then Alan Mann pointed out all I'd ever be was second driver to Jimmy Clark. He said 'What do you want to be, first driver in the European Championship or second in the British?'." Although he would sometimes stand in for Jim Clark in England, Whitmore therefore chose European racing and was rewarded with the championship in 1965.

He soon learned to master the Lotus-Cortina. "You had to grab the thing by the scruff of its neck and throw it around. It wasn't a particularly delicate car so you just had to be a bit brutal with it. When you got used to it – and I did so many

racing miles in it – I would do a long-distance race and have fun with it, be absolutely on the edge with it, but I could still wave to the crowd."

Whitmore remained great friends with Colin Chapman until the end, but disagreed with him on the A-frame suspension: in back-to-back tests the leaf-sprung Alan Mann cars were always quicker and more durable. "It probably cost Ford a great deal more than it need have done to get the success they had. He was very good with suspension in almost every

case but when you're like Colin you're not going to get it right every time, rather like the Lotus 30 race car, which didn't really work. The A-frame was the same – it certainly wasn't any better than the leaf springs."

Sir John Whitmore opted to drive for the Alan Mann racing team, in its red and gold livery, and was a real crowd-pleaser. In this 1964 race he is pursued by a Mini and an Alfa Romeo Giulia. The Alfas were to be the toughest competition for the Cortina in European racing.

mounting points for the leaf springs. To control sideways movement a triangular 'A' bracket was mounted at its tip under the differential housing with each end facing forwards and mounted on the bodyshell.

The Cortina was designed to have a big boot but the Lotus suspension dictated stiffening braces from the tail panel to the top of the wheelarches, displacing the spare wheel to the boot floor, while the battery was relocated from the engine compartment to help weight distribution.

The cabin was trimmed in appropriately sporty fashion for the time, with unique competition seats, lots of black vinyl, and a wood-rimmed steering wheel. A shorter-throw floor-mounted gearlever was fitted and a new instrument panel featured a circular speedometer and rev-counter

in place of the strip speedometer of early Cortinas.

The standard Ford Cortina range was launched in September 1962. Both the Elan and the Lotus-Cortina were intended to be available from January 1963, but deliveries didn't start until spring, when the rush was on to achieve to homologation. As it was a completely new line of cars, Ford initially played safe by badging early Cortinas as Ford Consul Cortinas, and the Lotus Type 28 became the Ford Consul Cortina-Lotus if you were a Ford dealer or simply a Lotus-Cortina to everyone else. It cost £1100 compared to the £639 of a basic two-door, but then it had twice the power-to-weight ratio.

Cars would arrive at Cheshunt fully painted and trimmed and Lotus would fit the engine, transmission and

suspension. Ford had a Lotus liaison manager on site to keep the link between Cheshunt and Dagenham sweet, but relations became strained as delivery dates strayed. The Elan was proving difficult to get into production and held up by the last-minute change in engine capacity from 1498cc to 1558cc to take advantage of the new racing regulations.

"In practice it didn't work out very well. Indeed, it was twelve months until the Lotus-Cortina came into production and even then they only came out in dribbles," says Sir Terence Beckett. "We gave Chapman a pretty free hand but he had a lot of difficulties getting it into production – the availability of materials he did or didn't want, tapping into a large organisation from a small one. He was developing it as he went along."

The Lotus-Cortina was built for competition and in 1964 racing customers were offered a power boost to 140bhp from a twin-cam stretched, at 1593cc, to the class racing limit. The conversion cost an extra £600, bringing the total price to £1725.

Still full of black vinyl, the facelifted Lotus-Cortina shared the improvements introduced on the 1965 Cortina range, including the round 'Aeroflow' air vents either side of the restyled dashboard: the instrument panel, with its alloy facing, is unique to these Lotus-Cortinas.

With the Elan's closer gear ratios, testers found that while the Lotus-Cortina wasn't especially quick from rest, its 105bhp was impressively delivered from 3500rpm. *Autocar* found 0–60mph came up in 13.6 seconds and 100mph in 43.1 seconds, with a top speed of 108mph. 'The car has an entirely different ride and feel from the standard product. Everything feels more firm and taut. It is more susceptible to minor bumps; on the other hand it remains glued to the road when driven fast in a way not normally associated with live rear axles,' commented the magazine, which had lost the 'The' from its title in 1962.

At a rate of five cars a day, homologation for Group 2 racing was achieved by the end of 1963. But 1964 was the year the Lotus-Cortina made its impact on road and track. Specifications also changed as the result of racing knowledge and following Ford's updates to the Cortina range. In July 1964 the road cars started to lose some of the weight-saving material (less important with homologation achieved), with the alloy transmission castings being replaced by cast-iron items and the aluminium panels becoming optional. To cure vibration, a two-piece propshaft replaced the original single-piece unit

and the close-ratio Elan gearbox was swapped for a Cortina GT unit. In 1964 Cortinas were raced by Team Lotus, with Jim Clark winning the British Saloon Car Championship, and also in Europe in the red-and-gold livery of Alan Mann Racing; in race trim they had 140bhp and a top speed of 128mph. Although the mainstream Cortina was not sold in the States the Lotus-Cortina was US-available – as a costly import – and here again it was raced with some success.

On road as on track, the Lotus-Cortina got a bit of a reputation. Early cars were sometimes down on power and although they could be serviced

While it excelled on the racetrack from the start, rally success eluded the Phase 1 Lotus Cortina because of the fragility of Chapman's rear suspension design. For 1965 this was replaced by simpler but more robust leaf springs, and thus improved the cars remained rally-competitive after the Mk1 Cortina had ceased production in 1966.

at Ford dealerships they were costly prospects to run. 'Unfortunately, 'Lotus' also spells 'racing' to the insurance man. The premiums are pretty high, and there was a lot of truth in the quip heard at the Motor Show – "it's an old man's car. No young man can afford the insurance",' said *Practical Motorist* in February 1965,

when it tested the facelifted Lotus-Cortina. 'As soon as you take off in first gear you realize that there is a little bit of Formula 1 buried somewhere in this car.'

The 1965 model year brought in changes from the facelifted Cortina range, such as a new dashboard with 'Aeroflow' ventilation and a new grille.

The biggest change was reserved for the latter half of the year when the Chapman-designed rear suspension was dropped for a version of the original leaf-spring set-up. The Lotus design put a great deal of stress on the differential housing and the racing teams found that this needed constant checking during a race and had to be

Crayford convertible Lotus-Cortinas

In the 1960s Crayford Auto Developments in Kent would chop the top from just about any car, but were most closely linked to Ford, often having access to early

prototypes. The convertible Lotus-Cortinas are the rarest of all Crayford's Ford conversions, few having been made and few surviving.

Accounts differ as to true numbers, but it is believed that no MkI Lotus-Cortina convertibles were produced. On the other hand around 200 soft-top MkII Cortinas were built, in two configurations: on the convertible, the hood folded down to sit on top of the parcel shelf, while on the more costly cabriolet a narrowed rear seat enabled the hood to sit flush with the bodywork. An extra crossmember had to be fitted under the dash to brace the front bulkhead. In total, only 20 MkII Lotus-Cortinas are thought to have been converted by Crayford.

A very rare breed: Crayford soft-top conversions of the MkII Lotus Cortina needed substantial bracing. By the time of this 1969 car, Ford was using Cortina 'Twin Cam' badges on the bootlid. (Andy Morrell)

Above: Although the Lotus-Cortina became a mainstream Ford-built car as the 1967 model-year MkII, Ford still played up the sports connection in its advertising (here with a McLaren Formula 2 car). Available only as a two-door, Ford gave the Lotus-Cortina an optional sill stripe inspired by that worn by the GT40.

Right: The interior of an early MkII Lotus-Cortina; only minor changes were made during its production run.

frequently topped up with oil. Left unchecked this movement could lead to the rear suspension collapsing or the suspension bushes becoming contaminated by oil leaks. The protruding brackets also made the Lotus-Cortina vulnerable to damage from rough roads and it was the leaf-sprung Cortina GT that gained a fine

rally reputation rather than the Lotus version. "The diff moved so much there was a 'top hat' in the boot it could go up into," says former export sales manager Roger Putnam.

Nonetheless, spurred on by its adoption for racing, from June 1965 Lotus-Cortinas reverted to standard Cortina GT rear suspension, with semi-

elliptic springs and additional location by twin radius arms. Another change, in October 1965, was to switch to the gearbox ratios from the Corsair 2000E, along with self-adjusting rear brakes. As with the Elan, a Special Equipment Lotus-Cortina became available, with a 115bhp engine. "The SE had adjustable shock absorbers, which

The Escort Twin-Cam

In 1968 Ford replaced the Anglia with the Escort. The competitions department soon spotted that the lighter Escort would 'go like hell with a twin-cam engine in it'. Intended primarily to create an effective rally car, the Lotus engine was duly fitted to a strengthened bodyshell with flared wheelarches and homologated for Group 2 and Group 3 in 1968. Ford offered a limited run to private customers, up to June 1971, when its AVO section took over to produce the RS range of Escorts.

Launched in 1968, the Ford Escort provided the basis of Ford's performance and competition cars for many years and was briefly offered with the Lotus twin-cam – although it was never badged as a Lotus. Quarter bumpers became an identifying feature of Ford's fast Escorts.

The characteristic green striping of the MkI was still available on the MkII, even though the car lacked the MkI's concave pressing in the body flanks.

Chapman hated," recalls Putnam. "He said 'Why should I allow anyone to play with the suspension on a car that I've designed? They're bound to get it wrong.'. . ."

Racing successes continued to mount during 1965, with Sir John Whitmore winning the European Touring Car Championship in an Alan Mann car. There was still more to come from the twin-cam, and for 1966 Cortinas raced in Group 5 with BRM dry-sump engines and fuel injection, these improvements giving 180bhp and a potential 150mph.

But the paths of Ford and Lotus were starting to diverge. 1966 marked the move to Hethel, the announcement of the Europa – and the arrival of a new, larger MkII Cortina which carried over the floorpan and other key components from the first model. A new Lotus version was more part of the marketing mix than a racing necessity, and Ford declined the offer of car assembly at Hethel. The MkII Lotus-Cortina thus became a

Without a stripe and available in the full range of Cortina colours, the MkII Lotus-Cortina was the ultimate 'stealth' car. Always built by Ford itself, the Lotus identity was dropped in 1970 and the car simply badged 'Twin-Cam'. The Lotus emblem on the grille of this car is a later fitting.

production model at Dagenham, with twin-cam engines supplied from Hethel; now the car was all-steel, it could easily be built on a Ford production line.

The MkII – now firmly called Cortina-Lotus by Ford – appeared in March 1967, still only a two-door but with a choice of colours and with the green flash an option on white cars. With only the black front grille of the Cortina GT and wider wheels to distinguish it, a MkII could really sneak up on you

unawares. It was heavier, but with the 115bhp Special Equipment engine as standard it was still good for 104mph and 0–60mph in 11 seconds, while being more comfortable – and more benign to drive fast – than its more track-orientated predecesssor. Essentially a Lotus-engined Cortina GT, this second-generation Lotus-Cortina ran through until the end of the 1970 model year. It changed little in this period, the principal modifications being a revised dashboard and a floor-mounted handbrake for the 1969 season.

Meanwhile, Team Lotus happily moved over from the now-obsolete MkI. Graham Hill gave the MkII its first outing, in 200bhp Cosworth FVA form, and it also continued to cut a swathe through British saloon car racing with Alan Mann's team. Used in rallying before the arrival of the Escort, it won the Canadian Shell 4000

Rally, the Gulf London Rally and the Scottish Rally in 1967.

According to historian Graham Robson, an estimated 2894 MkI Lotus-Cortinas were assembled by Lotus at Cheshunt between 1963 and 1966. To put its rarity in context, production of the standard Ford Cortina had hit one million by 1966. As for the MkII, something of an orphan these days, in its time it more than paid the rent, with a total of 4032 being made, the last in July 1970.

For a limited-run image-booster the Lotus-Cortina had punched well above its weight. "The entire Lotus-Cortina project, and our involvement in it with Ford, did a great many good things for Lotus," said Fred Bushell to Chapman biographer Jabby Crombac. "They gave us support with buying and taught us such things as quality control, and they virtually forced us into developing the management structure."

Lotus and the Ford GT40

Ford's obsession to make it big in motorsport knew no bounds. In 1963, with an eye to winning Le Mans, Uncle Henry went shopping in Italy and was only thwarted in a bid to buy Ferrari when founder Enzo Ferrari established that he would not have autonomy over the racing team. When the deal collapsed in spring 1963, Ford of America looked to England for the builder of what was to become the Ford GT40 Le Mans car.

The week after the Le Mans race, a Ford delegation took in a tour of likely candidates: Cooper, Lola and Lotus. Ford even considered taking over Lotus completely but at that point the company had no experience of building V8-engined GT cars; also Chapman would have been unwilling to sell. The business eventually went to Lola – already developing its mid-engined Mk6 with a Ford Fairlane engine – and the whole operation was snapped up by Ford.

US author Leo Levine, who has chronicled the GT40 story, writes that

The GT40 in action, at the 1967 Nürburgring 1000kms; this is the car driven by Colin Crabbe and Roy Pierpoint.

although Lotus, with its existing British and American contracts, seemed such an obvious choice, there was a concern that Colin Chapman would rub up against the equally strong-willed Carroll Shelby who was responsible for the Ford-powered V8 Cobras, and Ford would emerge the loser in the publicity stakes. Shelby later took over the GT40 programme but the cars were built in

England. Although he continued to do well out of Ford, Chapman was considered to have been sufficiently annoyed by losing the deal that he planned to offer a GT version of the ill-fated 1964 Lotus 30 racing car.

Buying Hints

1. The Lotus-Cortina has long been regarded as a valuable classic and it is still popular in historic motorsport, therefore there is an interest in faking one. Later cars with fewer Lotus-only parts, such as alloy casings, are easier to fake, and a run-of-the-mill Cortina GT can thus provide the basis for a convincing Lotus clone. The Lotus Cortina register – www.lotuscortina.net – can help to identify a genuine car.

2. As a steel-bodied car, any inspection has to start with a hunt for corrosion, which can be extensive. Look everywhere, including the door posts, around the rear suspension,

and around the front suspension turrets inside the engine bay, an area which can however be repaired. A leaking battery can cause the boot floor to corrode.

3. Outer panels are common to the standard Cortina, so if you can find them they will fit straight onto a Lotus. Make sure unique Lotus trim parts such as the badges and the quarter-bumpers are present. Look also for unique items of interior trim: the dash binnacles were Lotus-only, as were the front seats on the pre-facelift MkI. Both steering wheel and gearlever should be finished in wood.

4. The engine advice for the Elan also applies to the Lotus-Cortina's twin-cam. It will start to smoke if heavily worn and the timing-chain tensioner screw should be inspected to see how much thread is showing. Water pump failure presents the same problem of having to remove the cylinder head and sump. Note that the radiator is unique to the car.

5. Suspension and steering components give little trouble and can all be rebuilt, but work on the 'A' frame will cost more. Specialists can supply rebuilt braking components.

The Europa

From drawing board to production in around 18 months, the Lotus Europa followed the exotic mid-engined principles of the Lamborghini Miura, the Ford GT40 and of course the Lotus Type 23. This is a British-market Series 2.

Britain's first mid-engined sports car had a turbulent production cycle, even for a Lotus. A low-cost car that never was cheap, it was denied to home-market buyers for over two years, and only when substantially redesigned after five years did it redeem itself and become hailed as 'the poor man's Ferrari Dino'.

Like the Elan, the Europa sprang from the feeling that the Seven didn't fit Lotus's new sophisticated image and should really be pensioned off. In 1963 there had been thoughts of a glassfibre Seven with a pushrod engine but although Ron Hickman carried out a study of costs and some basic designs, the Lotus-Cortina was a more pressing project and the idea progressed no further.

However, in early 1964 Colin Chapman once more turned his attention to the P5 project, for a car planned to be built by Lotus Components at the rate of five a week.

The concept was for a sophisticated GT car using as many proprietary components as possible and offering a first for Lotus road cars and for British buyers: a mid-engined confuguration. In fact the Europa, as the P5 became, was one of the world's first mid-engined production sports cars – ahead of the Lamborghini Miura and its true rivals the Matra M530 and Volkswagen-Porsche 914.

The genesis of the shape is a little unclear but Ron Hickman says he provided the initial inspiration in 1963. At that time Lotus was in the running for the Ford GT40 contract and a Ford team arrived at Cheshunt for a look round. "I'd done a drawing to impress them," Hickman remembers. "It had Lotus badges on it, engine trumpets sticking out of a rear duct and eight pipes. I wanted it to scream V8 and stuck it on my office wall, to give the impression that was what we were going to do at Le Mans. Colin said 'If we don't get the job, we'll make it ourselves one day'. . ."

This is what came to pass. But the car needed the right engine and transmission combination at the right price. The Ford 105E engine and the Lotus twin-cam had been designed to be front-mounted, transmitting power

Lotus Europa
1966–75

Models quoted: Europa S2, Twin Cam and Special

ENGINE:
Four cylinders in line, aluminium block and cylinder head (iron block on Twin Cam/Special), water-cooled

Capacity	1470cc/1558cc
Bore x stroke	76mm x 81mm
	82.6mm x 72.8mm (Twin Cam/Special)
Valve actuation	Pushrod
	Twin overhead cam (Twin Cam/Special)
Compression ratio	10.25:1
	9.5:1 (Twin Cam)
	10.3:1 (Special)
Carburettor(s)	Twin-choke Solex (SE)
	2 x Dellorto 40 DHLA
Power	82bhp at 6000rpm
	105bhp at 5500rpm (Twin Cam)
	126bhp at 6500rpm (Special)
Maximum torque	79lb ft at 4000rpm
	103lb ft at 4500rpm (Twin Cam)
	113lb ft at 5500rpm (Special)

TRANSMISSION:
Mid-engined, rear-wheel drive; four-speed gearbox (S2 and Twin Cam) or five-speed (Special)

SUSPENSION:
Front: Independent by coil springs and twin wishbones; telescopic dampers; anti-roll bar
Rear: Independent by coil springs and lower wishbones, fixed-length driveshafts; location by diagonal radius arms and lateral lower link; telescopic dampers

STEERING:
Rack-and-pinion

BRAKES:
Front: Disc
Rear: Drum
Servo-assistance standard on Twin Cam and Special

WHEELS/TYRES:
13in steel (optional Brand Lotus alloys for Twin Cam/Special)
Tyres 4.5 x 13in

BODYWORK:
Glassfibre reinforced plastic; steel backbone chassis
Two-door coupé

DIMENSIONS:

Length	13ft 1in
Wheelbase	7ft 7in/7ft 8in
Track, front	4ft 5¼in/4ft 6¼in
Track, rear	4ft 6¼in
Width	5ft 4½in
Height	3ft 6in/3ft 7¼in

KERB WEIGHT:
13.1cwt (S2)
14cwt (Special)

PERFORMANCE:
(Source: *Motor/Autocar*)
Models quoted: S2 and Special

Max speed	114mph/121mph
0–60mph	9.5sec/7.7sec
30–50mph in top	9.2sec/10.9sec
50–70mph in top	10.4sec/10.9sec

PRICE INCLUDING TAX WHEN NEW:
£1667 (S2, 1969)
£2471 (Special, 1973)

NUMBER BUILT:
9887

The prototype shown at the 1966 launch: Lotus made no bones that it designed the Europa shell around available mass-produced bumpers rather than tooling up for a bespoke design. The drive for aerodynamic efficiency and the resultant use of double-curvature glass led to fixed windows – but these had to be made removable for reasons of practicality and cabin ventilation.

Clan Crusader: the real 'New Seven'?

If the Europa and the Elan were never quite budget sports cars, the short-lived Clan Crusader made a reality of the M2 concept.

Lotus engineers Brian Luff and Paul Haussauer were determined to pursue the idea of a glassfibre monocoque and, with a band of after-hours helpers, devised their own sports car, based around rear-mounted Hillman Imp Sport mechanicals. Europa and Elite stylist John Frayling was brought in to fashion the shape using strict cost parameters such as flat side glass and fixed-height headlamp pods. Clever details included foam-filled bumpers that were the same front and rear.

In 1970 Haussauer left Lotus to set up a new factory in Washington, County Durham, encouraged by generous regional assistance. Launched in 1971 fully-built, and then as a kit, the Clan Crusader was well received and was regarded as a quality car, but the project foundered

The Imp-based Clan Crusader was created by a group of Lotus engineers, as their idea of a 'New Seven'; it was a glassfibre monocoque with local timber reinforcement.

only two years later in the wake of the three-day week, the imposition of VAT, and production problems at the factory. Around 320 had been made.

The factory contents were sold to a Cypriot industrialist in 1974 but lay idle after the island was partitioned. Ten years later the Crusader was revived in Northern Ireland, updated with pop-up headlamps and latterly with Alfasud power. This rebirth lasted for only two years and some 40 cars.

Interior designer Peter Cambridge designed an alloy-faced dashboard for the Europa but for the S2 it was given a wood-faced item in line with those used on other Lotus models. The switches for the electric windows are on the centre console and the seats are now adjustable, rather than one having to move the pedals with a spanner.

rearwards into a gearbox, then through a propshaft to the rear wheels. Losing much of this hardware, the P5 demanded a combined gearbox and final drive unit and it seemed that there was nothing suitable readily available at the right price.

It has also been said that Chapman did not want to be entirely dependent on Ford for all his engine blocks and be vulnerable to sudden changes in price and supply. BMC and Vauxhall engines were researched but dismissed as too expensive and too heavy. A more obvious choice was the 875cc Hillman Imp engine, which could trace its ancestry to the Coventry Climax FW series, but the Rootes Group had rushed the Imp onto the market and a string of quality problems had ruined its reputation.

Chapman immediately spotted the

Opposite: Shown to the press just before Christmas 1966, the Lotus Type 46 was presented as the Lotus Europa or the Lotus-Renault GT. The first export-only series quickly changed in detail as production got underway. Here the engine cover is held on by Dzus fasteners and the rear light clusters are ex-Lancia Italian Carello units. These gave way to less expensive items before British sales began with the Series 2; also the door buttons were replaced by handles.

The move to Hethel

Lotus has been synonymous with Norfolk since 1966 but at the time the decision seemed perverse to industry observers. Norfolk has no history of motorsport manufacture and was well away from the motorway network and the traditional British motor industry in the Midlands.

Yet it did make sense on other levels. Cheshunt had run out of capacity and more space was needed for the Europa. Chapman wanted a new site within 100 miles of London with a landing strip for his aircraft and space for a test track. He and Fred Bushell narrowed the choice down to three sites before opting for Hethel near Norwich: grants were on offer to encourage business to take up where farming was tailing off, and the local council offered every assistance.

The land was acquired in 1965 and Chapman took a great interest in every detail of the factory – sometimes too much, as the building ran way over budget. Built through 1966 by Costain, it was a state-of-the-art facility which incorporated

much open-plan space – then almost unheard-of, but which Chapman had seen used by BP in Germany. It proved the perfect backdrop to the ultra-modern Europa placed in the foyer. At the same time the boss was able to buy nearby Ketteringham Hall and this later became home to Team Lotus and to the occasional more personal project.

To convince the nearly 500-strong Cheshunt workforce to move to Norfolk, Graham Arnold and the sales department persuaded furniture shops, estate agents, building societies and other Norwich businesses to mount an 'ideal home' exhibition at Cheshunt, and to show the financial advantages the team would buy £10 of groceries in Cheshunt and the same in Norwich. Company accountant Fred Bushell was induced to put down deposits on 24 bungalows in Wymondham and relocation allowances were provided. Staff transferred as parts of the site were completed and the move was finished by November 1966.

Superfast Europas

Making clear its racing pedigree, just six days after the roadgoing Europa was unveiled to the press its racing cousin the Lotus 47 made its debut at the Brands Hatch Boxing Day meeting on 26 December 1966. Driven by John Miles, the car, built from a prototype Europa, won first time out.

Although it bore a distinct resemblance to the Europa, and was sometimes referred to as one, there was very little the road car shared with this no-expense-spared racer. The much-lightened bodyshell sat on a backbone chassis but it held a 1594cc 160bhp Cosworth-Lotus twin-cam with fuel injection and a five-speed racing gearbox. The rubber suspension bushing was replaced by metal joints and disc brakes fitted all-round, with the rears inboard. The 47 also had

Above: Unlike the Elan, a competition derivative of the Europa, the Lotus 47, was ready as soon as the road car – but again for export only, as a fully-built car.

Right: Launched at the 1967 Racing Car Show, the 47 gave notice that a twin-cam would fit the engine bay; but road-car drivers would neither have afforded nor liked the Hewland transmission.

twin fuel tanks, and the entire nose space was filled with an oil tank for the dry sump, as well as the oil cooler and the master cylinders. It was priced at £2600 in kit form in 1967.

Lotus Components planned to

build 55 cars (it had to build 50 to qualify for the FIA Group 4 racing category of the time) but the exact number really completed is not clear. The 47's competition career lasted for the 1967 and 1968 seasons and it

engine he wanted when Renault launched its front-wheel-drive, five-door R16 at the 1965 Geneva Motor Show. Unusually, for a mass-produced family car, it had an aluminium cylinder block and gearbox casing, and the cylinder dimensions and shape of the combustion chambers meant it could be readily tuned. Unlike BMC's fwd cars, the R16's 1470cc engine was longitudinally mounted and took its drive forwards via a transaxle which combined the gearbox

and final drive. To fit it in a mid-engined car, all you had to do was rotate the whole unit through 180 degrees, although to prevent the car having four reverse gears and one forward ratio, the crownwheel-and-pinion naturallly had to be reversed.

Another plus was that the engine ancillaries such as the distributor were mounted on the gearbox end of the powerpack, and so would be easily accessible with the engine turned around in the Lotus. The Ford 105E

and the Lotus twin-cam had their service components at the front, and in the same situation would have been up against the bulkhead. The downside of this end-on gearbox was that the gear and clutch linkages had to be very long, travelling past the engine and into the cabin – resulting in a change that was a complete contrast to the short-throw shift of the Elan and the cause of much grumbling.

In 1965 Chapman enlisted the help of his friend the Paris-based motoring wedged the idea of a de-tuned version for the road in many people's minds, making the Twin Cam a foregone conclusion. Indeed, a number of people converted 47s into road cars, with engines ranging from twin-cams to BMW 2-litres. Lotus Components itself made up road cars using Ford Cortina 1600GT engines and one car, mated to a Renault transmission, became the one-off Europa twin-cam Type 52 of 1968.

For 1969 the Lotus Type 62 replaced the 47, marking the first outing for what was to become the 2-litre engine for the '70s generation of Lotus road cars – only tuned for 240bhp and given fuel injection. The Type 62 had a passing resemblance to the Europa (not least because the S2 was finally being promoted on the British market), but there the similarity ended. The 62 was a total racer, with a spaceframe chassis, and with many components from Lotus race cars. Only two 62s were built and they proved their worth by showing up weaknesses in the Vauxhall cylinder block.

The most impressive Europa was a 47-based road car with a 185bhp Rover V8, built in 1968 for British motor-component manufacturer GKN. As well as being MD Claude Birch's personal car, the GKN Europa was a promotional tool intended to use as many GKN components as possible. The use of a German ZF five-speed gearbox, however, meant the whole

powertrain was too long for the standard 47 chassis and this was solved by an add-on spaceframe and a custom-made bodyshell.

With new cylinder heads and the very best internal components for the Rover V8, performance figures were staggering, with a theoretical maximum of 154mph – drivers were warned not to blip the throttle on starting the engine or flames would come out of the carburettor intakes! The cabin was treated to a full re-trim in Connolly leather with a great deal of extra soundproofing. The final

Built as a publicity machine for GKN, this one-off Rover-powered V8 Type 47 needed extra aerodynamic aids just to keep it stuck to the road.

touch – the registration number GKN 47D – was found on a moped and duly transferred. For a few years the monster Europa was further developed and toured race circuits and shows on publicity trips; the car survives restored in the United States. Lotus Components turned down all requests to build a replica.

journalist Gérard 'Jabby' Crombac, to make an approach to Renault. At this stage he was still referring to the P5 as an 'inexpensive replacement for the Lotus 7' and proposed the idea of buying 500 engine/gearbox units a year. Renault's then head of PR, Bob Sicot, jumped at the chance of an association with Lotus's motorsport success – the company by then riding high with Jim Clark's many victories – and after various clandestine meetings in May 1965 a deal was done.

Even though the Renault agreement was right for the time, the Europa engine bay was designed from the outset to take a variety of engines. Early sketches by draughtsman Ian Jones show the twin-cam engine in silhouette with the outline of the Renault unit superimposed on it, showing that the Renault engine sat noticeably taller in the engine bay. The sketches also show a 'VW gearbox', typical of the Lotus talent for using components from other

manufacturers. In its standard form the R16 engine first developed 62bhp but Renault supplied a tuned 78bhp version for Lotus, this (net) output developed at 6000rpm by virtue of a higher compression ratio, bigger inlet valves and a single twin-choke Solex carburettor.

For comparison the standard Elan then had 105bhp. In the event the featherweight Europa still boasted a quoted top speed of 117mph. Being widely spaced, the Renault

The Europa GS

The Lotus Europa GS came about in 1974 when designer Mike Rawlings approached stylist William Towns (noted for his Aston Martin work), with an idea to produce a series of body conversions based on existing production cars, one of which was the Europa.

Towns is said to have sketched the shape on the back of a cigarette packet and with its pop-up headlamps and cut-down rear (said to improve visibility and aerodynamics) it took the Europa right into the wedge-shaped seventies. It was at first difficult to distinguish what was left of the Europa but as the conversion kept all the existing glass the centre section looked much the same.

Towns approached Bristol Lotus dealer GS Cars for a chassis and space to make up a prototype and take a set of moulds, and soon GS Cars joined the venture. The first car was completed in July 1975 with a second said to have been produced in consultation with Colin Chapman – who approved enough to allow Lotus badges to be used. The design had a great boost when *The Daily Telegraph* approached Lotus for an Esprit to put

on its stand at the 1975 London Motor Show. No Esprits were available, but Lotus pointed the newspaper in the direction of the GS Europa.

Put forward as a way of recycling a Europa into something that looked like an Esprit for less than half the price, the GS conversion involved cutting down the tips of the front wings, reskinning the doors and fitting an all-new rear section: the new sections were bonded and riveted to the existing bodyshell. The

If you couldn't run to the cost of a new Esprit, the GS Europa was a re-skin of a new or used Europa. With pop-up headlamps and slim rear pillars, GS Cars claimed it was more streamlined and easier to manoeuvre than the original.

cost for the body conversion was £1300 excluding VAT and the extensive options list included a 165bhp Cosworth-Ford BDA dry-sump engine for £2000. Around 8–10 cars are thought to have been built, the last in 1980.

gear ratios were seen as slightly unsporty but were deemed as acceptable.

The prospect of more powerful Renault engines from French sports-car maker Alpine was held out, but after Bob Sicot moved to Ford-France, Renault came under pressure from Alpine's Jean Rédélé not to be so obliging to a rival. There had even been talk of Alpine building the Europa under licence but in the end, from the moment the Europa adopted the twin-cam, the Lotus link with Renault tapered down solely to the use of the R16 transmission units.

The P5 project was not to have the stamp of Ron Hickman on it. Soon after the launch of the Elan he became

fully occupied with the +2 and argued with Chapman (one of the few people prepared to do so) over the development money and time on offer for the Europa, which he felt inadequate. So Chapman decided to head the team himself and took the job over to Lotus Developments. Taking 18 months from design study to prototype, development of the Europa was rapid. John Frayling, who had co-styled the Elite, was brought back as a consultant on the shape, Derek Sleath engineered the production car, Martin Waide the chassis and suspension, and Peter Cambridge was contracted to work up interior proposals. At launch it was openly admitted the Europa had been styled around its

bumpers – Ford Anglia front and Ford Cortina rear – because tooling costs for bespoke units would have been prohibitive. Headlights were standard 7in units from the Mini and taillights were initially Lancia items.

By 1965 it was clear the backbone chassis concept of the Elan was a great success and the Europa used a simpler version, with a truncated 'T' section at the front and a straight section running through the cockpit and widening out to a generous 'Y' at the rear. The engine bay was cooled by ducts in the rear wheelarches and the front-mounted radiator had coolant pipes running through the backbone, the fuel tank being placed to one side of the engine bay. Because the Europa

Above: Although the interior changes solved most early niggles, the Series 2 retained the high-sided fins and consequent poor rear vision when parking. However, some road testers praised the panoramic sweep of the flat rear window, unaffected by reflections.

Left: Compared with the Elan, the Renault-engined Europa was down on power at 82bhp but compensated for this with its light weight and clean shape. Nonetheless, this gave rise to a short-lived trade in tuning options, such as this 1969 conversion from Derbyshire dealer JA Else.

For 1971, a new bodyshell with cut down fins, a lower floorpan and the adoption of the Lotus twin-cam answered in one the major criticisms levelled at the Europa. There was an inevitable increase in price over the S2 but the new engine – coupled to a four-speed gearbox – offered 46 per cent more torque.

was conceived as a fully-built car, the chassis was designed to be bonded to the bodyshell rather than bolted in place, a move which increased rigidity but was to prove a mistake.

Front suspension was similar to that of the Elan, by wishbones and coil springs with Triumph uprights and disc brakes. The rear used a system similar to that found on the Lotus Eighteen racer, with a single tubular lower arm each side, pivoting from the gearbox, and the driveshafts serving as the upper links. Fore and aft location was provided by long box-section radius

arms running diagonally from the bottom of the wheel hubs to the centre of the backbone chassis, and a steel crossbeam ran across the rear of the chassis, between the upper mounting points for the coil springs. To remove the harshness from the ride a lot of rubber bushes had to be used and the suspension became very sensitive to being knocked or to being poorly adjusted. Rear braking was by Vauxhall Viva drums conventionally mounted outboard.

John Frayling is said to have taken his inspiration from the 1961 Ferrari 250GT 'Breadvan' which took the Kamm tail theory to its limits. Once more for Lotus the Europa's aerodynamics were impressive, with a drag coefficient of 0.29, although this was only achieved after windtunnel work brought the figure down from an initial 0.36. The full-sized plaster buck was built by Specialised Mouldings, of Crystal

Palace, South London. Using Frayling's fifth-scale clay P5 model, glassfibre casts were taken, then split into sections and scaled up to make the buck, then the full-sized body mould.

"I did drawings of the front and back half and drawings of the door trims," Peter Cambridge recalls. "They were all based on the fact it had to be dead cheap – this was a Seven replacement. We were going to try moulding a leather texture into the glassfibre and dodges like that, and the instrument panel was very very basic." When Chapman, Ian Jones and Lotus buyer John Standen went to France to collect the first engine for the prototype they were invited to rifle the Renault parts bin for any other smaller items, and door pulls from the French maker were factored in, as were suitable air vents.

The Elite idea of fixed side windows resurfaced, as they appealed to Chapman both on cost and

aerodynamic grounds, and this
demanded some serious thought as to
ventilation. Two electric fans were
fitted in the front compartment, one
to push air through the radiator and
another to help with passenger
ventilation. Two vents were fitted
either side of the dash and these
supplied air independently from the
heater. The theory was that when the
car was moving a ram air effect filled
the small 'boot' behind the spare
wheel and the brake and clutch master
cylinders. This then acted as a plenum
chamber – or air reserve – where
outside and inside air was mixed for
heating and cooling. In motion, the
depression created by this air
movement pulled air through the
cabin from the front to exit through
extractor slots above the rear window
– unless you were sitting in traffic,
when the owner's handbook advised
you to switch the fan on. Without even

quarterlights, the interior quickly
became fuggy or fume-filled, as the
car was low enough to score a direct
hit from the exhaust pipe of the car in
front. It also presented an
insurmountable problem when the
driver drew up to a toll booth and was
forced to open the door to pay –
especially if there were a kerb high
enough to prevent the door from
being opened . . .

For all that, the little car was not
entirely impractical. The interior was
always a tight squeeze and getting in
was like trying to post yourself through
your own letterbox, but brochures
showed a couple of modest weekend
bags in the front luggage compartment
and there was also a reasonable space
at the rear in a tray behind the engine
and transmission that could be taken
out for service access.

The first Renault engine and
gearbox were fitted to a running

*The black and gold livery of John Player Team
Lotus mark this out as the final Europa
derivative, the 1972 Special, fitted with a
Renault five-speed gearbox and the 126bhp
Big Valve engine. A chin spoiler arrived with
the twin-cam to improve stability.*

chassis on an aluminium platform,
known as 'the roller skate'. Two
prototypes were running by mid-1966,
when it was decided that the car
would no longer be a Lotus
Components product and would join
the Elan and the new +2 being
finalised for production at Hethel.

The name is said to have come from
Chapman initially wanting to call the
new car the Elfin or the Concorde, or
so he told the press, but the Europa
tag was settled on as being suitably
Anglo-French. In mainland Europe the
car was initially badged Europe and
only adopted the Europa name in all

Driving a Europa Special

Rewind an Elise thirty years and you have a Europa Special, with its 126bhp twin-cam engine and five-speed gearbox. From the driving seat, with the engine and weight behind you, the car feels as if it has a slight nose-up attitude and, like the Elise, the tops of the wings are easily visible so you can place the car accurately as you flick it round corners.

There is instant direction change via small movements of the standard thin-rimmed wheel, but the Europa doesn't feel nervous, just agile and eager. Proving the virtue of the separate chassis and supple suspension, the Europa is also surprisingly refined in some respects, shrugging off minor potholes without sending judders through the cabin.

The roadholding and handling are of course the aces in the Europa's pack. Even in this, the most powerful variant, the driven wheels always feel planted securely on the road in the dry – unless there's a loose surface at a junction. Cornering is as exciting today as it ever was: almost flat and always secure, so you can accelerate hard and hear the growl of the twin-cam as you surge ahead. For more relaxed progress, once fifth is found the revs drop to around 2500rpm.

However, unlike an Elan, this driving pleasure may not be available until the gearchange has been mastered. Although Lotus tried hard to improve the Europa's gear linkage, any Europa still benefits from specialist adjustment. Driving an original (and now very rare) Special, you can soon lose momentum while fishing for the right gear. In neutral the gate has a lot of sideways movement and until you get a 'feel' for the gear positions, you can even lose your way on the straight downwards movement from third to fourth, while fifth can seem a long way over and up to the right. Not only

that, but as the lever is moved the rods can be heard clicking away.

Still, at least the experience isn't as hair-shirt as on the first Europas. Once you've manoeuvered yourself in, the cockpit is a snug but not claustrophobic fit: by the Special enough footwell space had been squeezed out for six-footers. Hustling round corners, the well padded doors, seat bolsters and central tunnel hold you in place, while the padded top of the tunnel provides a natural rest for the left arm. If however you wear the wrong shoes, or just have big feet, the tiny Europa pedals become a challenge and your clutch foot will rub up against the steering column. Such imperfections remind one that Lotus was still emerging from the kit-car sector with the Europa, but nevertheless the later cars constitute a huge step forward from the purer but less practical S1 and S2.

Trimmed in the characteristic Lotus pale oatmeal trim of the time, the Special had become a mini luxury GT car, and thanks to its new gear ratios was now fit for cross-continental travel. Note the umbrella handbrake under the steering column.

markets with the change to the twin-cam engine. In Lotus-speak this first car was the Lotus 46, the Type 47 being the race version.

In September 1966 the tie-up with Renault was announced, and the Europa was launched on 20 December, as the first new car from the new Hethel factory in Norfolk. At the press presentation it was announced that the first 500 cars were to go to France, thereby taking up the first year of production, and that English sales were not a foregone conclusion. The French price was set at 21,700 francs fully-built, in comparison with the new-for-'67 Matra M530 at 16,490 francs. The price was quoted as likely to be around £1000 when the Europa was eventually put on sale in the UK – a long way from the original target of £650.

Roger Putnam, who joined Lotus as export sales manager in 1965 and went on to become chairman of Ford of Great Britain, was a fluent French

The Banks Europas

Europa Engineering, based at Banks Service Station in Southport, is a long-established Europa specialist which can source new components or remanufacture just about any part. It also runs a Europa-based race series.

Starting with a number of modifications such as new damper kits, it has developed its own custom-built take on the Europa. Created by owner Richard Winter, the Banks 47R is based on a remanufactured version of the Lotus Type 47 shell and the 62S race car which succeeded it. Owners can choose to upgrade their own Europas with some of the parts, or have a full car built for them using a spaceframe chassis which includes twin-wishbone rear suspension. This can accommodate virtually any power unit, including some transverse installations. Vauxhall units are a common choice but cars have been fitted with Alfa Romeo V6 engines and even a Mazda rotary unit.

Over 400 Banks spaceframes have been built and they finally caught the attention of Lotus after exposure on the TV show *Top Gear*. A meeting followed between both companies and an agreement was reached that the cars were worthy to become Lotus Europas 're-engineered by Banks' and wear the Lotus badge – provided a record was kept of the numbers produced.

Right above: While it looks like a '70s original at first glance, the Banks Europa is a re-engineered car built to the customer's specification.

Right: Chapman intended the Europa engine bay to accept a number of power unit: Banks cars have most often used contemporary Vauxhall units.

speaker and so was frequently sent across the Channel on Lotus business. "The Europa was impossible to drive in the summer, and extremely noisy with a very poorly conceived gearshift. It had no feel, like pushing against a sponge," he recalls. "The Renault-engined car was never a great success. It was pre-launched. We had all sorts of interim measures – funny windows and circlips that dropped into a slot into the door. The car was very basic, there was no trim on the doors, just glassfibre painted black, and it would steam up at the slightest drop of rain."

British road tests took some months to emerge, with one of the first being by Doug Blain in *Car* magazine for June 1967. He likened the feeling of being in a Europa to 'lying down in the bottom of a light bulb, gazing at the

Minor chassis modifications were needed to accommodate the Lotus twin-cam and five-speed 'box. Ahead of the engine, a glassfibre luggage box could be removed for maintenance. Owners of well-used Europas wrapped their luggage in case the engine developed an oil leak.

road beneath one's toes'. He soon spotted the many flaws such as poor rear visibility, the tendency to suck in fumes and the relaxed gear ratios. He also suggested that a Ford-powered Europa should be a logical replacement once the car entered the British market. Nonetheless, like other enthusiasts Blain recognised that Lotus had pulled off something special and nobody doubted the way the Europa went round corners. He recorded the highest ever g-force figure for the magazine to that date, and a top speed of 108mph.

With the April 1968 launch of the Series 2 – still export only – Lotus said it had acted on comments from dealers and owners and incorporated over 50 refinements including better soundproofing and electric windows ('to further the image set by the Elan'), plus adjustable seats. Under pressure from the insurance industry the bonded chassis was abandoned, too, in favour of a separate unit, as in the event of an accident owners could otherwise be faced with having to replace the whole shell and chassis.

Front indicators were moved to sit between the headlamps, the rear light units were changed, and the dash was now mahogany-faced marine ply instead of being aluminium-faced.

Lotus had been selling the Series 1 Europa in America with a typical dodge to get past regulations. In standard form the car's fixed headlights were too low for US regulations so cars were shipped with the front lower wishbones set up to make the front ride 1½in higher. This ruined the handling and made the car quite unstable at speed so owners were advised to swap the wishbones back to their original settings. Once the Series 2 was established, Lotus tried fitting longer springs at the front but then designed a revised bodyshell for the US market with a raised wing line. The Federal Europa S2 also had its own engine, Renault's enlarged 1565cc unit, to help comply with emissions targets; power was down a little, all the same, to 80bhp.

In July 1969 the Series 2 Europa was launched on the British market, two-and-a-half years after Europa exports to 35 other countries had begun. The company announced that it would only be available as a fully-built car but that it did not threaten the Elan, of which production was set to continue well into the 1970s. However, the Europa soon joined the price list as a component car. In 1970 the Europa S2 was listed at £1345 in kit form, when an Elan Coupé kit cost £1440.

The Renault engine remained at 1470cc and in the same state of tune, but a number of British dealers offered to boost power with off-the-shelf conversions. Hermes in Wimbledon, South London, offered a conversion to give a claimed 138bhp and Derbyshire dealer Else and Sons offered a number of changes covering the engine and gear ratios. With a big enough budget, Else conversions could become quite elaborate, with a new cylinder head, twin fuel tanks, alloy wheels and custom paint. There was also a BRM-branded conversion along the same lines.

Soon Renault engine tuning was made redundant by the inevitable twin-cam Europa. The project started

Buying Hints

1. With its chassis sandwiched into the bodyshell, the Series 1 Europa poses a particular problem if rust has set in. The chassis is bonded and riveted into the shell and has to be cut away, which is not a DIY job. With their low value, it is possible but not economically feasible to convert a Series 1 car to the later bolt-on chassis.

2. As for the chassis, rust starts in the front box section and the suspension pick-up points. At the rear the chassis can corrode beneath the battery tray. Replacement chassis are available as well as the Europa Engineering spaceframe conversion.

3. Europa rear suspension is very sensitive to wear and damage as the driveshafts form an active part of the suspension. Suspension bushes need to be in top condition to enjoy best handling and tyre wear will be heavy if the suspension is not correctly set up. If all is not well the car will weave all over the road.

4. If a handful of joints become loose, Europa gearchange quality can become very tricky – although if well set up by a specialist the later cars can be very good. The five-speed is more troublesome and it is possible to mis-select ratios, dropping from third to reverse instead of second. The linkage can come apart with wear, leaving you unable to select any gear.

5. Unlike the Elan twin-cam, the Europa twin-cam installation has separate drive belts for the water pump and the alternator, and these accordingly are less prone to knock out their bearings. Judging a twin-cam's condition is the same procedure as for an Elan (smoke and rattling), while the Renault engine's main problem is overheating.

6. While the Lotus twin-cam engine is still well supported by specialists, finding parts for a Renault-engined car is extremely difficult as there is no Lotus support for them and Renault dealers are not interested. Sourcing Renault 16 components is not always an answer, in any case, as the Lotus unit was tuned and modified in a number of ways, but specialists can come up with some parts swaps.

7. Look for accident damage and the inevitable gel cracks. Painting fibreglass is a specialised job on all Lotus shells, so if they have been restored check the standard of paint and preparation. Replacement bodyshells are available.

---

in earnest with the 1969 arrival of Mike Kimberley. He took a hard look at the Europa's flaws: the cockpit was too cramped, rear visibility was appalling, acceleration was lacking, and the gearchange was too stiff. Tony Rudd worked out a reasonably-priced way to mate a twin-cam to a Renault four-speed gearbox and transaxle but was limited to the 105bhp version because the gearbox had not been designed to cope with so much power. To overcome the problem of access to the twin-cam's ancillaries, Kimberley remounted the alternator with its own belt drive but the water pump had to stay in its original position. The gearbox linkage was re-routed and twin fuel tanks fitted.

The biggest body change was to cut the rear side panels down to the level of the engine cover and this lessened the blind spot a little. Inside, changes to the footwells boosted interior space, these mods being designed around the tall frame of Mike Kimberley, and the wheelbase was extended by an inch. Compared to the 1966 original the car was more luxuriously trimmed inside and while steel wheels were in theory standard, the optional Brand Lotus alloys invariably specified set off the new-look Europa Twin Cam a treat. Launched in late 1971, by this stage the rethought Europa had serious – and better-built – competition from the Volkswagen-Porsche 914, especially in the US market, so these changes came none too soon.

The Europa Twin Cam was to last a little over a year before the availability of the stronger five-speed gearbox of the Renault 16TX made it possible to fit the 126bhp Big Valve engine. The resultant 1972 Europa Special was named after the Team Lotus John Player Specials and a version was made available in the black and gold livery of the sponsor's cigarette packs.

The new five-speed transmission gave a much better set of gear ratios for long-distance cruising, and at last the Europa was loved by the road testers without too much qualification.

'The Europa is getting better all the time and no doubt it will become an even more successful car than its predecessor,' wrote John Bolster in an *Autosport* supplement. 'The Lotus Europa Special is a high-performance sports car with superb handling and roadholding'.

In 1973 *Autocar* recorded a best top speed of 121mph, yet was impressed by a fifth-gear fuel consumption of 30mpg. The same year the Elan was dropped from the range but the Europa Special, having been passed for another year under US safety legislation, continued. At £2708 it was considered expensive but desirable and even though the price had risen to £3209 by 1974, with the Fiat X1/9 snapping at its heels, *Car* magazine was moved to call the Special 'the most potent cheap sports car money can buy'. Europa production ended in March 1975 but there was to be a long delay before the Esprit surfaced as its would-be replacement.

The Elite and Eclat

'Now, the exhilaration of Lotus performance comes to four-seater motoring', said the glossy brochure for the 1974 Elite. It was a big-risk venture to aim at prestige car buyers.

It may be the least-loved model now, but Lotus bet the bank on the new Elite of 1974. This was the complete break with the kit-car past, the curtain-raiser to a range of larger and more sophisticated cars for the '70s and '80s. Project M50 was a car of many (perhaps too many) firsts for Lotus: the first to offer four genuine seats for adults, the first to use the new VARI vacuum resin-moulding process, the first to use the all-Lotus 2-litre 16-valve engine, and the first to be aimed straight at Britain's executive car market. This Elite had to work.

Planning had started by late 1967,

when the +2 had only just gone on sale, and continued fitfully until 1970. Chapman reasoned that, like himself, many Lotus customers had become successful professional people with no time to spend tinkering with cars they had built themselves. They also had bigger children and bigger salaries. The +2 was a clear nod towards this type of buyer, and the +2S was another move upwards, in that it was not offered in kit form. It was important that the M50 marked a further step forward, as well as that it would seat four adults.

In 1969 two key personalities arrived who were virtually to run Lotus for the next decade. Mike Kimberley, an ex-Jaguar engineer, became 'Engineer in charge of Continuous Development' and Tony Rudd was recruited from the BRM grand prix team, initially as manager of the Powertrain Engineering department. They were joined in 1971 by stylist Oliver Winterbottom.

While one of Kimberley's first jobs was to look at the entire Europa and Elan range for limited re-engineering, Rudd turned his attention to an engine for the new generation that would be all-Lotus, rather than half-Ford. Chapman would not consider Lotus to be a proper carmaker until it could build its own engines and be as self-sufficient as possible. In 1966 a project had started to develop a 150bhp four-cylinder 2-litre engine which could be slanted at an angle of 45 degrees, enabling it to fit under a low bonnet line. It was to have twin-overhead camshafts driven by a toothed belt and four valves per cylinder: a very sophisticated specification at the time.

The new Lotus engine was conceived as a series of six racing and road versions culminating in a V8, as the second half of the 'V' could be added without changing the bonnet line or the space available in the engine bay. All of the '70s models were designed to accommodate the V8, but only the Esprit was ever to receive it. Additionally a V6 was considered; this was not pursued with any enthusiasm, as Lotus was able to design a four-cylinder with a higher output and

Lotus Elite/Eclat/Excel
1974–92
Models quoted: Elite 2.0/Eclat S2.2/Excel SE

ENGINE:
Four cylinders in line, aluminium block and cylinder head, water-cooled

Capacity	1973cc
	2174cc (Eclat S2.2/ Excel HC)
Bore x stroke	95.3mm x 69.2mm
	95.3mm x 76.2mm (Eclat S2.2/Excel SE)
Valve actuation	Twin overhead cam, 16 valves
Compression ratio	9.5:1
	9.4:1 (Eclat S2.2)
	10.9:1 (Excel SE)
Carburettors	2 x twin-choke Dellorto DHLA
Power	160bhp at 4900rpm
	160bhp at 6500rpm (Eclat S2.2)
	180bhp at 6500rpm (Excel SE)
Maximum torque	140lb ft at 4900rpm
	160lb ft at 5000rpm (Eclat S2.2)
	165lb ft at 5000rpm (Excel SE)

TRANSMISSION:
Rear-wheel drive; five-speed gearbox (Lotus/Getrag/Toyota); optional four-speed automatic

SUSPENSION:
Front: Independent by coil springs and twin wishbones; anti-roll bar; telescopic dampers
Rear: Independent by coil springs and lower wishbones, fixed length driveshafts; location by radius arms and lateral link

STEERING:
Rack-and-pinion, optional power assistance

BRAKES:
Front: Discs
Rear: Inboard drums (Elite); inboard discs (Eclat S2.2); outboard discs (Excel SE), servo assisted

WHEELS/TYRES:
14in alloy wheels; 13in steel on basic Eclat 520; 15in on Excel SE
Tyres 14in x 7in (15in x 7in on rear of Excel SE)

BODYWORK:
Glassfibre-reinforced plastic moulded by VARI process; steel backbone chassis
Two-door coupé

DIMENSIONS (Elite):

Length	14ft 7.5in
Wheelbase	8ft 1.8in
Track, front	4ft 10.5in
Track, rear	4ft 11in
Width	5ft 11.5in
Height	3ft 11.5in

KERB WEIGHT:
21.7cwt (Elite 501)
23.0cwt (Excel SE)

PERFORMANCE:
(Source: *Autocar* & *Motor*)
Models quoted: Elite 503, Elite S2.2, Excel SE

Max speed:	124mph/127mph/ 131mph
0-60mph	7.8sec/7.5sec/6.8sec
30-50mph in top	14.4sec/11.9sec/11.1sec
50-70mph in top	13.7sec/9.2sec/9.8sec

PRICE INCLUDING TAX WHEN NEW:
£5857 (Elite 502, 1974)
£15,842 (Eclat S2.2, 1980)
£17,980 (Excel SE, 1985)

NUMBER BUILT:
6213 (all types)

better fuel economy than the six-cylinder engines of many rival cars.

As with the first Renault-engined Europa, the 900-series 2-litre engine project gained momentum after a Lotus visit to a motor show. Vauxhall introduced a fourth-generation Victor at the 1967 London show, with a new slant-four two-litre engine of 1975cc. The Lotus team spotted that its internal dimensions matched exactly those which they were planning and although the Vauxhall cylinder block was in cast iron, it was a simple job to match the Lotus head to the top for development and then enlarge the cylinder

dimensions to 1995cc. The first 900-series engine, the 904 of 1968, was built in low volume for racing and appearing in the Europa-like Type 62. An aluminium version was promised for later and when the production run of 50 LV/220 racing engines was announced in 1968 Lotus was careful to quash any idea that it would fit in the current range of road cars.

The production road-car engine was designated 907 and the line at Hethel was set up to produce 15,000 units a year. Claimed to be the first engine to pass US pollution standards without modification, it went on to be the

Every aspect of Elite production brought a new challenge, from the all-Lotus engine to a new method of body construction, and even down to the extent of the bright metal trim used around the windscreen – some of which became detached on a car used at the press launch.

cornerstone of all Lotus road cars until the last four-cylinder Esprit of 1999. In its launch form the 907 produced (in European tune) 155bhp at 6500rpm, and was matched to the five-speed transmission of the +2S 130/5. North American cars, with different carburation, ran at 160bhp, and this specification was soon standardised.

Whereas Chapman had been outvoted by the Lotus board on having a wedge-shaped +2, the new Elite faced no such hurdle. The 1968 Lotus

Ital Design was brought in for the upmarket Elite interior, and for 1974 that spelt veneer-effect fake wood trim. Some details weren't quite right, such as the radio hidden behind the gear lever. Note the dash-top mirror and the curled wire in the driver's footwell for the map-reading light.

56 was the first of the wedge-shaped Lotus grand prix cars and in the same year Bertone's wedge-shaped Alfa Romeo Carabo concept turned supercar design on its nose. Wedge was the way to go but early rear styling ideas for the Elite by John Frayling and Oliver Winterbottom were along conventional coupé lines. The wedge-shaped front was present but the rear had a gentle slope like that of a Maserati Ghibli. Once the styling developed to the model stage the problems began. "As the design went on and we began to make various quarter-scale models it became clear to us we'd overdone the aerodynamic efficiency," Tony Rudd confessed to the BBC in 1974. "Although the car had a very low drag factor it was a little too much like an aeroplane and had considerable lift, in fact dangerously so on the rear wheels."

It was back to the drawing board for Winterbottom who had to completely re-shape the back end of the body, the passenger compartment and the arrangement of the petrol tank. The resulting squared-off hatchback shape with its continuing roofline gave better rear headroom and certainly improved aerodynamics. Windtunnel testing revealed it had a drag coefficient of 0.30, not unusual for a Lotus but still exceptionally low for the day. The airflow was calculated so that air hitting the front of the car not only kept the nose down by use of a small spoiler but was forced through the radiator before exiting via ducts in the bonnet. Air was also directed into the backbone chassis to cool the transmission.

By late 1971 Winterbottom's full-scale Elite was recognisable as the final shape, although wearing conventional chromed bumpers. Anticipating the new VARI (Vacuum Assisted Resin Injection) moulding process, it was also styled for a bodyshell of two halves with a join in the middle. Even though Winterbottom had started work on an interior, his team was stretched and Chapman brought in Giorgetto Giugiaro's Ital Design to work on it. "It was very traditional," Winterbottom recalls. "The seats were thicker than

Seen here on a testbed, the Lotus 907 engine was designed to be fitted canted over to one side but there was only a marginal offset in weight distribution. Additional belts could be fitted to drive air-conditioning and power-steering units – another first for Lotus, and as promised by Chapman.

the originals so there was less space, and getting the design to work nearly killed Colin Spooner and his lads. It took ages to perfect and was ever so expensive with all the finishers and bits of artificial wood trim." All the same, the marketeers knew Ital Design sounded good in the brochure.

The Elite was not a true hatchback like the similar Reliant Scimitar GTE, as the rear seats did not fold. The cushions were secured in mouldings that were a fixed part of the lower half body. But four adults into an Elite would go – just. The seating was divided by the central backbone and the rear places so deeply set that you didn't need too much legroom as your knees were kept comfortably bent. The boot was reached by a hinged glass tailgate and an inner fixed window kept rear passengers dry when it was opened. With no load cover, luggage was on view to the rest of the world.

Although the idea of a monocoque glassfibre shell had been flirted with in the early stages, the production Elite was reassuringly familiar underneath, with a pressed-steel backbone chassis carrying the engine, transmission and suspension. Front suspension was by coil springs and wishbones with an anti-roll bar, and at the rear there were fixed-length driveshafts, a lower transverse link, and radius arms

mounted on the backbone. Front disc brakes were fitted but at the rear were inboard drums. Initially the rack-and-pinion steering was not power-assisted but this option appeared later in 1974. Alloy wheels were especially designed by GKN for the Elite and Dunlop also developed a new tyre with a tread pattern offering substantial amounts of grip.

The Elite was to have a full quota of luxury items such as electric windows and the option of air conditioning – although despite the up-market aspirations, the Elite owner was not offered the option of a leather

interior, these having briefly passed out of fashion. The distinctive single wiper was another solution to Federal regulations which required a large area of the windscreen to be swept: two-wiper and three-wiper combinations had been tried but neither worked. Headlamps were vacuum-operated on the Series 1 Elite, only changing to electric motors on the Series 2.

By 1972 Hethel was committed to full-scale production of the Elite, and it was late. 1970 had seen pre-tax profits nearly halve over the previous year and M50 development had to

The VARI process

Before the 1974 Elite, Lotus bodyshells had been laboriously made by laying glassfibre and resin into a mould by hand, often meaning no two cars were alike. Chapman had long envisaged a process where a nozzle could be plugged into a mould, the mixture fired into it under pressure and a self-coloured bodyshell be pulled out of it. The Vacuum Assisted Resin Injection or VARI process made this possible, but although the idea was floated that cheaper Elites might be self-coloured if customers could be persuaded to live with a choice of two finishes, they never were; all the same, early Esprits were self-coloured in bright plain shades until the practice was abandoned as not giving an appropriate finish for this sector of the car market.

VARI sprang from Chapman's boat-building companies, these ventures beginning with the 1971 purchase of Moonraker Marine, then the acquisition of JCL Marine and a number of smaller concerns. Bringing boat design into hangars at Hethel, Chapman embarked on a serious programme to make the existing products more technically up-to-date. The chief change was from wooden hulls to glassfibre, using VARI, which had been developed in great secrecy by Technocraft, a

Hethel-based research company formed to explore glassfibre moulding of boat hulls, car bodyshells, shower cubicles and baths, and even grp coffins. Over a decade after the first Elite experience, Chapman had become a leading expert on the use of glassfibre and the sheer size of the single-piece hull mouldings broke new ground.

The VARI breakthrough not only increased the quality of Lotus cars (subsequent models were awarded coachwork medals at motor shows) but additionally the perceived technological advance brought in extra business. "Without the VARI process Chapman wouldn't have been able to do the DeLorean deal," says

former JCL director Roger Putnam. "The DeLorean was launched on the back of a process called ERM, which didn't exist. It was a completely untried, untested process." VARI was refined further with the 1989 M100 Elan, its multitude of panels being set in heated moulds with pre-shaped sheets of glassfibre, and it was still a valid technique used for a number of panels on the Series 1 Elise and its optional hardtop until Lotus outsourced the panels for the Series 2.

Colin Chapman's dream of injecting resin into a mould and pulling out a bodyshell was fully realised with his VARI process. Here the upper half of a late-model Excel emerges, to have its door and glass apertures removed by hand.

The Jensen-Healey

The Jensen and Lotus tie-up was a neat solution for both companies. Jensen had a new sports car under development but no engine supplier, while Lotus knew the 907 engine would be production-ready before the Elite.

Jensen was originally a small coachbuilding company formed pre-war by two brothers. Based in the West Midlands, it had expanded to manufacture commercial vehicles and cars. By the late '60s it was making a name for itself in the expensive GT market with the highly-praised Interceptor model launched in 1966, with its Italian styling and American Chrysler V8 engine.

Jensen's staple income, however, had come from the building of the body for the Austin-Healey 3000 and the assembly of the V8-engined Sunbeam Tiger for the Rootes Group. However, in 1967 both cars were axed by their makers and Jensen's business was thrown into turmoil. Donald Healey failed to interest BMC – let alone its successor British Leyland – in replacing the 3000. Subsequently, wealthy Californian importer of European cars Kjell Qvale spoke to the Healey family about the loss of the 3000, which had been a big money-spinner for him. The upshot was that Qvale became the majority shareholder in Jensen in 1970 and Donald Healey joined the board, the two having decided to make a replacement for the 3000 at Jensen.

Jensen hoped to use a great deal of Vauxhall parts for the new car but late in the day it was found the Vauxhall

2.3-litre engine was severely hampered once bolt-on emissions equipment had been added. There was a panicked search for a replacement engine, including a bid to use the BMW 2-litre 'four', but the high-spec, well-publicised and US-ready Lotus engine fell into place.

Qvale insisted on a deal for up to 200 engines a week. Chapman explained that his engine was not going to be in a car for some years and was still in the development stage; he was also unwilling to offer a comprehensive warranty. This was to cost Jensen dearly as just to keep goodwill it paid for early car faults beyond the warranty period. By 1973 Hethel was producing 120 engines a week for Jensen, with a potential for 200 to 250.

But the lack of engine development started to show after the Healey's 1972 launch. A flow of letters from Jensen to Lotus bemoaned high oil consumption, carburettors which leaked petrol if the

The Jensen-Healey provided a testbed for the 907 engine – at the expense of Jensen's unfortunate customers.

car were parked downhill, and underbonnet fires. The car gained a poor reputation that it never really shook off, although Lotus did remedy many of the engine problems by the time of the 1973 Healey MkII, which had a new block casting for better oil flow and improved oil seals. At one point, indeed, Jensen looked into the idea of GKN making the engine rather than Lotus.

Jensen, with its gas-guzzling Interceptor, was hit hard by the fuel crisis, and matters were not helped by the three-day week and in-house labour problems; ultimately the company closed its doors in May 1976. By that stage the Lotus engine had redeemed itself, but plans to use the V8 in the Interceptor replacement and the 2.0-litre in a gull-winged coupé were left at the prototype stage.

take a back seat. By 1972, too, Mike Kimberley's team was also being stretched on making the Giugiaro Esprit concept car a production reality. With a new engine and no car for it, the 1972 Jensen-Healey deal provided a financial lifeline and saw that some of the bugs were ironed out at Jensen's expense.

1974 was a disastrous year to launch an expensive luxury car. The fuel crisis of 1973 and subsequent petrol price rises had sent car makers into a spiral and buyers gravitated towards fuel-efficient cars. The Elite started to become a badly-kept secret. The launch was scheduled for March 1974 and a new slogan, 'Join the Elite',

was agreed, along with a marketing campaign. However the British miners' strike and subsequent three-day week meant that the factory could not build up a sufficient reserve of cars for launch: even though Lotus was becoming less reliant on parts from other manufacturers, supplies of items such

The right ending? Unlike the Elite, the Lotus Eclat, launched in 1975, was praised for its looks: all that had changed from the Elite, though, was the tailgate, rear roofline and glass. This is the basic 520 model.

as windscreen-post trim started to dry up. The launch was postponed until mid-May but it was famously too late to stop a pre-paid advertisement appearing in *The Sunday Times* in March.

Undeterred, Chapman the salesman made a virtue out of the crisis. "I think in the long run this energy crisis might be a bit of an advantage to us in a way," he said. "We are offering a prestige car which has very low fuel

Lotus reacted to customer comments and improved the 907's low-speed torque with a new camshaft. After testing this Eclat 523 (a 522 with power steering) Autocar magazine pronounced it 'the best Lotus in years'.

consumption and so therefore is perhaps a lot less anti-social than some of the bigger-engined, larger and shall we say old-fashioned prestige cars." But the Elite needed more than just a spot of Chapman 'spin', as the planned price on introduction had soared. The 1974 Elite 502 cost £5857, or £5445 as the 501 without air conditioning, stereo or a heated rear window. To gauge the size of the jump, an Elan +2S 130/5 had been £2974 the previous year and a Reliant Scimitar GTE retailed at £2363.

Nonetheless, the initial reception to the Elite was good, with commentators appreciating its engineering, even if they were not united on its styling. 'At long last we have been given a low-built low-drag small-engined and efficient roadburner that is a true four-seater,' said LJK Setright, writing in *Car* magazine. "There was tremendous pent-up demand for the car and to be

fair when it came out it was an incredible car for that period. It had been really a very ambitious project for Lotus," recalls long-established Lotus dealer Bobby Bell of Bell & Colvill. "Elan +2S people moved into the Elite. We had a good number of orders. Demand was very very hot."

For a period the Elite was the only new Lotus on offer, while Europa sales petered out and the Esprit sucked up development time and money. A year later Lotus unveiled the Esprit and the new Eclat coupé, although the latter was the only model ready to go on sale. The Eclat was one more choice for buyers, but not a radical one. The plan had been that the M50 design would spawn a derivative (M52) which would use as many of its parts as possible and broaden the front-engined range. The initial look was a notchback design with a separate boot and would not have seated four. "Chapman wanted a design with just door glass, no rear quarter glass because he said that was sporty," says Oliver Winterbottom. "My design was sent to John Frayling who made a full-size model. I don't think Chapman liked that either! It came to Hethel and was immediately scrapped." Instead the production design, sketched in 1973, comprised merely an attractive change to the rear roofline so it sloped down into a conventional coupé shape with its own bootlid. The first prototype of November 1973 was badged 'Elite Coupé', which was pretty

Designing in safety

American legislative safety culture started to impose itself on the Lotus design process as the '60s drew to a close. The Elite was the first Lotus to be designed for a new set of rules and boasted a number of firsts. The windscreen was bonded to the body so it formed a structural part of it. The laminated Belgian glass, Glaverbel VHR, was only 5mm thick and in those pre-airbag days if an unrestrained passenger struck it, the screen was claimed to be slightly more flexible than a conventional laminate. The Elite was also the first Lotus, and one of the first British cars, to use impact-resistant plastic bumpers. These would deform slightly to absorb minor parking knocks.

To give some protection against a side intrusion, steel sections were built into the doors, with an anti-burst door lock. This was allegedly the result of Chapman sketching a bar about six inches deep, with hinges at one end and the lock at the other end, the whole clad in glassfibre. It in effect transformed the side-impact bar into the door and in production it was claimed the doors could take approximately twice the rated force

required by US Federal laws to achieve the standard lateral intrusion. The door reinforcement also formed the start of the roll-over hoop bonded into the shell and immediately obvious to the passengers as a big padded bar in the centre of the roof.

In 1975 the Elite was awarded the British Don Safety Trophy – previous winners having included the Rover 2000. The citation praised the Lotus for 'successful use of grp body construction plus the wide margin by which the Elite meets the US and

European Legal Safety Requirements, and the emphasis placed on the reduction of the risk of fire in the case of a collision, allied to the good fuel economy and low emission of pollutants, [which] added up to a substantial improvement of both primary and secondary safety in a high-performance car.' .

In 1974, the Elite's impact-absorbing bumpers predated those of the Triumph TR7 and looked far better than the add-on items given to the MGB at the same time.

accurate as it retained the lower half-body moulding, doors and windscreen of the M50. There were still four seats and there was little loss of headroom over the Elite.

When announced in autumn 1975 the Eclat was initially marketed as a cheaper alternative to an Elite. The basic 520 model had a four-speed Ford gearbox, steel wheels and no power steering, and buyers could save a useful £754 over an equivalent Elite. Other Eclats offered the same range of equipment including automatic transmission. In practice few buyers opted for the Eclat 520 and for those who felt the car looked a little unsporty, the 1977 Eclat Sprint, available only in white with matt black

detailing, had no more power but went a little faster in its five-speed form thanks to a lower axle ratio.

There were few complaints about Elite and Eclat performance and fuel economy relative to the engine size, but it was clear that torque could be better at lower revs. The initial attempt to rectify this was a change in camshaft profile to what was called the 'E' camshaft, as also fitted to the Esprit. When *Autocar* tested an Eclat 523 in July 1977, maximum power was delivered at 6200rpm with peak torque at 4900rpm and the magazine observed that 'the unit pulls strongly from low engine speeds.' In fact it liked it so much that it dubbed the Eclat the 'Best Lotus in Years'. However, a move

to increase engine capacity had to come to keep the range competitive and meet changing emissions standards. Chapman is said to have been asked in the early '70s to back an engine range stretching from 1.8 litres to 2.4 litres, but decreed capacity had to stay at 2 litres. However, once Chrylser had paid for the 1979 Talbot Sunbeam Lotus to be up-engined from 1973cc to 2174cc, Lotus was encouraged to go the same way.

The first Lotus 2.2-litre was built for Chrysler in 1978. Chrysler added parts to its own specifications, but common to both the Lotus-Chrysler and the subsequent Lotus engine was a lengthened stroke, increasing from 69.2mm to 76.2mm; it was not feasible

Above: The interior of the 2.2-series cars lost much of the fake-wood decoration and gained redesigned front seats.

Below: By 1980 the Elite's time was marked and it became a special-order car. The 2.2 car was launched in the midst of a recession and was comfortably outsold by the Eclat.

outright increase in power, which in non-turbo Lotus cars was unchanged at 160bhp while the Sunbeam 911 produced 150bhp. 'Overall performance has benefited considerably from the greater torque offered by the new engine although the standing-start acceleration figures are not startlingly different,' *Motor* found when testing an Elite 2.2 in November 1979. For the record the figures were 0–60mph in 7.5 seconds and a top speed of 132mph, although the car was too fast for the chosen test track. The magazine said 25mpg was achievable.

The 2.2-litre was fitted to Elite, Eclat, and Esprit ranges in May 1980 and the cars relaunched as the S2.2 series in tandem with a number of other detail changes. For the Elite/Eclat the major change was the adoption of a German Getrag five-speed gearbox rather than the Maxi-derived Lotus unit. Otherwise, after six years on the market, it was the normal Lotus tactic of little tweaks in response to customer niggles, as the money wasn't there for a great deal more. Thus there were re-spaced pedals, a much-needed exterior catch for the tailgate, and rearranged switchgear. The range was simplified by dropping the '500' designations for the various specification packs and letting customers pick their own options. At £16,433, the cheapest Elite was now competing with the Porsche 911SC at £16,732 and, at the top end, the £19,187 Jaguar XJ-S.

This was another turbulent time for carmakers. The 1980 '2.2' cars were launched into a recession and some shrewd business decisions had to be made to revive sales, which had plunged in 1980 and dwindled almost to nothing in 1981. In autumn 1981, therefore, the Riviera Eclat and Elite were launched, offering a dose of fresh-air motoring, thanks to their large lift-out sunroof; at the same time the factory cut prices, first on the Eclat and then on the Elite.

A decent revival was made possible by the 1981 agreement with Toyota to co-operate on engineering new

to increase the bore, as there was insufficient space within the engine block. Externally the two power units were very similar but Lotus was at pains to stress its version had many detail differences and was called the 912, wheareas the Sunbeam unit was tagged the 911. However, both engines aimed at better torque rather than an

Driving the Elite/Eclat/Excel

A good Elite has a hint of the continental GT about it and still turns heads. By modern standards the Lotus 2.2 is an agreeably gruff four-cylinder and happy to rev towards 6000rpm. Wind it up to motorway speeds and it still stands up as a comfortable long-distance cruiser. Because the gearing isn't all that long, fifth gear will still pull at the legal limit: the tail sits down slightly and you power away. The gearchange is short and firm, the clutch effort acceptable, but the pedals are still closely spaced with nowhere to rest the left foot.

Suspension is supple and well controlled and although there is some body roll, you have to push an Elite

quite hard to reach the rear end's limits of adhesion. Common to the majority of survivors, the power steering is well-judged and offers just about the right amount of assistance.

In an early Elite or an Eclat, the rear view mirror sits atop the dash but you soon learn to drop your eyes down and find a view through the letterbox rear window. It can be difficult to judge the width front and rear, all the same, as the wheelarches flare out beyond the width of the cabin.

When they are on song, these are easy cars to get along with, perhaps too easy. You climb straight in and down through wide doors with no stooping. While the tunnel covering

the chassis backbone is a defining feature, there's the right amount of room and an easily adjusted driving position.

Even given that the Excel retains the slight fastback of the Eclat bodyshell, two adults would not be happy for long in those deep rear seats. You choose whether to manoeuvre yourself in backwards or go in forwards bent double. The knees-up seating position is comfortable but you'll most likely be touching the headlining. Nonetheless, an Excel can be a family-friendly Lotus, even a practical one – and you know that it won't fall apart if hurled round a race circuit.

models and which allowed Lotus to buy in components from Japan. On the one hand this fruitful alliance led to development of the Toyota Supra and MR2 and to the M90/M100 sports car projects detailed in Chapter 12. On the other, it allowed Lotus to raid the Toyota parts bin, a prospect which pleased Mike Kimberley, by now managing director of Lotus Cars, because it gave both cost and quality benefits. "If you can take to somebody's parts bin for those items which the customer never sees or feels

but which have to give reliability, you can get them at a massively reduced cost from somebody producing half a million instead of our little 500 or 1000. That was our philosophy."

The Toyota link provided the best means of rejuvenating the Eclat range. The Lotus engine remained but the Getrag gearbox was replaced by the light and robust Supra unit and the Salisbury differential – which had always been noisy – also went, in favour of a Supra unit. The Supra also donated its driveshafts, and outboard-

mounted Toyota disc brakes replaced the first generation's awkward inboard-mounted rear drums, while the chassis – now galvanised – incorporated improved rear suspension. Externally, the Eclat responded well to a new design of front bumper with a blended-in spoiler, along with new sill mouldings and a reshaped rear bumper, while the profile of the side glass and doors changed, losing the 'dip' behind the door mirrors and the backwards kink upwards to the rear pillar. The 1970s

In 1982 the Elite and Eclat were replaced by the new Excel, based on the coupé bodyshell. The matt-black trim was very period but the best changes were the use of reliable Toyota parts and a lower price than preceding models.

Above: Without the funds for any radical development, Lotus successfully updated the Excel for most model years in the '80s. Thus 1983 saw a new rear spoiler, a revised bonnet, and a fresh choice of wheels.

Below: Looking surprisingly contemporary for 1986, the Excel's last major styling change was a new upper bodyshell moulding with flares above the wheelarches. Wind-tunnel testing gave rise to new front and rear spoilers.

chrome trim also vanished. The revised car was introduced in October 1982 as the Eclat Excel – although it soon lost the Eclat tag.

By this time the Elite, latterly built only to special order, was being phased out. Although it had come to be outsold by the Eclat, in the troubled years of 1981 and 1982 the gap had widened – even if in the former year the question was almost academic, with the 31 Eclats made

being barely a less misererable statistic than the 13 Elites that left Hethel. In 1982 only 14 found homes, against 162 Eclats and Eclat Excels, and after a sole example had been built in 1983 the model was laid to rest, with 2535 cars having been made.

Coupled with another reduction in price, the front-engined Lotus was given a new lease of life by the arrival of the Eclat Excel. This now appeared to be somewhat of a bargain; not only that, but the Toyota parts were soon seen as bringing increased reliability. In the end the Excel was kept in production for a further ten years, during which the Esprit came in for a serious redesign and the Elan project unfolded and collapsed. Styling tweaks became more frequent and the Excel's first cosmetic update was the work of newly-arrived stylist Peter Stevens. Taking advantage of the fact that the shell was made of a top and bottom moulding, efforts were concentrated above the waistline, and in 1983 the Excel gained twin bonnet louvres and lightly flared wheelarches. A more radical upper body moulding, with a modified glass area, followed in 1984.

1986 brought a long overdue new dashboard design and the only power boost the non-turbo 2.2 Elite/Eclat/Excel range ever benefited from, in the form of a 20bhp hike to 180bhp for the Excel SE, thanks to high-compression pistons, enlarged inlet ports, reprofiled camshafts and different carburation. A four-speed automatic also appeared in the range as the Excel SA – for 'Sports Automatic'. That was it for engine changes and with its lack of fuel injection the car was now no longer for sale in US markets. An Oldsmobile engine was tested but was no cheaper than the Lotus unit. The Excel was finally killed off in 1992 by the need to be re-engineered for a catalytic converter, coupled with a steady downturn in demand for what was essentially an 18-year-old design. Over 6200 cars had been built, not quite the figure which might have been hoped for, given the once-forecast rate of 25 units a week.

Buying Hints

1. Although groundbreaking at the time, the Elite has not been popular with classic-car enthusiasts. Many are in poor condition and sell at low prices, but they cannot be restored economically. If you want an original '70s car go for the latest you can find, ideally a '2.2' where somebody else has picked up the bills. The same goes for early Eclats. The better-built and younger Excel, however, represents a relatively practical and cheap way into Lotus ownership.

2. Engines have a poor reputation unless well maintained, and conversions to other engines such as the Rover V8 are not uncommon. Oil pressure should sit at 35psi at 3500rpm, rise to 45psi at 6500rpm but be negligible at tickover when the engine should be quiet. As with most aluminium engines, cooling is vital but the early cars had an inadequate water pump and owners tend to have fitted manually-switched electric fans. Excel engines have had less time to wear, but when they do the price of new pistons and liners will be steep. The cambelt should be changed every 24,000 miles or two years.

3. The Elite and Eclat use three different types of gearbox and the first Maxi-derived five speed is the oldest and most troublesome – but this is usually confined to worn syncromesh and bearings. The Getrag and Toyota manual and automatic 'boxes are very durable.

4. If a Series 1 car has not had a replacement chassis by now it will almost certainly be badly corroded and will need replacement, which given the low value of Elites may write it off. Rust starts from the top part of the chassis and seeps downwards. The crucial point is the rear crossmember between the damper mounting points; this is hard to see, but if it goes completely, so does the suspension. Fortunately, Series 2 cars have a galvanised chassis.

5. Clonking from the front and rear suspension is an indication that the bushes are worn – these should be replaced as a set. The Elite and Eclat inboard rear brakes are difficult to work on and major work means the driveshafts have to come off. The Salisbury differential on early cars can become noisy; the Toyota item is far more durable.

6. If there are problems with the vacuum-operated headlamps they will rise when the engine is turned off and fall when it is back on. Series 2 headlamp-motor repairs entail major dismantling of the front end and failure of the wiper motor requires dashboard surgery.

7. Many trim parts on the Elite/Excel are no longer made or re-manufactured. Headlinings often droop, and the materials used are not hugely durable; it is thus worth paying more for a good interior. Check to see that items such as windscreen trim and the small glass inner window on the Elite are still present. Switchgear is from the parts bins of companies such as British Leyland but bear in mind that the donor cars themselves are by now long gone. On a good car, all electrical items should work.

8. Bodywork is unlikely to be a problem apart from stress cracks around door handles and cracks from accident damage. Shell quality improved progressively but the doors are heavy and you should check that they haven't dropped: they are supported by the steel anti-intrusion bars, which can rust away unseen and let the doors sag. The front screen can leak into the front footwells if it no longer seals properly – rebonding is expensive and so a degree of dampness is not unusual. The small spoiler fitted to Series 1 cars is important for cooling but can be caught on kerbs and snapped off.

A modified dashboard moulding was belatedly introduced for 1986, with the dials angled towards the driver. As on the Esprit, the square light switches were sourced from Austin-Morris cars.

The Esprit

Simply beautiful but only for show; the 'N' at the end of this Lotus Cars UK-registered Series 1 Esprit is from 1975, but buyers would have to wait until summer 1976 before the car was production-ready.

When Italian stylist Giorgetto Giugiaro broached the idea of a Lotus-based show car to Colin Chapman at the 1971 Geneva Motor Show, it was the start of a line that would be with us for nearly 30 years, in the form of the Esprit.

A Europa chassis was duly provided and work started on the Italian Lotus in mid-1971. Ital Design was also hired to style the forthcoming Elite interior. However, the 'Lotus dream car' was going to be much more than motor show decoration. The Europa chassis

Lotus Esprit
1976–87

Models quoted: S1/S2/S2.2/Turbo/S3

ENGINE:
Four cylinders in line, aluminium block and cylinder head, water-cooled, longitudinally mounted

Capacity	1973cc
	2174cc (S2.2/Turbo/S3)
Bore x stroke	95.3mm x 69.2mm
	95.3mm x 76.2mm
	(S2.2/Turbo/S3)
Valve actuation	Twin overhead cam, 16 valves
Compression ratio	9.5:1
	9.4:1 (S2.2/S3)
	7.5:1 (Turbo)
Carburettors	2 x twin-choke Dellorto DHLA
	2 x twin-choke Dellorto DHLA, Garrett AiResearch T3 turbocharger (Turbo)
Power	160bhp at 4900rpm
	160bhp at 6500rpm (S2.2/S3)
	210bhp at 6000rpm (Turbo)
Maximum torque	140lb ft at 6200rpm
	160lb ft at 5000rpm (S2.2/S3)
	200lb ft at 4000rpm (Turbo)

TRANSMISSION:
Mid-engined, rear-wheel drive; five-speed gearbox (Citroën/Maserati)

SUSPENSION:
Front: Independent by coil springs and twin wishbones; anti-roll bar; telescopic dampers
Rear: Independent by coil springs and lower wishbones, fixed length driveshafts; location by radius arms and lateral link; telescopic dampers
Rear (S3 and Turbo onwards): sliding driveshafts, upper and lower transverse links

STEERING:
Rack-and-pinion, unassisted

BRAKES:
Front: Disc
Rear: Discs (inboard) servo assisted

WHEELS/TYRES:
14in alloy wheels; 15in alloy optional on S3/Turbo
Tyres(front/rear) 6in x 14in/7in x 14in; 7in x 14in/7.5in x 14in (S2/S2.2/S3); 7in x 15in/8in x 15in (S3 optional/Turbo)

BODYWORK:
Glassfibre-reinforced plastic moulded by VARI process; steel backbone chassis
Two-door coupé

DIMENSIONS:
Length	13ft 9in
Wheelbase	8ft
Track, front and rear	4ft 11.5in
	5ft 0.5in/5ft 1.2in (S3 option/Turbo)
Width	6ft 1.2in
Height	3ft 7.7in

KERB WEIGHT:
19cwt (S1)
21cwt (S2)
21cwt (S2.2/S3)
24cwt (Turbo)

PERFORMANCE:
(Source: *Autocar*)
Models quoted: 1977 S1/1981 S3/1981 Turbo
Max speed	124mph/134mph/148mph
0–60mph	8.4sec/6.7sec/6.1sec
30–50mph in top	13.9sec/10.4sec/10.4sec
50–70mph in top	12.9sec/9.9sec/8.5sec

PRICE INCLUDING TAX WHEN NEW:
S1, 1977: £7979
S3, 1981: £13,461
Turbo, 1981: £16,982

NUMBER BUILT:
4860

Lotus Esprit (X180)
1987–2003

Models quoted: Turbo/Turbo SE/V8

ENGINE:
Four cylinders in line or 90-degree V8, aluminium block and cylinder head, water-cooled, longitudinally mounted

Capacity	2174cc
	3506cc (V8)
Bore x stroke	95.28mm x 76.2mm
	83mm x 81mm (V8)
Valve actuation	Twin overhead cam, 16 valves
	Twin overhead cam, 32 valves (V8)
Compression ratio	10.9:1
	8.0:1 (Turbo SE/V8)
Carburettors/fuel system	2 x twin-choke Dellorto DHLA (Turbo/SE) Garrett AiResearch T3 turbocharger Fuel injection, 2 x Garrett T25 turbochargers (V8)
Power	215bhp at 6500rpm (Turbo)
	264bhp at 6500rpm (Turbo SE)
	349bhp at 6500rpm (V8)
Maximum torque	192lb ft at 5000rpm (Turbo)
	261lb ft at 3900rpm (Turbo SE)
	295lb ft at 4250rpm (V8)

TRANSMISSION:
Mid-engined, rear-wheel drive; five-speed gearbox (Renault)

SUSPENSION:
Front: Independent by coils and twin wishbones; anti-roll bar; telescopic dampers
Rear: Independent by coil and lower wishbone, upper and lower transverse links; location by radius arms; telescopic dampers; anti-roll bar

STEERING:
Rack-and-pinion (assisted on V8)

BRAKES:
Front: Disc
Rear: Disc
Servo assistance: anti-lock on all models from 1990

WHEELS/TYRES:
15in alloy wheels; 16in rear on SE, 17in front/18in rear V8
Tyres (front/rear) 7in x 15in/8in x 15in (Turbo); 7in x 15in/8.5in x 16in (Turbo SE); 8.5in x 17in/10in x 18in (V8)

BODYWORK:
Glassfibre-reinforced plastic moulded by VARI process; steel backbone chassis
Two-door coupé

DIMENSIONS:
(Turbo)
Length	14ft 2.5in
Wheelbase	8ft 0.76in
Track, front	5ft 0in
Track, rear	5ft 1.2in
Width	6ft 1.2in
Height	3ft 8.8in

KERB WEIGHT:
25cwt (Turbo)
27.1cwt (V8)

PERFORMANCE:
(Source: *Autocar*)
Models quoted: Turbo (1988)/SE (1989)/V8 (1996)
Max speed	150mph/159mph/172mph
0–60mph	5.4sec/4.9sec/4.2sec
30–50mph in top	9.6sec/6.1sec/8.1sec
50–70mph in top	6.3sec/6.3sec/6.0sec

PRICE INCLUDING TAX WHEN NEW:
£35,660 (Turbo X180, 1991)
£47,310 (Turbo SE, 1991)
£58,750 (V8, 1996)

NUMBER BUILT:
5816
Total Esprit production 10,676

In translating from show car to reality, the Esprit retained the essential look of the 1972 Ital Design proposal but was modified in many details. The side crease line adapted well to the body being split into two halves for the VARI process. The vents behind the rear window reappeared behind scoops on later Esprits.

supplied was longer and wider than that of the standard Twin Cam – wide enough in fact to take the new 2-litre engine – and its provision was part of the Lotus masterplan for the '70s that had already been laid out: a family of cars based around the all-Lotus 2-litre 907 engine. The styling of the M50 Elite had just been signed off and the next car in line was the mid-engined M70. Lotus stylist Oliver Winterbottom had already gone so far as to make a model and sketches for the Europa replacement, and they tended towards a wedge-shaped two-seat coupé.

The still-unnamed full-sized show car from Ital Design was presented to Lotus later that year and of course it looked fantastic. It made its public debut at the 1972 Turin Motor Show, the name Esprit having been chosen by Giugiaro. Chapman was keen to emphasise to the press that it was just a styling exercise on the Europa but it wasn't hard to read between the

lines that this was the way that Lotus was heading.

Mike Kimberley installed Oliver Winterbottom in Turin to supervise a second prototype while the specification was being decided at Hethel. The move to a production car had its own problems, one of which was the windscreen. "The one thing that made the Esprit such a sexy car was that it had a very fast 19-degree screen which we were told was impractical," says Kimberley. Chapman's solution was to keep the angle of the pillars but change the profile of the screen glass to meet the 24-degree angle required by regulations. "We had a great long argument about whether you would see that the glass started in the middle as it should do but then instead of going on a curve out and curling back at the ends it went out and then came back as two wings, making it almost like a flat screen at the bottom," explains Kimberley. "Colin was determined it was right – and nobody ever did notice it."

By late 1973 the second prototype body was ready and in September Kimberley and Winterbottom made a full presentation of the M70 to the Lotus board, right down to the trim fasteners. The Esprit had a factory cost

estimate of £1238 in standard UK specification with alloy wheels, a five-speed gearbox, a quoted top speed of 136mph and a 0–60mph time of 6.5 seconds. Bodywork was to be self-coloured, and moulded in two halves using the VARI method, with a trim strip covering the join. The brief was to use as many M50 Elite parts as possible, mixed – as usual – with components from other manufacturers; one example was the tail lights, which came from Fiat's X1/9.

The Esprit adopted the same principles as the Europa, with a mid-mounted engine set longitudinally in a backbone chassis and driving the rear wheels through a combined gearbox and final drive unit. However, as the 907 engine was to be in the same 160bhp tune as in the Elite and was set for more power, the Renault transaxle of the Europa would have been unable to cope with the torque. Once more, Lotus found just the right type of ready-made unit in France, installed in the front-wheel-drive Citroën SM coupé introduced in 1970. Promised continuity of supply was to prove crucial, as the Maserati-powered super-Citroën was killed off before the Esprit got to market; happily Lotus was able to continue using the SM transmission until the end of the 1980s.

Left: The striking instrument pod also made it from show car to production car but the effect of using parts from other manufacturers was a little messy and the cockpit was cleaned up on subsequent series of Esprit.

Above: As tested by Autocar magazine in 1976, the first Esprit drew praise for its looks but the writers noted that visibility suffered from reflections and from the thick 'A' pillars. No rear wiper was necessary, thanks to good airflow management. Early cars were self-coloured.

Below left: Unlike the plush Elite, the 1976 Esprit struck out with a simpler cabin design, with very of-the-moment tartan seat trim. Note the fly-off handbrake on the sill. Scuff marks on the seat show how agile the occupants needed to be.

Below right: A true mid-engined car, the Esprit's 907 engine sat in the middle of a trimmed luggage compartment insulated by the bulkhead and the cabin glass. The straps held a plastic cover and bags could be hidden with a blind. The battery is in the top right-hand corner.

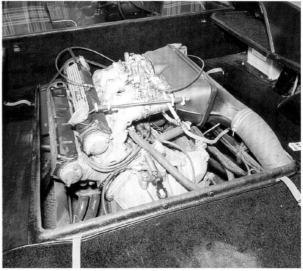

The first James Bond Lotus

James Bond did not swap his Aston Martin for a Lotus by happy chance: it was down to the sheer doggedness of Lotus PR Don McLaughlan who parked one outside Pinewood Studios (or a restaurant by some accounts) until somebody took notice. Production designer Ken Adam subsequently recognised it as the most beautiful car in England. The effort was said to have cost £18,000, according to Lotus author Jeremy Walton – peanuts compared to the subsequent Bond BMW deals.

For the filming of *The Spy Who Loved Me* in 1976 Lotus supplied two road cars and six shells. Various effects were built into the shells at Pinewood, with Lotus help, to simulate the transition of one car into a submarine as it sprouted fins. Meanwhile, Perry Submarines in Miami converted a full-sized shell into a sub with two divers for the sequences filmed in the Bahamas.

In Sardinia an Esprit was mocked-up around a spaceframe cage so it

could be shot off a pier and Lotus drivers including Roger Becker obliged as 007 stand-ins with the road cars. As nothing could keep up with the Esprit the second car was also used as a camera vehicle. During one sequence a pyrotechnic charge in the road blew a 'bullet' hole in the rear valance of one car and McLaughlan painstakingly recreated it on his group of 'PPW 306R' stand-in show replicas.

A whole generation of men have marked their childhood with the James Bond Lotus Esprit submarine car. As well as road cars and working submersibles, dummy cars were hurled into the sea and pulled out of it – on a cunningly hidden piece of wire.

Esprit suspension was a cautious evolution of Lotus practice, with twin wishbones and coil springs at the front (from the Opel Ascona) and with the rear using the driveshafts as the upper links in conjunction with combined coil/damper units and semi-trailing arms. Braking was by discs all-round, with the rears inboard since the SM's transmission featured inboard (front) brakes. Although air conditioning was designed-in as an option, the Esprit did without power steering as it had little weight over the front wheels. A great deal of work was done to stop front-end lift, and the road car consequently sprouted a front spoiler. Although the bodyshell had the appearance of an 'all in one' shape, lifting the tailgate revealed that the passenger compartment was sealed from the engine/luggage bay by a bulkhead window.

In Norfolk the project was diverted to Team Lotus headquarters at Ketteringham Hall, under Tony Rudd and Colin Spooner, as the rest of the team was so stretched on the Elite and Eclat. Kimberley was already concerned that the programme was 'too short for a high degree of refinement' and his 'pessimistic' programme envisaged the first running prototype being completed in October 1973. In the event it did not run until late 1974 and Rudd recounted how he picked Chapman up from Heathrow Airport in January 1975 to some disbelief that he had actually driven there in the car, only for the suspension to fail on the return journey.

Like many car-makers hit by the energy crisis, Lotus was once more struggling to stay in business during 1975, at the expense of mass redundancies. The Esprit was ready for a debut at the Paris *salon* but the company did not have the tooling

ready to put it into production. It was just as well that the Eclat, shown at the same time, was ready for sale, as the very last Europas had already left the factory. Customer Esprits were finally ready for delivery in June 1976, by which time the price had risen from a claimed £5844 in Paris (in line with the cost of an Eclat) to £7883.

However, the motoring press was by now happy to accept that the era of kits was long gone, and that Lotus was nipping at the heels of Porsche and Ferrari for a lot less money. *Autocar* did not publish its first test of an Esprit until January 1977 and noted that while it had a much smaller engine capacity than its rivals, its lightweight construction gave it a competitive power-to-weight ratio. The shape seemed to raise expectations of towering speed but the actual performance of the test car was at odds with the Lotus claims of

138mph. *Autocar* returned 124mph (albeit on a wet day), which was barely more than the Europa Special tested by *Motor* four years earlier. However, the car did return a commendable 23.3mpg on test.

There were still rumblings that the design was not all it should have been, as there was little more cabin or luggage space than a Europa and rear visibility was poor. Other road tests remarked on the amount of noise and vibration that was transmitted to the cabin, echoing some of the concerns that had been picked up by Mike Kimberley in 1973. More seriously, by 1977 a crash programme was underway to cut warranty costs: among other problems Californian cars overheated, prompting the addition of a third fan, while fuel

leaked onto engines, and interior mirrors and Lotus badges fell off.

Nonetheless, 1977 was a great year for the Esprit, with its best-ever sales of 580 cars and a prominent role in the James Bond film *The Spy Who Loved Me*. To tackle the problems of the early cars, a revised model, badged as the S2, was launched in 1978. The engine received the new 'E' camshaft design of the other cars, which improved engine flexibility, while outside there was a more integrated design of front spoiler, bigger rear cooling vents, Rover SD1 tail lights, and Speedline alloy wheels. The headlamps were raised by electric motors rather than vacuum and the interior received redesigned instruments and wider seats. Early Esprits had been given self-coloured bodywork but this led to colour

mismatches and paint was soon used. 1980 also saw the first Esprit special edition, in JPS racing livery to celebrate the Formula 1 wins of Mario Andretti. However, the genuinely 130mph S2 was short-lived, as in early 1980 the range gained the new 912-series engine of 2.2-litre capacity: while power was

Below: Outwardly no different from a standard Esprit, '600 LOT' was a turbocharged conversion by Lotus dealer Bell & Colvill. It was rapid but suffered from cooling problems. The later Lotus turbo was a more thorough redesign.

Bottom: The first factory special edition came in 1978, being applied to the short-lived 2-litre Series 2. Black and gold echoes the cigarette-box colours of Team Lotus sponsor John Player.

Above: With its stripes and spoilers there was no mistaking the 1981 Esprit Turbo; this was all the same, more restrained than the livery of the Essex Petroleum cars that preceded it.

Left: The 1980 Esprit Turbo was first seen as a limited edition in the colours of new racing sponsors Essex Petroleum. Sumptuous (and creaky) ruched leather became a Turbo feature – but the roof-mounted graphic equaliser for the stereo was deleted.

unchanged at 160bhp, the driving experience was again improved.

That was nothing compared to the impact of the Lotus Esprit Turbo. It burst onto the scene in February 1980 with the most lavish press launch Lotus had ever attempted – a dinner party at the Royal Albert Hall where Shirley Bassey provided the cabaret. Although the car was not yet in production, this spectacular was down to new Team Lotus sponsor Essex Petroleum being keen to make a splash. Enter the Turbo through dry ice alongside the Formula 1 Lotus for 1981. . .

Lotus dealer Bell & Colvill had already been producing an

aftermarket turbo conversion for the Esprit 2.0 (and one had paid a visit to Hethel) but the Lotus car was substantially different. The new backbone chassis, now galvanised, was wider and stronger to cope not only with the new engine but with a future V8. With fewer Opel parts, the front suspension now resembled that of the Elite/Eclat and at the rear a radical change was made: new upper transverse links – in conjunction with wider lower wishbones – relieved the driveshafts of their dual role, which lessened the amount of stress and vibration transmitted to the interior. The Turbo sat on wide Goodyear NCT tyres wrapped around 15in alloy road wheels with 7in front and 8in rear rims, setting a trend for ever-fatter tyres on the Esprit.

The engine was thoroughly reworked even in relation to the still-new standard 912 unit. There was great concern that it should be durable, well-cooled and well-lubricated, and the first Esprit Turbos accordingly

used a dry-sump lubrication system, this being retained until 1983. The camshaft profile was altered and the compression ratio reduced – because Lotus was obliged to use carburettors, as no manufacturer would supply fuel injection in the small quantities required by Hethel. Power was boosted from 160bhp to 210bhp at 6250rpm by the addition of a Garrett AiResearch turbocharger set up to deliver its punch from low revs. With experience of client cars, Lotus opted for a smaller unit to lessen lag – the sudden power surge that so plagued early turbo installations.

The Esprit finally began to be talked about as a 150mph supercar that went as fast as it looked. Giugiaro contributed to a distinctive restyle which blended the spoilers and extra cooling ducts into the body, and 'venetian blind' rear louvres marked out the Turbo even further. The interior was retrimmed in plump-looking leather. The first run of 100 Esprit Essex Turbos was dressed in the racing

team livery and priced at £20,950, but this dropped to £16,197 when the car appeared in standard colours for 1981 minus some of the Essex options. The standard Esprit 2.2 gained the new chassis and several cosmetic modifications which echoed the Turbo, becoming the Esprit S3. A price cut made the improved range even more appealing and a Lotus once more appeared in a Bond film: *For Your Eyes Only*. In 1983, meanwhile, a federal specification Esprit Turbo reintroduced Lotus to the US market on the back of a new distribution arrangement.

As the sales of the Elite dwindled, the Eclat turned into the Excel, and the projected new X90/X100 two-seater bumped along the ground, the Esprit Turbo became the company's best seller. The years following Colin Chapman's death in 1982 were yet again a time of financial trauma, as American Express called in a £2.2 million loan and for the first time Group Lotus had to allow a major

Esprit convertibles

While Lotus tinkered with targa Esprits and did its best to open up production cars with glass roof panels, a couple of firms went one stage further in the 1980s and offered an Esprit convertible conversion.

Hamburg firm Kollinger produced an Esprit Turbo Roadster which removed the roof from the screen backwards and replaced it with a remodelled rear deck which included fairings rising up to meet the rear of the head restraints. A purpose-built hood or hardtop was then added.

In the UK, the St Tropez Spyder featured a similar double-skinned rear body panel incorporating engine cooling vents, mounted on two-stage self-supporting hinges which were intended to aid engine maintenance. The A-posts, screen surround, doors and rear chassis were reinforced, and there was claimed to be no loss of rear

luggage space. The engine bay had extra air ducts designed to improve induction and engine cooling and a number of body-kit options were offered. Only three St Tropez Esprits are thought to have been built, one being used as the basis of a conversion kit to Rover V8 power.

The Paul Bailey (PBB Designs) Esprit convertible offered a choice of bodykit options and could be applied from S1 to S3. (Club Lotus)

Turbocharging took Esprit performance into the supercar league. The 1986 HC had 215bhp, in contrast to the 160bhp of the original Esprit. Body-coloured bumpers were also adopted for the non-turbo Series 3 cars, but not the Turbo's venetian-blind rear window.

Getting tighter: turbocharging called for a wider rear chassis, although the exterior dimensions of the car did not change. Compare this engine-bay shot to that of the earlier car to see that baggage space has been lost either side of the engine.

Esprit reinterpreted. Having succeeded in keeping the project under wraps, the new Esprit (codenamed X180) surprised the motoring press at its October 1987 launch. Sitting on the same chassis, it was a familiar shape yet one that was ready for the 1990s.

outsider to take a financial interest in the company. In 1983 British Car Auctions took a majority share alongside the holdings of the Chapman family, Fred Bushell and Toyota. The next year JCB took a stake, and Toyota further increased its interest until the shock sale of the whole company to General Motors in 1986. The car ranges received little real development during this period and only the growth of Lotus Engineering consultancy work, such as a contract to develop a family of engines for Chrysler, kept Lotus Cars afloat.

The Etna concept car

History repeated itself in 1983 when Giugiaro met Mike Kimberley and chairman David Wickins (of new shareholder British Car Auctions) at the 1984 Geneva Motor Show. He had sketches and was looking for a platform for his next show car and Lotus was trying to attract funding for a new car and the V8 engine.

Lotus concept cars were still rare and the Etna was duly unveiled to rave reviews at the 1984 Birmingham show. At the time Lotus was keen to emphasise that it had serious production potential to sit above the Esprit, rather than replace it. Although engineless, the Etna was also touted as the first application

of the V8 and production was said to be two to four years away if backing could be found. With a suggested price of between £30,000 and £35,000 in 1984's money, it was seen as a replacement for the Excel, to be offered in both V8 and four-cylinder versions.

The Etna was based on a standard Esprit Turbo backbone but Lotus told Car magazine that it was looking at moving to monocoques, still using composite materials. The imagined specification was a shop window for the talents of Lotus Engineering, the Etna being said to have the potential for including active ride, continuously-variable transmission,

From most angles it's clear that the 1984 Etna concept influenced the Peter Stevens Esprit; stillborn versions of the new Elan had an even closer resemblance.

four-wheel drive, traction control and anti-lock brakes, while the dash was shaped to have electronic gizmos such as a TV screen for 'direction-finding equipment'.

As smooth as the then-current Esprit was sharp-edged, the Etna created expectations that came to nothing. Car put its finger on the crux of the matter: 'Just how Lotus intends to finance this car alongside their X100 small Elan, about two years away from production, is far from clear.'

When the Excel gained the High Compression engine for 1986, its next destination was bound to be the Esprit. Installed in the standard car, power was boosted from 160bhp to

172bhp and in the Turbo the increase was from 210bhp to 215bhp. The gains for the Esprit were not as great as those for the Excel as the car had a more restrictive exhaust system, but

tested in early 1987 the HC Esprit Turbo was found to have an actual top speed of 141mph. There was a fuel-injected derivative for the US market, the HCPI, which had a catalytic

Above: The 1987 Stevens design toned down the Turbo exterior to the extent that it was hard to distinguish from the standard model (here in red). Note the glass 'bridge' across the silver Turbo's rear deck.

converter, while the home-market Turbo HC retained carburettors. Finally there were some changes to the interior and bodyshell to squeeze out a little more interior space.

The HC models were the last fling for the original Esprit shape, which looked even more out of date once the smooth Etna concept car had been

By the 1990s, Lotus was expert at turbocharged engine installations. Charge-cooling and ignition changes made up for the fact that the engine was still a four-cylinder unit when most Esprit competitors had V8s or V12s.

shown in 1984. The matter was in hand. Designer Peter Stevens had been working on a new shape with design director Colin Spooner since late 1985, with the brief that the existing chassis be retained, and by the time GM took the reins there was a full-scale glassfibre model to show them. "I started work with a fairly clear idea of what I was aiming for," Stevens told writer Mark Hughes in 1989. "Giugiaro's design had so much that was good, so I knew that I should not be seen to be throwing any of it away. Nothing about it can be criticised."

A new model was a dire necessity – the Excel was on its last legs and the X100 sports car project was in limbo as Toyota had pulled out when GM arrived. "I was suddenly left with no product," recalls Mike Kimberley. "I had to do a crash programme. Our guys did a fabulous job on the Esprit – 12½ months to soften the shape – and we took the opportunity to refine the vehicle, make it more reliable, and that gave it a new lease of life." In fact from concept approval to production took only 15 months, with cars ready for sale from the October 1987 launch.

A 1998 *Esprit Turbo limited edition produced for the US market only. The X180 was purpose-built in one body configuration for all markets – the non-turbo cars were not offered to American buyers, and later phased out altogether.*

The chassis was largely as the S3, and at first the same engines were carried over in the same stage of tune, with a mixture of carburettors and fuel injection. Eventually, supplies of the Citroën gearbox had started to dry up and so the new Esprit moved over to the five-speed unit of the Renault 25 and Alpine GTA: this brought with it the use of outboard rear disc brakes.

The new Esprit, codenamed X180, was designed to be easier to manufacture. The old car's evolution had given rise to three sets of body moulds, whereas the new model was designed around the federal Turbo specification. The shell was still made in two halves by the VARI process but Stevens and the team worked to change the moulding process to flatten the centre ridge. The exterior dimensions changed very little, as did the other body 'hard' points – the windscreen A-frame angle, in particular, had to stay the same even though all the glass was new. There were no funds to change the interior radically but a lot of work went into new trims, a seat redesign and different materials, to give a fresher feel. To help bring in a little light there was a panel in the roof finished in a honeycomb pattern, or a lift-out glass sunroof.

Gone were the skirts, spoilers and decals of the S3 and the first Turbo. In fact it was hard to tell a normally-aspirated 1987 Esprit from the Turbo continued on page 126

As turbo power was boosted even further (264bhp on the SE), the glassback tail was lost for 1991 and a high-mounted spoiler fitted for a claimed improvement in downforce. The SE's top speed was in excess of 160mph.

The SID research vehicle

It looked like an Esprit (well, a bit) but it wasn't an Esprit. In the early '90s Lotus Engineering was keen to showcase its talents and went public with a demonstration of its work into Structures, Isolation and Dynamics – or SID. At the same time it was developing anti-noise technology and drive-by-wire steering.

Instead of a Lotus engine a 300bhp V6 from a Metro 6R4 rally car was used to propel a glassfibre-and-Nomex honeycomb monocoque centre section sitting on a backbone chassis under parts of an Esprit shell. The entire front and rear halves were removable, and hid four-wheel drive, four-wheel steering, and experimental Michelin tyres.

But SID's most apparent feature was the active suspension system, whereby suspension loads could be fed into the central structure or into Elan-style suspension 'rafts' as required and computer-controlled electro-hydraulic actuators

could change the suspension's reactions in microseconds. Drivers were astonished by the car's ability to glide over poor road surfaces at high speed yet corner almost completely flat.

Active suspension was also applied to Lotus Formula 1 cars and to a tank that could move at high speed without shaking its crew up. But while a prototype was produced, no

With a passing resemblance to an Esprit, SID was a shape to clothe the work of Lotus Engineering, its suspension electronics controlled with the aid of a laptop computer.

production Esprit was ever fitted with active suspension. However, the technology was sold by Lotus to most of the world's manufacturers and today's top-line systems can trace their lineage back to Hethel.

Above: Although Esprits had been tending to become more luxurious, the limited-edition Sport 300 of 1993 took its lead from the US racing X180R, with a tough body kit and various race-inspired options.

Opposite above: In 1996, when all had lost hope of seeing it, Lotus introduced an Esprit V8; but road-testers found it to be heavy to drive and not as good on the ears as they expected a V8 to sound.

Opposite below: Lotus effectively produced a MkII V8 for 1998, with many detail improvements such as a new clutch mechanism and better gear linkage. The following year, it became the only Esprit engine choice.

Driving a late Esprit Turbo

continued from page 123

The feeling from inside a 'Stevens Esprit' is essentially the same as a 'Giugiaro Esprit' as the positions of the dash, screen and side windows don't change. It's easy to be comfortable although you may find the sunvisor brushing your forehead. Although alterations were made to enlarge the footwells, the pedals on all Esprits remain small and angled slightly towards the centre of the car.

The clutch can feel heavy, and with both Citroën and Renault gearboxes you can feel the linkage working. The gearchange has long and slightly rubbery movements, but the positions are easy to find.

With their cosseting interiors and well-insulated engines, Esprit Turbos can actually be driven quite languidly and are easily suited to long-distance drives: in an SE 60mph equates to a relaxed 2500rpm. However, relentless urge is available in all gears when the turbocharger comes into play, the power being delivered smoothly with hardly any lag. This also makes for a flexible engine in low-speed traffic. The intercooled (or 'charge cooled') SE cars have a transient 30 second overboost facility which momentarily allows a claimed 280bhp. In any Esprit Turbo you can of course watch the power hike in front of you on the centrally-placed boost gauge – which normally sits at 0.5bar but flicks

across towards 1.0bar when the engine is given its head. After this excitement, careful owners allow the car to idle for 30 seconds after a hot run, to prolong turbo life.

This kind of power above all gives you confidence for straight-line overtaking, rather than powering out of corners, because there is no way of seeing the Esprit's nose unless the headlamps are raised. However, familiarity breeds a greater sense of ease: fears that the car is too wide are largely a function of sitting so close to the ground.

With low-profile tyres, some bumps are transmitted through the steering wheel and make a leather interior creak, but Lotus revised the X180's suspension settings from model to model so some are harsher than others. There is virtually no sensation of roll through bends or that grip will even twitch unless the car is being hurled round a racetrack. The steering is responsive and true (and heavy at parking pace in cars without assistance), but there isn't quite the agility of the smaller Lotus cars. Braking power is reassuring, as you'd expect. Considering the basic design goes back to the mid 1970s, all-in-all the later Esprits acquit themselves very well: indeed they just went on getting better and better.

other than by the Turbo's decals behind the doors and its lower body mouldings with more ducting. From the rear it was easier to distinguish the two as the standard Esprit had a flat rear deck and Europa-style 'flying buttresses' while the Turbo filled in the gap across the deck with a glass panel similar to that on the Etna concept. The new look was well received.

Although a V8-engined Esprit seemed even further away, there was a lot more potential for Turbo development and no fewer than ten different versions of the Turbo were made between 1987 and 1991, thanks to various changes in the fuel injection system. Early changes coaxed 228bhp out of the turbocharged engine (for the Esprit S) but the first significant development of the X180 Esprit – or 'Stevens Esprit', as it has become known – was the 1989 Esprit Turbo SE. A four-cylinder Esprit now had performance to worry a Ferrari, with 264bhp and 0–60mph in 4.7secs. The air entering the engine from the turbocharger was now forcibly cooled (charge-cooled), which boosted efficiency, and the chassis was designed to take advantage of Goodyear Eagle tyres. Additionally the first free-standing spoiler on an Esprit appeared at the tail. At £42,500 the SE was the most expensive Esprit to date and it was the first to be raced by the factory, in 1990, in a successful campaign to boost US sales.

The performance drive continued as the 16-valve engine proved itself capable of yet more development, although it was now a very different animal from the 1970s original. By 1990, in fact, it made sense simply to drop the normally-aspirated Esprit and concentrate on the best-selling Turbo in a number of states of tune and equipment. Anti-lock brakes also made an appearance for the first time. For 1991 a further attempt was made

Ten years after the Peter Stevens Lotus Esprit, for 1998 the V8 was treated to an all-new dashboard and centre console with a much more contemporary feel. Note the thin racing-style seats.

The Lotus V8

The all-Lotus road-car V8 engine was so long coming it began to assume the status of a unicorn. Plans had been laid down when the 900-series engine was being developed in the late '60s and the new generation of cars was designed to accommodate it. By 1970 it had even been allocated a type number – 909.

Colin Chapman asked for a Rover V8 to be trial-fitted to an Elite but at the time the fuel economy of the standard engine proved to be a good selling point – and that was aside from the cost of a new unit. Nonetheless, Chapman was determined that Lotus should eventually produce its own V8-engined four-door saloon to rival Mercedes.

The V8 seemed to return to favour when times were good and in 1978 Chapman gave Tony Rudd the go-ahead on the basis of 320bhp and 300lb ft of torque. A fuel-injected Esprit V8 was duly built and run by Tony Rudd's development team in 1982, two years before the Etna concept was shown to the public. It was claimed to produce 350bhp, although the results with fuel injection were far from satisfactory.

By the time the Etna show car was ready, Lotus was also in a position to spill the beans on the V8 – said to be 'the lightest V8 ever produced' – and a prototype engine was shown to the outside world. Tony Rudd envisaged 100 a month being produced and the plant was said to be ready. But for that, Lotus needed to have at least one other major buyer which would take a reasonable quantity. Ford was rumoured to have an interest and then Aston Martin was suggested – even Rover, for its 800 due in 1986.

The backing was not forthcoming, either for the Etna or the V8, and luckily Lotus engineers proved adept at developing the four-cylinder engine and turbocharging it. Ironically the company was commissioned to design the 5.7-litre LT5 V8 engine for

use in the Chevrolet Corvette ZR1, this sophisticated lightweight unit being unveiled in 1989.

For the '90s a new team applied its mind to the V8, armed with the knowledge from previous attempts and with the intervening experience in turbocharging that they had acquired. Finally, in 1996, Lotus at last unveiled its own twin-turbo V8, only for it to have a life of barely seven years in the Esprit. The V8 was now less about a Lotus road car than a technology project. It was designed to be packaged for rear-wheel or front-wheel drive, longitudinal or transverse installation, and a 4-litre non-turbo was said to be under consideration, while a V4 or V6 could be derived from the design. In 1996 the potential Esprit V8 build rate was 400 cars a year but total V8 engine manufacturing capacity was a potential 1500. While at Lamborghini, Mike Kimberley had bought the engine's intellectual property rights from then Lotus boss Romano Artioli. "We wanted the V8, but with a lot more torque," he recalls. "So we gave Lotus the project of doing a turbocharged intercooled version." However, the eventual beneficiary was AC Cars rather than Lamborghini.

Talked about for four decades but never seen in public, the Lotus V8 went through several concepts and design teams.

John Owen, formerly of the Lotus V8 design team, joined AC cars as chief engineer and the Lotus V8 engine was offered as an engine option for the 1998 Ace and Aceca, then from 2000 in the 212 S/C (a version of the Cobra); but the Lotus engine was displaced by a Ford V8 as AC went through another turbulent period in its history.

Had the money been there, the V8 could have powered the Lotus Eminence, a luxury saloon that remained a 1984 paper publicity exercise. The sketch is by Harris Mann, better known as the stylist behind the Austin Allegro and the Triumph TR7.

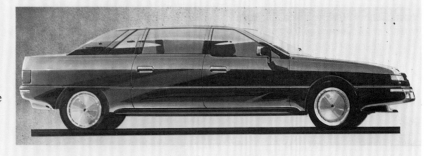

Having had one last restyle with Elise-like rear lights, the last X180 Esprit left the factory in 2003.

to increase cockpit space by introducing a repositioned cabin bulkhead, revised pedal box and a slimmed-down transmission tunnel; meanwhile the 'glassback' styling was deleted, to be replaced on the SE by that free-standing rear spoiler.

By 1992 the first run of the M100 Elan had abruptly ended but the Esprit hung doggedly on. Lotus promised a new generation of 'Super Esprits' and there was talk of a new General Motors V6 version to run alongside the Turbo. Sure enough, the 1992 British Motor Show previewed an exciting hardcore Esprit, the Sport 300. This was a lightweight version of the US racing X180R Esprit, with 300bhp, racing options and a menacing body kit. Having had its first facelift – subtly different bumpers – by

Lotus stylist Russell Carr, 1993 saw the Esprit move to its next incarnation, the S4. The limited-run Sport 300 entered full production and for the first time power steering was introduced on the S4, although a one-off assisted Esprit had existed as a result of Hazel Chapman having told her husband that she found her car too heavy to drive. The assisted steering was also long overdue, as the Esprit had sprouted wider tyres with each passing year; also it facilitated improvements to the steering geometry. Introduced for 1995, the £51,995, 300bhp Esprit S4S was seen by many as the best-handling Esprit ever.

At long last the 1996 Geneva Motor Show ushered in the Esprit V8 and an engine all set for emissions requirements into the next century. Worked on by a new team since 1993, the V8's specification was now totally contemporary, with a displacement of

3.5 litres and with 32 valves and twin turbos; it was good for 349bhp and 0–60mph in 4.8 seconds. Maximum torque was developed at 4250rpm, and in race tune the engine was delivering 520bhp. The chassis was modified at the rear to suit the new engine's dimensions and the suspension stiffened to help traction, yet the newcomer was only roughly 1cwt heavier than the S4.

Naturally, the arrival of the V8 created a stir, but it seemed to have come too late. The new Lotus was astonishingly quick but testers observed that the power unit wasn't a hugely sophisticated design and didn't sound particularly exciting in the way a Ferrari or a TVR engine did. They also found themselves unable to hold off criticising the cabin, the jerky driveline and the heavy gearchange. But it was still a British supercar, and at £58,750 it cost over £30,000 less than a Ferrari F355.

However, the four-cylinder Esprit was not quite dead – as was proved by the arrival at the same time of the GT3. Henceforth the sole four-pot variant, it employed a 240bhp 2.0-litre turbo engine developed from a tax-saving Italian-market engine; while in an attempt to appear pared-down, the interior was treated to composite shell-type competition seats and a body-coloured glassfibre strip around the centre console.

The V8 received remedial action for 1998. This was chiefly to answer complaints of its heavy clutch, and involved fitting a smaller-diameter twin-plate AP Racing unit, halving the effort needed; additionally the gear linkage was re-worked, and earlier cars had this mod retro-fitted. The 1997 Motor Show also saw an

additional GT version of the V8, and all Esprits at last received a new dashboard and improved heating and ventilation.

As the year 2000 loomed, Lotus was fully owned by Malaysian carmaker Proton and the Elise had proven to be a runaway success, although finances were far from stable. For the time being the fortunes of Lotus Cars were dependent on featherweight two-seaters but the Esprit remained a small-volume favourite, built largely for appreciative US customers. Another 'Super Esprit', the limited-edition Sport 350, arrived for the 1998 British Motor Show, with a carbonfibre rear wing, magnesium alloy wheels and racing brakes. Although power was unchanged, it was 110lb lighter and could reach 175mph. The four-cylinder Esprit hung on until 1999

when it could no longer comply with emissions regulations: 9438 four-cylinder Esprits had been produced and the Lotus 900-series engine had lasted for 27 years if you counted its Jensen-Healey debut and had grown from 140bhp to 300bhp in production form.

In 2000 the 10,000th Lotus Esprit was produced and the following year Russell Carr gave the car one more gentle revision – proving how durable the Stevens X180 shape had been – endowing the car with Elise-style round tail lights and some mild interior restyling. As the final Esprit V8s rolled off the production line in February 2004 – by which time 1237 had been made – rumours of an all-new Esprit were already starting to circulate, but the new supercar was not confirmed until autumn 2006, for a 2009 introduction.

Buying Hints

1. If you are of an age where the S1 'James Bond' Esprit was your pin-up car, most specialists have one word about buying one: don't. With the oldest at least 30 years old, they look great but now require a lot of pampering for regular use. Of course the line steadily improved and the choice between a late S3 and a 'Peter Stevens' car can be made on the basis of personal choice. Esprits from 1983 onwards are considered best, as they have a galvanised chassis, with the HC Turbo being the pick of the S3 cars. The majority of post-1987 Esprits for sale will be turbo cars although they are not badged as such.

2. V8s are in a different category of purchase and running costs. Although the V8 Esprit is the youngest in the range it is a complex car and a lot can go wrong. Clutches can fail and gearboxes can be stripped by the huge amount of power they have to handle. There were a number of early cars with porous engine blocks and consequent warranty claims.

3. Esprits are often not regularly-used cars and some owners only cover 2000–3000 miles a year. With a lack of regular use, brake callipers can seize.

4. Steering racks can fail after 50,000 miles. If there is perceptible play in the steering wheel while the car is moving, replacement will be needed. The unit is based on a Ford Granada component and is not expensive. Power steering was only introduced on 1994 GT3/S4 cars and makes a big difference at low speeds.

5. Turbochargers are reliable on the whole and benefit from being allowed to warm up to operating temperature before heavy use and from a 30-second period of idling before switching off the engine. Failure is signalled by plumes of smoke from the exhaust.

6. Check that the heating system works, as it is complex and difficult to work on. If fitted, air conditioning should be run at least once a month

even in winter. It will need re-gassing every couple of years. To test the system, run the engine and turn to the maximum cold setting and you should hear the compressor cut in. The system should be very efficient.

7. Electrical systems are reasonably reliable but the passenger-side electric windows can stick through lack of use. The system can be overhauled. Dashboard warning lights, especially on cars with anti-lock brakes, can be misleading.

8. Engine cooling is managed by three cooling fans in the front compartment. Check that they cut in when the engine has been left to idle.

9. As with Elite/Eclat/Excel family, Esprit interior trim can become quite shabby and if mechanical matters are in good order and you have the choice between two examples, go for the car with the better interior. However, being a snug two-seater there is less to retrim than with an Elite/Eclat.

The *Talbot Sunbeam Lotus*

Born to slide: a Talbot Sunbeam Lotus in its natural environment. Lotus supplied an engine that punched above its capacity in terms of torque and power, and Talbot supplied a tough rear-driven hatchback. It is seen here in Britain's 1980 RAC rally, in which works cars took first, third and fourth places.

In 1977 struggling British carmaker Chrysler UK seized on the sophisticated Lotus 907 engine as a way to boost its flagging motorsport programme and model image.

Chrysler was in a bad way. Formerly the Rootes Group, until the American manufacturer took control in 1967, the range comprised the antique Hillman Hunter, the last gasps of the Imp, and the ageing mid-sized Avenger launched in 1970. Production of the Imp had been dogged by government encouragement to locate the factory in Linwood, Scotland, inconveniently hundreds of miles away from the main Rootes plant at Ryton, and Linwood was to be the eventual home of Chrysler

UK's make-or-break model, as without the new model it would face closure.

A £35m Government loan for a new small car was secured in double-quick time and work started on the Sunbeam, Project R424, in January 1976. While it had to look appealing, there was no time for complication and it had to use as many existing proven components as possible. With UK assembly of the front-wheel-drive French-designed Simca/Chrysler Alpine and Horizon some way off, the stop-gap Sunbeam was rushed into the showrooms in about 18 months.

The new Chrysler was a smart but unadventurous car, part of a dwindling band of rear-wheel-drive superminis along with the 1975 Vauxhall Chevette and the 1978 Toyota Starlet. It used a shortened Hillman Avenger floorpan and the Avenger engines, with the addition of a 928cc version of the Hillman Imp unit in the base model.

As the Sunbeam took shape, competition manager Des O'Dell was well aware that the Hillman Avenger's motorsport career was fading fast. Competition versions had won the RAC British Saloon Car Championship three times in four years but the final development, the Avenger-BRM, had suffered a number of teething troubles and was disadvantaged by a change in the regulations. By 1976 the factory team felt it wasn't going to attract big-name drivers without a new car.

While not the latest word in technology, the Avenger-derived

For such a hot hatchback, the Sunbeam Lotus was restrained for its day. Wheels were of a unique design and if the headlamps look too small for the grille it's because they were borrowed from the Avenger, as was the floorpan.

Talbot Sunbeam Lotus

1979–82

ENGINE:
Four cylinders in line, aluminium block and cylinder head, water-cooled

Capacity	2172cc
Bore x stroke	95.2mm x 76.2mm
Valve actuation	Twin overhead cam, 16-valve
Compression ratio	9.4:1
Carburettors	2 x twin-choke Dellorto
Power	150bhp at 5400rpm
Maximum torque	154lb ft at 4800rpm

TRANSMISSION:
Rear-wheel drive; five-speed gearbox

SUSPENSION:
Front: Independent by MacPherson struts; anti-roll bar
Rear: Live axle with coil springs, four-link location; telescopic dampers

STEERING:
Rack-and-pinion

BRAKES:
Front: Disc
Rear: Drum
Servo assistance

WHEELS/TYRES:
13in alloy wheels
Tyres Pirelli 185/70HR13

BODYWORK:
Steel monocoque
Three-door hatchback

DIMENSIONS:

Length	12ft 7in
Wheelbase	7ft 9in
Track, front	4ft 3.8in
Track, rear	4ft 3.1in
Width	5ft 2in
Height	4ft 6in

KERB WEIGHT:
18.8cwt

PERFORMANCE:
(Source: *Autocar*)

Max speed	121mph
0-60mph	7.4sec
30-50mph in top	8.1sec
50-70mph in top	9.0sec

PRICE INCLUDING TAX WHEN NEW (1979):
£6995

NUMBER BUILT:
2308

Sunbeam had a sturdy coil-sprung live-rear-axle layout, which lent itself to easy engine and transmission swaps for rallying, just as the similarly arranged Vauxhall Chevette HS proved. Four-wheel drive in rallying was yet to come and small hatchbacks could put more power out at the tail than at the front.

O'Dell's shopping list was for a proprietary engine that could give 240bhp, had an appropriate torque curve for rallying, and could mate to the five-speed ZF gearbox of the Avenger-BRM. There was no suitable larger engine available in the Chrysler Europe range, a bespoke engine from an outfit such as Cosworth was unaffordable, and so the Lotus 907 became an obvious choice. With its all-aluminium construction it weighed little more than a 1600cc Avenger unit but had the potential for 50 per cent more power.

The Lotus-Chrysler connections were already there. Lotus had previously indicated a wish to work with Chrysler in 1971 when the latter was seeking more power from the Avenger Tiger 1600, also an O'Dell creation; but the Tiger ultimately stuck with the Avenger engine and the idea went no further. There was also a personal connection. Chrysler competition manager Wynne Mitchell had been at technical college with Mike Kimberley, and it was he who brokered the Lotus deal. Early in 1977 O'Dell went to Lotus with an order for two engines: one 2-litre 907 giving the standard Lotus 160bhp, and one rally version to be built and delivered later.

Chrysler reasoned that as well as providing the basis for a homologation run of 400 cars to qualify for Group Four, a roadgoing version would perk up a brand image that was nearly on the floor. Any possible car would have a wide market in France, Belgium and Spain, it was thought, and Chrysler optimistically ordered 4500 Lotus engines, the European dealers believing they could sell that number of cars.

The rally engine was a curtain-raiser for the next generation of Lotus road cars. Capacity was expanded to 2173cc, keeping the existing bore of 95.2mm but increasing the stroke from 69.2mm to 76.2mm. The new Lotus 2.2-litre had a new crank, connecting rods and pistons and the block was strengthened at the bottom end. When delivered, it was giving 234bhp but after a pre-rally rebuild it ended up with the 240bhp that had been sought. Chrysler fitted some of its own components and the production engines differed in a number of details. As per Lotus models, fuel was fed through twin Dellorto carburettors, with a unique Janspeed twin exhaust system built to Lotus and Chrysler specifications.

Waiting for the 2.2 Lotus engine to arrive, the standard Lotus 2-litre was put to work in an Avenger used by O'Dell himself thorough 1977 and the results were enough to enable him to come away from the Linwood factory with one of the first Sunbeam rolling chassis. The Chrysler Sunbeam range

The Isuzu Piazza

If few manufacturers opted for a Lotus engine, many more took advantage of Lotus Engineering's expertise in suspension and handling to enliven otherwise stodgy models. The Isuzu Piazza was a typical example of what was to become a well-trodden path to the Lotus door.

Based on a 1979 Guigiaro show car, the Japanese Isuzu Piazza coupé did not appear in the UK until 1985, by which time it was out of date, especially with its live rear axle. With a limited budget to play with, Isuzu took the Piazza to Lotus to sort ride, handling and road and tyre noise, obviously whilst retaining the live axle. Lotus Engineering was reported to have gone through 150 damper settings, as well as reducing the ride height and changing spring rates, mountings and bushes. The revised Piazza Turbo was relaunched with 'Handling by Lotus' badges, a policy

which Mike Kimberley was happy to see applied, and Lotus went on to sort the Trooper off-roader. However, despite Lotus help, the Piazza merely limped on until 1990, by which time the next Isuzu link was as the engine supplier for the new Elan.

Isuzu had no track record of selling performance cars in the UK, and ultimately became better known for off-roaders. The Piazza coupé needed as good a reworking as Lotus could give it before it had acceptable handling.

The Vauxhall Chevette HS and Lotus

A few years ahead of the Sunbeam, Vauxhall made more limited use of the Lotus connection in its rally campaigns with the Chevette.

To face the rallying might of Ford, Vauxhall first used the Viva-derived Magnum coupés then switched to the 1975 Chevette hatchback. The 2.3-litre four-cylinder Magnum engine was still a distant relative of the Lotus Type 907, which had borrowed its dimensions and internal architecture during development of the Lotus unit. Following on from this, Vauxhall used a small number of Lotus 16-valve cylinder heads on Magnums before fitting one to a rally Chevette in 1976 and achieving homologation on the basis of this one prototype.

However, when the road-going Chevette HS models went on sale in 1978, the Lotus 16-valve head had been replaced by one of Vauxhall design which was claimed to provide better accessibility for maintenance in the engine bay because of the way the engine was canted over. This caused controversy in the rally world

as it made the road car significantly different from the homologation rally version, and in the end all the rally cars had to run with Vauxhall cylinder heads.

While the rally Chevette boasted 240bhp, the roadgoing 2300HS had 135bhp. It was priced at £5939 in 1979, easily undercutting the Sunbeam by over £1000, but was still a rare beast all the same. Vauxhall opted to deck it out with a more striking body kit than enjoyed by the Sunbeam Lotus and a London

Here being driven by Tony Pond, on the 1981 Scottish Rally, the Vauxhall Chevette rally car started with a Lotus cylinder head but road cars had a Vauxhall item of similar design. Pond was a top name who also helped hone the Sunbeam.

Vauxhall dealer offered a further luxury styling upgrade called the HS-X. Vauxhall additionally developed a limited run of 150bhp Chevette HSRs, which were available until 1980 and featured glassfibre panels including flared wheelarches.

proper was launched in spring 1977 and to make it clear that something sporting was in the pipeline, the car O'Dell had managed to secure was dressed up and fitted with a BRM 16-valve Avenger engine, as the first Lotus rally engine had not yet been delivered. This Sunbeam – registered WRW 30S – was set for a gruelling life as a development car, and was eventually to receive the 2.2-litre Lotus engine.

Later in the year Sunbeams were rallied fitted with Avenger-derived pushrod engines and competition customers were offered 1300cc, 1600cc and 2000cc versions, the last-mentioned being a Brazilian-sourced unit; meanwhile, Henri Toivonen took ninth place in a 160bhp 2-litre Sunbeam in the RAC Rally. However, customers were not offered a conversion pack to re-engine their

cars with the Lotus power unit, as Chrysler intended to market the Sunbeam Lotus as a 'high-performance luxury saloon'.

The Sunbeam Lotus was unusual in that the car was homologated after having competed successfully as a prototype, so it could first prove itself to the management and begin attracting top drivers. The traditional way, in contrast, was to build the homologation run first then rally the car, following up with it being released for road sale.

The Lotus 2.2 was not fitted into a Sunbeam until February 1978 and it was an exceptionally snug fit in the little car's engine bay, slanted as it was to one side; indeed, the Chrysler motorsport team had to machine 80 thou off the top of the cylinder head so the Lotus cam covers didn't hit the inner wing. At the end of March 1978,

the engine ran its first rally in the much-used prototype, 'WRW 30S', and the drivers found it instantly potent – if challenging to keep on the road. It was tested by Triumph driver Tony Pond, with permission from British Leyland, and Pond's input played a key part in further developing the car: it is said to have gone through 17 different rear suspension layouts. The rear was certainly subject to many changes but in the end it retained the Sunbeam's conventional coil-sprung live axle, but with disc brakes and a Salisbury limited-slip differential; at the front there were ventilated discs.

In July, once more driven by Tony Pond, the Sunbeam Lotus took a second place in the Mille Pistes, a rough road-rally in the South of France, and this was a resounding enough success to help O'Dell convince Chrysler Europe that the

The Lotus-Horizon and Lotus Esprit Visa

After the Sunbeam contract, PSA had Lotus work on an altogether more radical rally car inspired by the mid-engined Renault 5 Turbo and based around the Horizon shell. Named after the rally class it was intended for, the Horizon Group B had a mid-mounted 210bhp Esprit Turbo engine and two prototypes were built. Lotus also constructed a similar car for Peugeot's sister company Citroën, using the Visa hatchback, but nothing came of either project, as Peugeot perhaps more logically put its money behind the 205-derived T16.

Hoping to boost the image of the Citroën Visa, the PSA Group sanctioned various rally derivatives. That with the Lotus Esprit Turbo engine was the most outlandish, the power unit filling the space behind the front seats. The car was rear-wheel-drive only.

Sunbeam did have a future in motorsport. In the next event, the Epynt Rally in Wales, the 2.2 finally blew up, having lasted longer than the team had expected. The car was not eligible to compete in the 1978 RAC Rally so Chrysler fielded the 2-litre

To fit the 911-series engine in the Sunbeam's engine bay, it had to be modified top and bottom; Chrysler made a number of detail changes. Lotus made it clear that the 2.2 fitted later to its own cars was a unit in its own right, calling it the 912.

non-Lotus Group 2 Sunbeam instead.

Meanwhile, the first fast Sunbeam road car, the 1600Ti, appeared in January 1979. With 100bhp it could hit 111mph and accomplish 0–60mph in 9.9 seconds, but it was considered to be a crude machine to drive compared to rivals such as the Volkswagen Golf GTi. Compared to the Lotus that followed it was also pure boy-racer, with stripes and spoilers more for decoration than function.

Not long after, in March 1979, the Sunbeam Lotus was launched at the

Geneva Motor Show to a warm reception. The Lotus badges lasted longer than the Chrysler items as the Sunbeam Lotus almost immediately became a Talbot Sunbeam Lotus and in France – believe it or not – a Talbot-Simca Sunbeam Lotus. This was because in August 1978 Chrysler had transferred all its European interests to the Peugeot-Citroën (PSA) group and consequently in July 1979 all European Chryslers became Talbots – until 1987 when the marque disappeared. The Talbot Sunbeam Lotus was sold and serviced through 61 selected UK dealers.

The Lotus production engine supplied to Talbot was designated '911', whereas the Elite/Esprit 2.2 was the '912'. The Lotus version differed in a number of details such as carburation and ignition, and cylinder head, sump and camshaft design. Compared to the '912', power was down in the Sunbeam by 10bhp, to 150bhp, but the torque was still there, peaking at 4800rpm compared to the 5000rpm of the Lotus unit, and was easily unleashed through the tough ZF gearbox. Drive was taken to the rear axle by a modified propshaft, the body structure was stiffened in places to accommodate the greater stresses, and a lot of detail surgery was required to the engine bay, with items such as the battery and radiator fan changing position. Additionally, there were modified front inner wings, wheelarch lips, and a larger transmission tunnel with extensions to the gearbox mountings. All the suspension settings were stiffer, and the car sat on unique alloy wheels with chunky Pirelli tyres. Compared to the rally cars, the road car lost the rear disc brakes and limited-slip differential, the brakes now needing a hefty shove. Performance was a claimed 0–60mph time of 7.5 seconds and a top speed of 123mph.

Exterior finish was any colour you liked so long as it was black with a silver side flash, and the car carried unmissable Lotus logos ahead of the doors. In some respects the Sunbeam recalled the days of the Lotus-Cortina and the production process was

Cortina-like too, although more complicated. Starting with a top-of-range Sunbeam GLS, the Linwood factory reinforced the suspension mounts, and fitted uprated springs and dampers and a front anti-roll bar. The engineless cars were then transported to a satellite factory at Ludham near Norwich that Chapman had acquired through his boat businesses. There the engines and transmissions were fitted, along with a larger-capacity radiator and the wheels. The completed cars were then sent to Chrysler/Talbot in Coventry for final checks before despatch to dealers.

The press took to the Sunbeam, as apart from the Vauxhall Chevette 2300HS there was no other unruly over-engined little hatchback to compare to it. Despite Chrysler's luxury aspirations for its high-performance newcomer, it came across as bouncy, brutal and fun. In November 1979 *Car* magazine revelled in its cornering powers – thanks in no small part to the fat tyres rather than the crude live axle – but found that 'its instincts are less well adapted to the straight and narrow, especially if the road surface is second-rate, because the car then has the wayward tendencies of a puppy on linoleum: not slipping about, you understand, but just not running true, so that one cannot sit back and luxuriate unless there's a fair bit of leeway.' Drivers paid the price for all that fun with fuel consumption in the low 20s and it soon became clear the nine-gallon tank didn't give a sufficient range to compensate.

For a while the Talbot Sunbeam Lotus was a marvellous British oddity, a blunt instrument of car with a far bigger engine than was good for it. Rally successes piled up from 1979 to 1982. In 1980 Henri Toivonen became the youngest-ever winner of the Lombard RAC rally, Sunbeam Lotus cars finishing first, third and fourth.

Talbot eventually won the World Rally Championship in 1981: the combination of Lotus power and Chrysler had proved an ideal partnership. However, you had to be a real fan to pay out for the road car. In

Buying Hints

1. The Talbot Sunbeam Lotus presents a problem to the classic car buyer. The survival rate is very low and despite the car's humble origins the best examples will fetch the price of a reasonable Lotus Excel; but if the engine is in need of a rebuild, walk away, as the economics will never add up.

2. Many cars will have been modified – better dampers are a popular improvement – but be wary of ex-rallycross cars as road prospects.

3. Similar rules apply to the engine as in the Elite and Esprit: watch for smoke, low oil pressure and signs of overheating. A straight engine swap from a terminally-ill Elite 2.2 is possible but the power unit may need modification to fit the Sunbeam engine bay – the engines are not identical. The ZF gearbox is bullet-proof.

4. Rust is of course a major issue although the Sunbeam is no worse than its Ford contemporaries. Check the tops of the front wings, the sills inside and out, the floorpan, the boot floor, around the battery box, and the front strut mounts.

5. Re-shells using a standard Sunbeam shell are not unheard-of: the chassis number on the strut mounting on the driver's side should match the engine number. If you can find a donor Sunbeam, some exterior panels are the same although the wheelarches and some other pressings were modified, as was the engine bay.

6. Smaller parts can be found on scrap cars and some service items may still exist as Peugeot-labelled parts. The engine is the costliest part of ownership. The best way to tap into spares and advice is via the Sunbeam Lotus Owners' Club – www.sunbeamlotus.com

late 1980 a Volkswagen Golf GTi cost £5700 and the newly-introduced Ford Escort XR3 £5123, whereas a Lotus Sunbeam had risen to £7205. Sales soon faltered, not helped by it being known that the entire Sunbeam range's days were numbered. For the 1981 model year a limited facelift took place across the range and the Lotus version gained a smoother Horizon-style front, extra front driving lamps, a larger 12-gallon fuel tank, striped seats and a remote-control driver's door mirror. There were slight modifications to the engine and Talbot also boasted of improved sound insulation and modified suspension, while alongside the established black finish the car could now be ordered in metallic blue with a contrasting side stripe.

The Sunbeam had been built to do a job and four years after its introduction the inevitable closure of Linwood was announced. The rear-

drive hatch became surplus to the UK model range once the Horizon had arrived, followed by the Peugeot-derived Talbot Samba in 1982. As sales started to tail off the last Sunbeam Lotuses proved difficult to sell, and to use up a run of 150 leftovers towards the end of 1982 the final fling was to have Warwickshire-based coachbuilder Avon retrim the cars; alternative paint schemes were also available and there was special badging and a sunshine roof.

When production ended in 1982, 2308 Talbot Sunbeam Lotuses had been built, way below the original estimate. The bulk of sales were to UK customers and the car retains a loyal following although surviving examples now only number in the hundreds.

Peugeot-Talbot's sporting future, meanwhile, was with the mid-engined Group B Peugeot 205 T16, which was also to prove a memorable rally car.

The new Elan

Enthusiasts had come to believe the open-topped Lotus sports car was a thing of the past and so the 1989 Elan created massive initial excitement. The top-down profile was designed to be as clean as possible.

In 1973, with the end of the classic Elan, it was predicted that the open two-seater Lotus had gone forever. The future seemed large, fast and luxurious. But within Lotus the Elan ideal would not lie down and die.

As early as 1975, Mike Kimberley put forward costings for a front-engined 2-litre sports car based on a combination of Elite, Eclat and Esprit parts. Discussed as an Elan replacement, it progressed no further, with Chapman showing no interest and the company at full stretch getting the Esprit to market. Kimberley and stylist Oliver Winterbottom were persistent. "From 1979 to 1981 we kept pushing Colin, presenting lots and lots of styling designs. He kicked and struggled and wouldn't even talk about it in the beginning, but after 18 months or so started to get interested.

Top: The M90 project, here as a 1982 mock-up, progressed to a working model. It was displaced by the Peter Stevens X100 (above), inspired by the Etna concept.

He didn't want to go downmarket. In those days he still wanted to go up against Mercedes – which I didn't feel we could do," says Kimberley.

The boss eventually relented, on condition that the car use as many parts from an established manufacturer as possible. Oliver Winterbottom returned to Lotus in October 1980, fresh from styling the TVR Tasmin, and the 1981 agreement with Toyota on model development

and component supply launched the M90 sports car project. The first mock-ups were closed coupés based on a modified Excel chassis with a reduced wheelbase. A soft-top styling model appeared in spring 1981 and full agreement to use Toyota parts – such as the Celica engine – was signed in September 1982.

However, progress soon became fitful and finally the M90 project was frozen in the aftermath of Chapman's death and the subsequent financial troubles. It also lacked direction. There was an assumption that rear-wheel drive with a grp body on a steel backbone was the way to go, even at a time when the world was going front-

Lotus Elan
1989–92

ENGINE:
Four cylinders in line, cast-iron block, aluminium cylinder head, water-cooled

Capacity	1588cc
Bore x stroke	80mm x 79mm
Valve actuation	Twin overhead cam, 16-valve
Compression ratio	9.8:1
	8.5:1 (SE)
Fuel system	Multi-point fuel injection
	IHI turbocharger (SE)
Power	130bhp at 7200rpm
	165bhp at 6600rpm (SE)
Maximum torque	105lb ft at 4200rpm
	148lb ft at 4200rpm (SE)

TRANSMISSION:
Front-wheel drive; five-speed gearbox

SUSPENSION:
Front: Independent by coil springs and twin wishbones; anti-roll bar; telescopic dampers
Rear: Independent by coil springs and lower wishbones; upper transverse links; anti-roll bar; telescopic dampers

STEERING:
Rack-and-pinion, power-assisted on SE

BRAKES:
Front: Disc
Rear: Disc
Servo assistance

WHEELS/TYRES:
15in alloy wheels
Tyres 6.5in x 15in

BODYWORK:
Glassfibre/composite and steel materials on steel backbone chassis. Two-door convertible

DIMENSIONS:
(Non-US version)

Length	12ft 5.7in
Wheelbase	7ft 4.6in
Track, front and rear	4ft 10.5in
Width	5ft 6in (incl. mirrors)
Height	4ft 0.4in

KERB WEIGHT:
21.3cwt (SE)

PERFORMANCE:
(Source: *Autocar & Motor*)
Model quoted: Elan SE

Max speed	136mph
0-60mph	6.5sec
30-50mph in top	9.2sec
50-70mph in top	7.7sec

PRICE INCLUDING TAX WHEN NEW:
£19,850 (Elan SE, 1990)

NUMBER BUILT:
3855

After years of false starts, Peter Stevens's Elan began with a clean sheet of paper and made the transition to production. Note the 'cab-forward' design, where a steep screen sits over a short bonnet; this was a trend beginning to catch on in car styling.

wheel-drive. Winterbottom argued that the car could have a steel bodyshell, but it was felt Lotus needed to stand out by its use of composite materials.

After the British Car Auctions refinancing of 1983, the M90 was left idle but revived later the same year. New chairman David Wickins came up with a new title for the project, X100, and the car was up and running again, this time reaching full prototype stage. With its two-tone silver paint and sharp edges, Winterbottom's shape was neat and versatile, with a hood folding in two stages and space inside for two rear jump seats. But Kimberley was not convinced, and reluctantly scrapped it as being 'a little bit too TVR-ish'.

"We couldn't find a direction to focus on," Lotus design director Colin Spooner told *Car* magazine in 1990. "We knew we wanted a new small car but we couldn't decide why. We went

through a number of iterations, none of which we were happy with. The trouble with the M90 was that it never went beyond what we'd done before. It was never going to have the technical quality and impact that the original car had."

Although not made public until the final Elan appeared, the axed M90/X100 had been much closer to production than most Lotus prototypes, and had been costed for sale by a Toyota accountant at £9990 for the coupé and £10,490 for the convertible – with more powerful variants planned with a turbocharged engine and the Lotus 2.2-litre unit. For a while, in fact, two X100 projects were running: one derived from the Oliver Winterbottom M90 and another from designer Peter Stevens – who was also to work on the Excel and restyled Esprit.

The surviving X100 project finally leant towards front-wheel drive, which was no longer uncharted territory as Lotus had taken on a number of projects to tame the handling of various client cars. It also opened up a wider choice of powerplants, while it

was felt that buyers would see a fwd car as more modern. The development engine was the 1587cc Toyota 16-valve unit used in the Corolla GTi and the MR2 (which Lotus had had a hand in developing), and gave 122bhp; transversely mounted, it had a compact end-on five-speed gearbox.

A 2+2 coupé X100 was developed, then a convertible, with full-sized models made by CECOMP of Turin. The brief for Stevens was to derive his designs from the 1984 Etna showcar but he became unhappy about this when the Etna itself was stillborn. "We weren't as fired up as we ought to have been. Then the Etna died, and X100 ended up looking like a car we weren't going to produce," he told *Car* at the Elan launch. A number of running prototypes were produced from 1985 to 1986 and the convertible, although it lacked the razor edges of the Winterbottom M90, was not dissimilar in profile: cue yet more agonising over its looks.

The February 1986 GM buyout brought swift and powerful backing to the Elan project, now codenamed M100: £16m for product development, £8m for tooling and £11m for increased capacity. Sales projections for the new Elan were 3000 cars a year when its namesake took 11 years to reach a total output of 12,000 units.

In March Kimberley yet again called for the X100 to be redesigned. To be sure of a quicker result, he initiated a styling challenge, asking Colin Spooner's team to compete with Ital Design and the GM design centre in Detroit. Much to Detroit's irritation, The Lotus team produced its design by November and won. It was radical compared to its competitors, with a squat, cab-forward stance and a wheelbase of 88.6in – longer than that of the original Elan – and minimal front and rear overhangs. Tail lights from the Alpine-Renault GTA blended in perfectly.

With Lotus now owned by a competitor, Toyota politely declined to provide an engine and after a worldwide trawl which included Vauxhall, the project team was delighted to find a unit with all the

Mazda MX-5 – the Elan influence

Having thrown all its efforts into producing a word-class front-driven sports car, it is a deep irony that the Mazda MX-5 walked all over Lotus by being a shameless copy of the rear-driven '60s Elan roadster.

The idea stemmed from automotive journalist Bob Hall, who went to work for Mazda in California in the 1980s having sold his bosses the idea of a roadster using parts from existing cars. To persuade them that this was the car they should make he produced an original Elan and the project was underway by 1984. An instant hit, the 1989 MX-5 (Miata in the US, Eunos in Japan) wasn't a complete Elan clone – Mazda examined a number of classic sports cars, down even to their exhaust notes – but the end result had a central subframe not dissimilar

to the Lotus backbone (isolating the engine and driveline), the tiniest gear lever you could imagine, and a suspiciously authentic exhaust note. But there it ends: even the first series MX-5 was close to the size of an MGB and every new generation has become that little bit bigger.

The original Elan was an acknowledged starting-point for Mazda's MX-5 (Miata in the States), a bold reinvention of the traditional rear-wheel-drive sports car.

right ingredients still in development at GM affiliate Isuzu. Its iron-block/alloy-head 4XE engines were conceived to power a whole family of cars in the US and Japan, as single-cam or double-overhead-cam units. All the ingredients for a high-revving Elan-like unit were in place in the 16-valve version, developing 135bhp at 7200rpm, while there was also a 160bhp turbocharged derivative on the cards. Working with Isuzu, the

Lotus team was able to put in its own requests such as reshaping the plenum chamber, so it would fit under the Elan's bonnet, and a change to the specification of the engine-management software. In other cars Isuzu eventually dropped the 1.6 in favour of a 1.8, but this was never fitted to the Elan.

The use of the Isuzu engine allowed the bonnet height and nose length to be reduced and Stevens accordingly

repackaged the car to emphasise cabin space. He was determined that the hood should not sit proud but would disappear under a hinged panel as on a BMW convertible. There were

Some called it dumpy, but the M100 Elan was neat, hood-up or hood-down. The first shutline on the rear deck opens a well for the hood to sit in, with a decent-sized boot behind. Unless the headlamps were raised, the driver had no hope of seeing the end of the bonnet.

Driving an M100 Elan

A well-maintained 1990s Elan is the easiest way into Lotus two-seater motoring – too easy for some, in contrast to the hardcore Elise. If you've been raised on front-wheel-drive hatchbacks the second Elan will be no step back in time and will flatter your driving style. You'll believe the road tests, which said it can be deceptively quick point-to-point on a good set of roads.

Over fifteen years on, the looks are coming into their own. It's a high-waisted car and you feel snug sitting low down in the cabin. The dash is as deep as on some modern MPVs and there's no reference point for the nose. If you have to have the driver's seat pulled forward, too, you'll notice the top corner of the steeply-raked windscreen isn't far from your head. For once in a Lotus, however, the pedals are straight ahead in a good-sized footwell.

Hood down (it folds into its purpose-built space in about 15 seconds) there's plenty of chance to hear the exhaust burbling away and all the better if somebody's fitted an aftermarket exhaust. Most models for sale are the preferred 165bhp SE turbos, while the Elan S2s were all turbocharged. The turbo can hardly be heard whooshing away up-front, although you may hear a little escape of air if a dump valve has been fitted, and the engine is very flexible and will pull strongly in all gears, while being happy to rev with a real feeling of Japanese durability.

It was a lot of power to put through the front wheels in 1989, but today the Lotus suspension still prevents the wheel writhing around in your hands as you pull away. The indirect cable gearchange can't hope to compare to the shift of a classic Elan and the throws feel long, but gear selection is quick and easy. The power-assisted steering is very subtle, very direct, and you can flick in and out of bends as the driver of a Lotus should. Overall, the sensation is of being planted to the road, with the expected Lotus compliance over all but the harshest bumps. Even years on, the average Elan doesn't suffer greatly from scuttle shake, although trim can rattle. It's a classy act, all things considered – what a shame the car's life was cut so short.

said to be influences of the old Elan in aspects of the styling, such as the front air intake and bumper profile, but these were subtle. The Elan was seen as a range of cars but a convertible was the main focus of the project, as US sales were envisaged. Simon Cox (who went on to work for Isuzu and GM) styled the cabin and sourced GM interior components such as air vents, stalks and switches to harmonise with it, going to the lengths of restyling the markings on the instrument pack to obtain the orange figures of the production car. Development of the German-sourced dash moulding alone cost £1m.

The M100 Elan retained a backbone chassis, but the structure was far more complex than on the 1960s original. For added rigidity and crash protection, steel frames were riveted and bonded to the floor to form sill members and for further bracing a tubular beam ran across the cabin, from A-post to A-post, with the windscreen attaching directly to the top of these. Similarly, the B-posts were braced by a square-section steel member. A detachable front subframe,

finally, allowed the transverse engine and gearbox to be parted from the backbone and dropped down for maintenance.

No question of then plonking the body on top: compared to the usual two-half VARI process, the new Elan's bodyshell was composed of 58 VARI-moulded panels water-trimmed by robots and of far higher quality than before. The aim was to build an Elan in 168 man-hours compared to the Esprit's 550, but the assembly process was still complex for its volume aspirations and price and could not be further automated. In compensation, the result of all these endeavours was a car with impressive torsional rigidity – showing how standards had moved along, it was more than twice as stiff as a Jensen-Healey.

Chassis dynamics were sorted by former Lotus F1 driver John Miles, and the solution to maintaining the correct wheel geometry, with wheels that both steered and transmitted power, was truly innovative. The Elan had the expected twin-wishbone front suspension, but the wishbones were mounted onto separate 'rafts' on each

side which were then bolted to the front subframe. Tested on hard-used Toyota hatchbacks before being transferred to the Elan prototypes, the rafts allowed the wishbone bushes to be made very stiff and a low castor angle introduced to tame torque-steer – common on powerful front-driven cars of the time, when the steering wheel would writhe as drivers pulled away quickly. Because the rafts were an extra mounting point, they also helped to isolate NVH (Noise, Vibration and Harshness) from the cockpit. Like the Excel, rear suspension was by lower wishbones with upper links, combined coil-spring and damper units and an anti-roll bar.

In 1988 M100 prototypes underwent full worldwide durability testing to GM standards (taking in Death Valley and northern Sweden) and the production car was unveiled in October 1989. It had long been an open secret that the Elan would be front-wheel-drive and the press verdict was that Lotus engineers had taken fwd handling to a whole new level. Press cars were invariably the turbocharged SE, this being reflected

Top: Lotus was able to spend a great deal on the dashboard moulding but the use of GM instruments was a necessity. The switch for the electric door mirrors is behind the gearlever and everything else is in the right place for the driver.

Middle: The Elan project would have foundered for the lack of a suitable powerplant, but with the General Motors takeover Lotus was able to search GM affiliates and to play a key role in the final development of the new Isuzu 1.6-litre to 1.8-litre engine family. Without the turbo or the Lotus badge the power unit was also used in some humdrum US-market saloons.

Bottom: In true Lotus tradition, the tail lights were from another car, the exotic Alpine-Renault GTA, but they blended in well. The transparent cover over the numberplate was prone to fogging up in wet weather and was later deleted.

in sales, and in tests a top speed of 136mph and a 0–60mph time of 6.5 seconds were recorded. The magazines concurred that while controversially styled, the Elan was of a different quality from previous models. "The new Elan was a fantastic success," Bobby Bell of Bell & Colvill remembers. "People couldn't believe how well it performed – and other than a very boring hood-sealing problem it was a very reliable car."

Serious production did not get underway until 1990, creating a two-year order book and helping early cars to change hands for an alleged £5000 premium. The normally-aspirated 130bhp Elan was priced at £17,850, the 165bhp Elan SE at £19,850. In the UK the Mazda MX-5 was initially only offered in one 114bhp state of tune which the Elan comfortably beat, and using the base car as a comparison its pricing was less at odds with the Mazda's £14,219 than it was to be in the US, where the Mazda sold for the equivalent of £9000. Even then, this mattered little, as the majority of buyers opted for the more expensive turbocharged car.

Mike Kimberley's Elan post-mortem

"Day one we lost," says Mike Kimberley today. "We lost the race on time and the material cost was too high. Some of the reasons were automotive industry black holes you can fall into. For example, when we started the design and development of the M100 under GM, its prognosis of future legislation in the USA was that three-point seatbelts would be made mandatory across every state rather than airbags, so we didn't design it for an airbag. Mistake number one. The net result was the nose was too short, the crash force was too high, and so we had to re-design the car when airbags suddenly became mandatory halfway through the Elan's development. We added ten inches to the nose and added a new structure for an American version, and that cost £5m on its own and delayed us for ten months. Then, under GM we adopted the Demming quality principles and added £7.5m implementing those through manufacturing. And on top of that we

had to adopt – because of insurance purposes -– all of the vehicle durability testing and engine testing that GM undertook. Our costs went off the clock, a classic case of being caught between a rock and hard place. Colin Spooner and all the guys did an exercise and took £2745 out the material costs, which would have taken it down to a very reasonable on-the-road price and a good profit margin but the Lotus directors wanted to kill it and convinced the GM people to go along with them, which was a tragedy."

A US-market Elan in an upmarket setting. Engineering to US specification led to delays in the car going on sale and it was then not helped by a high price. Note the longer front and rear bumpers designed to meet US regulations.

Note also how the spoiler is blended into the rear wing moulding compared to a UK car.

Forced suddenly to re-engineer the federal version when airbags became mandatory, the Elan was late reaching its key US market and only a handful arrived in summer 1990, and even then not for California where it did not yet meet emission laws. Only 22 US-market Elans were built in 1990 and 1991, which coincided exactly with a worldwide recession. The exchange rate had tipped against the pound and the US press, already sniffy over a Lotus with a Japanese engine driving the front wheels, seized on the $40,000 sticker price when the slower Mazda MX-5 Miata was $21,000. Hefty discounts ensued.

Back home, after tackling early problems with leaky hoods, detail changes were few, such as the deletion of the clear plastic cover across the rear numberplate, which would steam up in wet weather – although some said this was also because police cameras on bridges could not read through it.

In 1991 the Elan won a British Design Council award and spawned a concept car, the M200, styled by Julian Thomson, who was later to mastermind the Elise. Dealers looked forward to a facelifted version, perhaps with anti-lock brakes, but across the Atlantic storm clouds were gathering.

On 15 June 1992 General Motors pulled the plug on the Elan. The news stunned the world but had been planned in secret at Hethel for months: on the fateful day the workforce, the dealers and then the press were all told within the space of three hours.

"The vast sums this car is losing mean I cannot invest in the Esprit, which is a profitable car for us,"

managing director Adrian Palmer told the press. Team Lotus, Lotus Engineering and the Millbrook test track were safe, but Palmer expressed no hope of short-term economic recovery and said that he would be seeking buyers for the production line. "We were gutted when production was stopped," Bobby Bell remembers. "There was no warning. We were called to a meeting in Norfolk – we didn't know what it was about until we heard on the radio news on the way up. Elans weren't the latest thing, but they were still selling. We sold 120–130 in a year."

Just 3885 'new' Elans had been built.

Julian Thomson's M200 concept was shown at the 1991 Frankfurt Motor Show as a potential Elan competition car, but remained a one-off. Other proposals such as an Elan coupé remained paper projects.

The Kia Elan

There was a long search to find a buyer for the Elan production line and the deal was not concluded until Lotus was in Bugatti's hands and the run of S2s had been completed. A number of approaches were made (even Caterham made a bid), but the surprise buyer was Korean car-maker Kia, which had only just started to build a sales presence in the UK with cut-price hatchbacks. Nonetheless, it had been a client of Lotus Engineering and in 1996 was rumoured to be part of a consortium to buy the whole company before it was sold to Proton.

After a great deal of negotiation as to how the Kia Elan should differ from the Lotus original, the end result was fairly similar, only with the substitution of Kia's own engines. Shown first as the KMS-II concept car in 1995, where the Lotus pop-up headlamps were replaced by faired-in units, the production version was based on the federal Elan and differed only in the use of Kia's normally-aspirated 1.8-litre engine, along with redesigned tail lamps and a new numberplate housing, as well as re-sourced instruments and switchgear.

Available in left-hand drive only, the Kia car was known as the Elan on the home market, Vigato for some

export markets and Sports Car (rather than Elan) in the UK. It was never officially offered in Europe, although the UK importer brought in four press cars in 1998 and made noises about offering the car for £16,000. However, Kia also found the Elan was too expensive to build and this, coupled with a takeover by Hyundai, saw production end in 2000 after around 1000 cars had been made.

After negotiations regarding to what degree it would resemble the Lotus, the Kia Elan appeared in an almost identical form apart from the rear light clusters. This is a UK-registered car imported for road tests: the Kia was only sold in Korea and North America.

GM had bought Lotus for £22.7m, invested £67m and lost £12.7m in 1990 alone. It had to write off £24m on the Elan along with 300 jobs – and the Carlton was also axed later that year. In early 1993 Lotus was once more up for sale and this time was sold to an unexpected buyer, Bugatti International. GM retained the right to have first refusal if it were to be sold on again, as it was – and still is – a major client of Lotus Engineering.

But the M100 Elan story was not quite over. A stockpile of parts and engines was inevitable as the long supply chain from Japan could not simply be switched off overnight, so engines and transmissions continued

to arrive. Finding itself with 800 Isuzu engines and an empty production line, Bugatti unveiled the Elan S2 at the 1994 Geneva Motor Show. Sold only in turbocharged form, for £24,500, the limited-edition S2 gained an exhaust catalyst and lost 10bhp as a result. However, Lotus fitted wider 16inch wheels and tyres and revised the power steering, which some had found over-assisted on the first cars. Seats were improved as was the elbow room around the gearlever, and anti-lock brakes and an immobiliser was standard. Each car had a numbered plaque. Reviewing the car for *The Independent*, Roger Bell said the 'too easy to drive' critics were wrong. 'The

Elan may not be particularly macho but its huge ability is exhilarating. Such stability and poise permit brisk driving in safety.'

Production of the S2 ended in August 1995. Bugatti had said it was merely a curtain-raiser to its own two-seater but just how soon this would arrive was another surprise. One month later, at the Frankfurt Motor Show, the world had its first glimpse of the stunning new Elise.

Opposite: Improving on an accomplished package, there was little to outwardly distinguish an Elan S2, but minor handling changes were well received.

Buying Hints

1. The front-wheel-drive Elan represents a good secondhand prospect and benefits from being over-developed in some areas. Series 2 cars command a premium over the first production run, and turbo SE versions are preferred. The very rare non-turbo cars are considered poor performers and can feel heavy, as they lack power steering.

2. A car with a mileage of under 50,000 miles is ideal but the Isuzu engine can run to 75,000–80,000 miles without major attention. The cambelt should have been changed at 60,000 miles. A little oil leakage is usual around the cam-cover gasket and the engine should run fairly cool.

3. Gearboxes are durable although synchromesh can fail, giving a graunching sound when changing gear. Gear selector cables are prone to break and it is a plus point if a car has had its cables replaced.

4. Newly-fitted front brake discs and pads are desirable for optimum Elan braking and kits are available to upgrade the system. Dash warning lights for cars with anti-lock brakes can illuminate as a result of a loose wire.

5. Early Elan hoods had sealing problems and today a degree of leakage is common to all cars in poor weather. Specialists can replace hood fabric but replacing an entire mechanism is costly – make sure you fold the hood down and back up to check it is in alignment.

6. If you've ever owned a Cavalier or a Carlton, it's a trip down memory lane for the switches and handles. The upside is they should be reliable and are all available as used parts. Cars of around 130,000 miles tend to suffer from sagging seats.

7. The Elan bodyshell is sturdy and well built and gel cracks should be ancient history. Paint should still look good and the panel fit reasonably snug. Any accident repair should have been carried out by a known specialist as some chassis straightening requires specialist tools.

The *Lotus Carlton*

Menacing even when standing still, the Vauxhall Lotus Carlton (or Omega for Europe) came only in a shade of dark green which appeared black. Note the very necessary cooling ducts in the front spoiler.

Although GM had owned Lotus since 1986, there was little outward sign that any of its own cars had benefited while it invested in the new Elan. Nonetheless, Mike Kimberley was keen that the 'Handling by Lotus' badge would appear across the Vauxhall range and started to push the idea of a super-saloon.

"We had to work with the Opel guys to convince them it would be worth using the Carlton/Omega as the first trial to give what I thought were relatively bland cars a bit of sizzle," he recalls. "And I must admit we gave the same pitch to our friends at Holden who had things like the Commodore going. At the same time we were trying to do the same thing with other companies."

The time was right for an image booster for the Opel Omega and

Vauxhall Lotus Carlton

1990–92

ENGINE:
Four cylinders in line, cast-iron block and aluminium cylinder head

Capacity	3615cc
Bore x stroke	95mm x 85mm
Valve actuation	Twin overhead cam, 24 valves
Compression ratio	8.2:1
Fuel system	Multipoint fuel injection 2 x Garrett T25 turbochargers
Power	377bhp at 5200rpm
Maximum torque	419lb ft at 4200rpm

TRANSMISSION:
Rear-wheel drive; six-speed gearbox

SUSPENSION:
Front: Independent by MacPherson struts with twin-tube dampers; anti-roll bar
Rear: Independent multi-link with semi-trailing arms; coil springs; telescopic twin-tube self-levelling dampers

STEERING:
Rack-and-pinion, power-assisted

BRAKES:
Front: Disc
Rear: Disc
Servo assistance; anti-lock standard

WHEELS/TYRES:
17in alloy
Tyres 8.5 x 17in front and 9.5 x 17in rear

BODYWORK:
Steel monocoque
Four-door saloon

DIMENSIONS:

Length	15ft 6in
Wheelbase	8ft 9in
Track, front	4ft 9in
Track, rear	4ft 10in
Width	6ft 3in
Height	4ft 7in

KERB WEIGHT:
32.5cwt

PERFORMANCE:
(Source: *Autocar & Motor*)

Max speed	Over 164mph (actual maximum not recorded)
0-60mph	5.1sec
30-50mph in fourth	5.5sec
50-70mph in fifth/sixth	7.7sec/20.5sec

PRICE INCLUDING TAX WHEN NEW:
£48,000 (1990)

NUMBER BUILT: 950

Vauxhall Carlton ranges. In many ways the German-designed – and German-built – cars were equal to those of Mercedes and BMW but they were always seen as a poor relation by buyers swayed by a prestige badge: a Lotus emblem or two might be a help in the brand-conscious '90s. This was a problem shared by Ford, but after linking with Cosworth for the Scorpio 24v, Ford-Europe gave up building big saloons with its own badges: instead it bought Jaguar, while GM itself invested in Saab.

The Lotus Carlton project started in 1988, a maverick decision spurred on by the great rapport between Mike Kimberley and GM Europe president Bob Eaton, bucking against the analytical approach Opel engineering might have liked to take. "Our colleagues at Russelsheim were probably not as eager as we were," remembers Kimberley. "It was a question of 'who is this little company Lotus?' – which is understandable. The way round it was that we always worked on the basis of 'you're the guys responsible for the product, we're supporting you so you tell us what you want us to do. We'll recommend but it's your call'. . ."

However, during early development Lotus engineers encountered lubrication and distortion problems

with the cylinder block and it later transpired that the knowledge about the cylinder block was available but hadn't been passed over to the Lotus team. The solution was to use the block developed for the Omega diesel which was stronger and thicker. With its alloy head and iron block the

standard 3.0-litre 24-valve straight-six was upped to 3.6-litres and received new induction and exhaust systems (including twin closed-loop catalytic converters), Mahle pistons, new connecting rods and a forged steel crankshaft. To this, add the key ingredient of two Garrett T25 turbos,

Vauxhalls by Lotus

The one thing everybody expected out of the GM takeover was a string of Vauxhalls or Opels by Lotus, but the Carlton stood alone. "I wanted to use the Lotus name as much as possible, and together with our GM colleagues we picked out what we thought would be the best vehicles that would benefit. One I particularly would have liked would have been a Lotus Calibra," Mike Kimberley remembers. But such a car never emerged, even though the motoring press were crying out for Lotus to improve the Calibra's torque-steer. Kimberley would have been happy to apply 'Lotus Design' branding and handling right across the range, even to the Frontera, but it was not to be. GM remained a client long after the split but perhaps stung by the

The re-worked Isuzu Piazza needed to shout its Lotus input but Mike Kimberley's wish for similar Lotus badging on GM cars was not realised. Nonetheless, Lotus continued to have an input into Vauxhall handling from the Corsa upwards.

Carlton's bad press, preferred to revive the Vauxhall VX performance brand and even its own version of the Elise, the VX220, rather than sell Lotus-badged hatchbacks.

Above: By the late '80s Lotus had learnt a great deal about turbocharging and charge-cooling from the Esprit and it opted for twin turbos on the six-cylinder engine, giving the Carlton prodigious shove in all gears. The only GM gearbox able to cope was that from the fastest Corvette.

Below: As you might expect for such an exclusive car, each Carlton was given its own numbered glovebox badge at Hethel during the retrim. The numbers just fell short of four figures.

each with its own throttle body and water-cooled intercooler. The original engine-management system could not be adapted for the twin-turbo engine and was re-mapped by AC Rochester and all Lotus Carltons ran best on high-octane super-unleaded petrol.

A six-speed gearbox from the Chevrolet Corvette ZR-1 was needed to cope with the massive torque and only added to the exotic specification (a peculiarity of the gearing was that when put into sixth, the Carlton would slow down). The rear axle came from the Australian Holden and while four-wheel drive was tried during development, rear-wheel drive controlled by a limited-slip differential won the day. The standard car's Bosch anti-lock brakes were retained. In theory this provided the option of traction control but this was never fitted. The ventilated discs were made by AP and based on a Group C racing design. They were some of the largest ever seen on a production car, at 13in at the front, one inch more in diameter than an entire Mini wheel.

The wheels filling the bolt-on arch extensions were 8.5 x 17in at the front and 9.5 x 17in at the rear, respectively on 235/45-section and 265/40-section tyres. Naturally there were Lotus-inspired suspension modifications. At the rear an extra link was added to the semi-trailing arm each side, along with self-levelling dampers, and the front struts and steering geometry were redesigned to Lotus specifications.

When it appeared at the 1989 Geneva show, the Lotus Omega prototype drew the crowds with its aggressive bodykit and a rear spoiler which extended automatically to cut lift above 100mph. The first design brief was 100bhp per litre and at the time of the show power was quoted as 360bhp at 5800rpm. This and the torque figure were already headlines: maximum torque was 376lb ft at 3800rpm, much of it generated from a mere 2000rpm.

However, engine development had not been completed – in fact there was no official commitment from GM that the car would actually be built – and when it did appear the production

The Carlton controversy

Even before it had gone on sale, Vauxhall was taken aback by the backlash the Lotus Carlton created amongst road-safety campaigners. With over a year between the Geneva show and the first customer cars, it became well-known that the Carlton could achieve 176mph. Some felt that while that was fine for £200,000 Ferraris and Porsches, a much cheaper four-door from people's favourite Vauxhall should not commit the same sin. The chairman of the Association of Chief Police Officers said that he could not understand the thinking behind it, and the Royal Society for the Prevention of Accidents made it the focus of a campaign against car-makers extolling speed in advertising.

Forced onto the back foot by a popular-press outrage, Lotus argued that the Carlton had phenomenal braking and composure to match its speed, but Vauxhall felt obliged to announce it was dropping top-speed claims from all its car advertising (while retaining the 0–60mph figure) and that it was offering buyers high-speed driving tuition. Sadly, as its insurance rating reflected, the Lotus Carlton also had an irresistible appeal to car thieves hard-pressed to choose between it and the Ford Sierra Cosworth.

version boasted 377bhp at 5200rpm; this was 200bhp more than the standard Carlton 3-litre even though the cubic capacity had been slightly reduced from that of the show car. Torque was now 419lb ft at 4200rpm, sufficient for monstrous urge in any gear. In development, GM claimed the Lotus Carlton was a 176mph car, based on a test around Italy's Nardo circuit.

While power had gone up, the appearance of the show car had been toned down a little as the extending rear wing had gone (a fixed one had proved satisfactory) and there were bigger air intakes and another turbo cooling vent on the bonnet. Finished only in the very dark metallic Imperial Green, the production model was aggressive yet restrained.

Compared to the Sunbeam and Cortina contracts, Carlton production at Hethel was a great deal more involved, helping to explain why the car cost £48,000 in 1990 – comfortably more than twice the price of a fully-loaded Vauxhall Senator. Drivable Omega/Carlton 3000 GSIs, built on a dedicated line at Opel in Russelsheim, Germany, would arrive at what had been the DeLorean engineering centre at Hethel. They were then dismantled, with the engine and gearboxes being removed and sent back to the factory. These were then reused as 'shuttle' engines on the next batch of putative Lotus Carltons, allowed the electrics to be tested on the production lines in Germany and the cars to be moved about.

So instead of starting with a bare shell, Lotus had a complete car which it then had to strip down and rebuild. Although the engine and transmission units were continually recycled, other parts such as brakes and hubs were simply scrapped to avoid any liability should they be reused on customer cars. A great deal of cutting and welding was involved to widen the transmission tunnel for the new gearbox, strengthen the shell and prepare it for the body kit. The bodies were pre-painted but nonetheless cut

The standard Carlton GSI was already a well-equipped car but the Lotus was laden with equipment (weight was not an issue) and a CD player was an exotic fitment for the time. Note the six-speed manual gearbox.

The Pininfarina Chronos

Although destined to be a short-lived saloon special, the Lotus Carlton did donate its running gear to a semi-functioning sports car in 1991. Unveiled at the Geneva show, the Pininfarina Chronos was a front-engined two-seater designed to entice longstanding client GM into agreeing its production. Bob Eaton donated a Carlton which was then reduced to a platform retaining the engine bay and bulkhead but shortened by 11 inches. The Chronos was badged as a GM car rather than associated with any individual brand, so that it could be adopted by any division, but it remained a one-off.

At a time when most concept cars were barely able to move, the Pininfarina Chronos was based on a dismembered Lotus Carlton, although there were no exterior signs of its underpinnings. (Pininfarina SpA)

away to accommodate the wheelarch extensions and these, like the front and rear-bumpers, were custom-built in glassfibre.

Aside from the thorough re-engineering, the specification was exhaustive and included air conditioning, a CD player, an alarm system and leather and wood trim. The electrically-powered and heated front seats were custom-built using the frames of the standard car and the rears were reshaped to give the appearance of two club armchairs. The dashboard was as standard, with an extra dial for the boost gauge, and a plaque set into the glovebox lid announced each car's build number. Lotus badges appeared on the sides, boot and doorplates, and fans of the marque were pleased to note that the service book said 'Lotus Carlton', not 'Vauxhall Lotus Carlton'.

Production settled at around 13 cars a week, each taking 150 hours to build. Badged as either an Opel or a Vauxhall, the intended production run was 1100 cars, of which 440 would be destined for the UK, to be sold and serviced through 17 specialist Vauxhall dealers. In the initial excitement customers put down deposits before the car went on sale in November 1990. The major markets were the UK and Germany followed by other European countries: the Lotus Carlton was never sold in the States.

Before a wheel had turned, the Carlton was already being touted as the world's fastest four-door production car. At Geneva there had been talk that its top speed would be governed to 155mph as with the BMW M5; but this wasn't the case, and UK car magazines had trouble finding a track which would allow the car its full head of steam. Handily enough, in 1987 GM had sold (or offloaded) its Millbrook test track in Bedfordshire to

Opposite: The Lotus Carlton was a thorough and costly aftermarket conversion, with the Lotus styling kit blended into a body shell cut to fit in some places. Front and rear bumpers were new, as were the wheelarch extensions and side skirts. The boot spoiler was subtle compared to that on the Geneva show car.

Lotus. With its two-mile high-speed bowl, it provided a good launch and test venue. Road testers required nerves of steel as the mighty Lotus thundered round the banked bowl getting ever closer to the crash barrier at the summit and risking the rear tyres blowing under the unequal g-force or the suspension jacking itself up.

In its 1990 test, *Autocar* reached 163.6mph before it had to bring the test to a halt. It guessed the car was capable of achieving at least another 10mph, while 0–60mph had arrived in 5.1 seconds. The way the Carlton stopped was as impressive as the way it went: given the right conditions it could halt from 100mph in under six seconds.

Built as a flagship super-saloon with no racing ambitions, the Lotus Carlton was a different kind of animal from the rough-and-ready Cortina and Sunbeam. For a large car it could be hustled around a series of bends with very little drama, with understeer being the principal characteristic, but it wasn't light (32cwt) or obviously lithe. *Autocar* found something lacking: 'The Lotus Carlton is, of course, dominated by its vastly

powerful and impressive engine. But far from being a wicked, fire-breathing monster, it's as gentle and benign as a pussycat...The problem is the driver can only get so involved – with its dull-sounding engine, ponderous gearchange, feel-less steering and heavily damped responses, it is a little short on aural and tactile stimulation.'

The Lotus Carlton was unchanged for its production life, once more keeping Lotus afloat at a difficult time, and it proved a glorious folly for GM, by that stage greatly perturbed over the money pit that was the Elan. It had been intended to produce the Carlton through to 1993. But while it was admired, there were few buyers willing to spend more than the price of a BMW M5 on a big Vauxhall, even one with a Lotus badge. By 1992 a Lotus Carlton cost £5 short of £50,000 and, coupled with a downturn in the luxury car market, production ended in October – only months after the Elan had gone, and adding to job losses. Of the target 1100 cars, 950 were built and only 248 found UK buyers, but at least this meant the Lotus Carlton gained immediate classic status.

Buying Hints

1. The value of a good used Lotus Carlton is around that of a new family hatchback but running costs are not on the same scale. The used market is small but on the whole cars have been well cared for; if not, they can be more expensive to run than an Esprit.

2. As with the Lotus-Cortina, the first thing to be sure of is that you are buying a genuine car: compare markings on the bodyshell with registration and service documents and check with a vehicle identity company to see if the car has been crashed, and if so, if it has been properly repaired. A club can be of great help here.

3. Badges should all be present as should all the body kit. The fact that the original shells were cut into makes them even more vulnerable to rust and wheelarches can rot – as can door skins, the windscreen surround and the spare wheel well.

4. Providing the cooling system works, turbos rarely give trouble and nor do the strong gearbox and rear axle. Brake discs are costly to replace.

5. Engines should run beyond 100,000 miles without a problem but timing chains need replacement at around 65,000 miles. Look for blue smoke and rattling. Any performance modifications are best avoided.

Elise *and* Beyond

Lotus Elise S1
1996-2000

Models quoted: 1.8i/111S/Exige

ENGINE:
Four cylinders in line (Rover), aluminium block and cylinder head, water-cooled, mid-mounted transversely

Capacity	1796cc
Bore x stroke	80mm x 89.3mm
Valve actuation	Twin overhead cam, 16 valves
	Variable valve timing (111S)
Compression ratio	10.5:1 (1.8i)
Fuel system	Multipoint fuel injection
Power	118bhp at 5500rpm (1.8i)
	143bhp at 7000rpm (111S)
	177bhp at 7800rpm (Exige)
Maximum torque	122lb ft at 3000rpm (1.8i)
	128lb ft at 4500rpm (111S)
	127lb ft at 6750rpm (Exige)

TRANSMISSION:
Rear-wheel drive; five-speed gearbox

SUSPENSION:
Front: Independent by coil springs and twin wishbones; monotube dampers; anti-roll bar
Rear: Independent by coil springs and twin wishbones; monotube dampers

STEERING:
Rack-and-pinion

BRAKES:
Front: Disc (ventilated)
Rear: Disc

WHEELS/TYRES:
15in alloy (front) and 16in alloy (rear)
Tyres (front/rear) 185/55 VR15 and 205 50 VR16 (1.8i); 185/55 ZR15 and 225/45 ZR16 (111S); 195/50 ZR16 and 225/45 ZR17 (Exige)

BODYWORK:
Glassfibre-reinforced plastic panels, hand-laid and by VARI process, over bonded aluminium central chassis with galvanised steel rear subframe. Two-door roadster/coupé

DIMENSIONS:
Models quoted: 1.8i /Exige

Length	12ft 2in/12ft 8in
Wheelbase	7ft 6in
Track, front and rear	4ft 8in/4ft 9in
Width	5ft 11in
Height	3ft 11in/3ft 10in

KERB WEIGHT:
14.2cwt (1.8i)
15.1cwt (111S)
15.4cwt (Exige)

PERFORMANCE:
(Source: *Autocar*)
Models quoted; 1.8i/111S/Exige

Max speed	124mph/130mph/
0-60mph	5.5sec/5.6sec/5.4sec
30-50mph in fourth	5.0sec/5.3sec/7.9sec
50-70mph in top	8.3sec/7.1sec/10.1sec

PRICE INCLUDING TAX WHEN NEW:
£18,950 (1.8i, 1996)
£26,590 (111S, 1999)
£29,995 (Exige, 2000)

NUMBER BUILT:
10,619 (Elise), 583 (Exige), 340 (340R)

Lotus Elise S2
2000-on

Models quoted: 1.8i/111S/111R

ENGINE:
Four cylinders in line (Rover, or Toyota in 111R), aluminium block and cylinder head, water-cooled, mid-mounted transversely

Capacity	1796cc
Bore x stroke	80mm x 89.3mm (1.8i/111S)
Valve actuation	Twin overhead cam, 16 valves
	Variable valve timing (111S/111R)
Compression ratio	10.5:1 (1.8i)
Fuel system	Multipoint fuel injection
Power	120bhp at 5500rpm (1.8i)
	156bhp at 7000rpm (111S)
	189bhp at 7800rpm (111R)
Maximum torque	124lb ft at 3000rpm (1.8i)
	128lb ft at 4500rpm (111S)
	133lb ft at 6800rpm (111R)

TRANSMISSION:
Rear-wheel drive; five-speed gearbox (six-speed on 111R)

SUSPENSION:
Front: Independent by coil springs and twin wishbones; monotube dampers; anti-roll bar
Rear: Independent by coil springs and twin wishbones; monotube dampers

STEERING:
Rack-and-pinion

BRAKES:
Front: Disc (ventilated)
Rear: Disc (ventilated)
Servo-assistance (anti-lock on 111R)

WHEELS/TYRES:
16in alloy front and 17in alloy rear
Tyres (front/rear) 175/55 VR16 and 225/45 VR17

BODYWORK:
Glassfibre-reinforced plastic panels by RTM process over bonded aluminium central chassis with galvanised steel rear subframe
Two-door roadster/coupé

DIMENSIONS:
Model quoted 1.8i

Length	12ft 4in
Wheelbase	7ft 6in
Track, front	4ft 9in
Track, rear	4ft 11in
Width	6ft 2in
Height	3ft 11in

KERB WEIGHT:
14.7cwt (1.8i)
15.3cwt (111S)
16.9cwt (111R)

PERFORMANCE:
(Source: *Autocar*)
Figures for 1.8i/111S/111R

Max speed	124mph/127mph/143mph
0-60mph	5.8sec/5.0sec/5.1sec
30-50mph in fourth	5.3sec/5.2sec/4.4sec
50-70mph in fourth	5.3sec/5.2sec/4.5sec

PRICE INCLUDING TAX WHEN NEW:
£22,995 (1.8i, 2000)
£27,995 (111S, 2002)
£27,995 (111R, 2004)

NUMBER BUILT (to end 2005):
Elise 12,747; Exige 1335

Opposite: Right first time. Seen first as a limited-edition engineering showcase in 1995, the following summer saw the Elise enter series production.

In 2005, ten years after its debut, the 25,000th Elise was built. Jackpot: here was the fastest, best-selling Lotus ever. Initially intended to be a limited-edition technology showpiece, the Elise went on to be the mainstay – saviour, even – of Lotus Cars, as its versatile chassis spun off more and more variants, and even a whole new car for General Motors, the Speedster/VX220.

The idea of a back-to-basics, ultra-lightweight Lotus was being bounced around by the engineers even while the M100 Elan was in development. "We were looking at all sorts of ways of producing very small, very lightweight sports cars because we felt that was

Above: The hood will keep off a shower, but putting it up is a slow process involving a number of bars and clips.

Left: Perhaps the best view of an early Elise. Although mid-engined, visibility is good. Early styling models had a flat end to the rear deck but a spoiler was added close to production, to improve downforce.

the right way to go and we could use some of the microcar technologies that were coming out of Japan," recalls former Lotus engineer and communications manager Patrick Peal. "With the 600cc turbocharged four-wheel-drive mini cars of the time we could have had a car that weighed less than 600 kilos and would have been an absolute rocketship." However, seeking a convertible for the US market, General Motors played it safe and shied away from any real commitment to a doorless, Seven-type car.

So, like the M100 Elan, it took another new owner and desperate times to get the lightweight car project off the ground. When Romano Artioli took over on behalf of Bugatti International in 1993, he vouched that 'Lotus is a jewel of totally underrated value' and although the Italian parent company's troubles would eventually drag Bugatti down, Artioli was committed to a new range of Lotus cars including a 2+2 and a V8.

Ken Sears, chief engineer of vehicle design, put forward his suggestion for a stripped-down sports car in mid-1993 and, as detailed in the comprehensive book by Alastair Clements, Elise, rebirth of the true Lotus, project M111 was approved in January 1994. Producing a best-selling car in itself was not the initial aim. Rather it was to promote the more lucrative services of Lotus Engineering, which had long since become the backbone of the company, and as a result line up a major manufacturing partner. "From Elan experience we knew there was still a market," executive engineer Tony Shute told Complete Car magazine in 1996. "In addition, as I'd nicked all the engineering research budget to finance the project, Lotus Engineering wanted something in return – to

Some considered the extruded aluminium pedal boxes a work of automotive art but they were an elegant solution to the problem that no production car assemblies would fit the chassis tub.

demonstrate Lotus technology to clients worldwide."

The new car had rapidly to fill the void the Elan had left but, despite this, production was initially set at a run of only 2700 units over three years. This gave the potential for more unconstrained thinking. Having explored various engine and transmission configurations, the M111 became mid-engined for better front crash protection and for the ease of buying a readymade engine/transmission unit for transverse mounting.

After over thirty years, Lotus decisively broke with the backbone chassis for a new technology which would be the building block for generations of cars to come. Chassis engineer Richard Rackham had been working with Rover for some time, on aluminum structures, in partnership with Norwegian company Hydro Aluminium, which specialised in extruded aluminum and was keen to break into automotive work – it was also to provide parts for the short-lived Renault Sport Spider. The extrusion process of heating the alloy and then forcing it through a die had long been used in constructions such as greenhouses, but was new to cars. By the time BMW bought Rover in 1994, Rackham had learned a great

Lotus and Rover

In late September 1993 Rover expressed an interest in the M111 project, even mooting the idea of co-manufacturing, but after its January 1994 sale to BMW, Rover opted to let Lotus go ahead on its own with the Elise, while it forged on with bringing the MGF to production.

Lotus was back in the frame six years later when BMW finally despaired of Rover's losses and invited buyers to offer their plans. The final running came down to Phoenix, a group of ex-managers, and venture capitalists Alchemy Partners, headed by Jon Moulton.

By April 2000, the sale seemed set to proceed to Alchemy, with the company putting forward a plan to concentrate on the MG brand and abandon mass production. Moulton said Alchemy had approached Lotus to develop a new model, which naturally would be a lightweight sportscar with an 'aluminium chassis and plastic body' using Lotus methods. However, by the end of the month the risk-takers had decided that the cost of mass redundancies was a risk too far and pulled out, leaving the way open for Phoenix. Beyond the supply of engines, the Lotus link was lost.

"At the time of the Rover disposal there was limited contact with the then CEO and chairman of Lotus," Jon Moulton remembers. "Nothing of detail was ever negotiated – the obvious thing would have been to buy Lotus after Rover. I have worked to some extent with at least five relatively serious groups who wanted to buy Lotus and have been in negotiations three times. People wanting finance for a deal appear about once a month!"

The 1997 Elise Sport 190 gave notice that the little car was ready to race. The detachable doors were in Kevlar and an RAC-approved rollcage and racing harnesses were standard.

deal about working with aluminium as a base for a car rather than a cladding.

The aim was a crashworthy structure that was still light and rigid and required minimal production tooling. Because the components were extruded into a mould, they could include attachment points for other items such as suspension and doors without needing to add on extra parts. Working with European experts, Lotus developed and patented a system of riveting and adhesive-bonding the aluminum structure for a very strong but light join between the various elements. Because the load was spread more widely than a welded joint, the walls of the mated parts could be thinner ($\frac{1}{16}$th of an inch), adding to the lightness of the chassis. The bare tub weighed in at less than the average man – 64kg (141lb) – but was claimed to be as stiff as a BMW saloon, and the joins soon proved

their worth in durability testing.

There were 25 different sections: the side members of the chassis swept round in a gentle arc, narrowing at the front and acting as side crash protection, and further boxes were added at the front to provide the dashboard structure and footwell ends, while another shrouded the fuel tank with a steel rollbar on top. The transverse-mounted engine was held within a galvanised steel subframe. With no corrosion worries, the structure could be left unpainted and the minimal look became a design feature of the interior, including details such as the stylish sliced-section pedal arms springing from the extruded pedal box.

The suspension development team included John Miles, who had developed the M100 Elan 'rafts', and the Elise had classic double wishbones front and rear. A wide track was combined with stiff dampers to control roll and softer springs for an acceptable ride – one that was less yielding than on the M100 Elan, but tolerable for fast road use. With so

little weight, power steering was considered unnecessary, as was a brake servo. The notably large front brake discs were specially developed for the Elise, which was the first production car to receive Metal Matrix Composite (MMC) items composed of ceramic material and aluminium, which not only saved weight and better dissipated heat but also didn't develop surface rust when standing idle.

Parallel with chassis development, the body was designed as two large front and rear mouldings, which Lotus called clamshells. These were hand-laid glassfibre mouldings, rather than VARI ones, although this method was still used for the doors, bonnet and sills. With the chassis tub arriving ready-made from Denmark (production later transferred to the UK), Elise construction was simpler than had been the case with the M100 Elan, despite it being largely finished by hand.

Julian Thomson, who had worked with Peter Stevens on the Elan, now headed the Lotus design team. In evolving the style of the

Top: Once Rover was ready to provide its 143bhp K-Series engine from the MGF, Elise performance moved up a notch with the 1999 111S, shown here with a body-coloured hardtop.

Middle: The cabin of the 111S is standard Elise in all its simplicity. Note the depth of the sill projecting into the cabin, the manual window winders, and the coin trays built into the lower corners of the dashboard.

Bottom: The transverse engine is a snug fit, but makes a small luggage boot possible for a weekend away.

Chapmanesque original Elise, the stylists assembled a number of past cars, including an Elan, a Type 23 racer and a Caterham Seven. As Mike Kimberley had done for the M100 Elan, Artioli initiated a styling competition for project M111 among 11 design houses, including IDEA from Turin and Peter Stevens's own business. Thankfully the Lotus proposal was considered the most forward thinking, although the idea of a doorless bodyshell was discarded as too impractical. The winning design was neat and pretty, and although it had a number of styling features from older cars, such as the Europa's inset indicators and an Elan-like air intake, these were subtle compared to the later wave of 'retro' cars such as the new Mini and Beetle. Aerodynamics were closely studied, with a blended-in rear spoiler, a chin spoiler, and an optional underbody rear diffuser for racetrack-type downforce. There had to be some borrowing of other people's components, but Lotus was now a past master at blending them in: Rover Metro door mirrors and Peugeot 306 switches seamlessly joined Vauxhall column stalks. Interior furnishings were minimal, with no carpets on offer (mats were optional), a couple of storage pockets behind the gear lever and a small boot behind the engine. For a likely £20,000, this was outrageously uncompromising: a radio-fitting kit was extra and the passenger seat fixed in its rearmost

Proton and Lotus

Despite the rave reviews afforded the Elise, it became obvious that Lotus was in trouble again in 1995 when Bugatti International's parent company Bugatti Automobili was put into receivership.

Kia and then Daewoo were strongly rumoured to be in the frame but Artioli opted to sell an 80 per cent stake to Malaysia's DRB HICOM, makers of Proton cars. Although the deal was much more about buying engineering expertise and breaking free from Mitsubishi than taking on a famous sports-car marque, commentators have found the company's use of the Lotus name to be understated at the least, even if Proton has poured money into Elise derivatives.

In 1997 it said it would start production of the Elise in Malaysia (re-engineered to make it easier to build), and it promised a Proton version of the stillborn M250. Some knocked-down Elise Series 1 kits were shipped abroad, and the first real Lotus-badged Proton was a 1999 GTi version of its Satria 3-door hatchback, itself derived from the Mitsubishi Colt.

A 100 per cent stake in Lotus followed, but when the 2002 Impian saloon arrived only brief mention was

made of Lotus having sorted its handling. The 2004 Gen-2 was part-styled at the Lotus Design studio, however, and the 2006 Savvy minicar also played the Lotus-tuned suspension card, although not to any great effect: the press remain critical of the general refinement and quality of these latest-generation Protons.

Even with a combination of cost-cutting, the VX220 project, and the incredible success of the Elise, Lotus has relied on Proton's purse to stem

By 2006 there was little overt evidence of Proton's ownership of Lotus, and the fact that hatchbacks such as the Gen-2 have handling by Lotus and partial styling by the company is no doubt lost on buyers. (Proton Cars)

its losses, although in 2005 it made more than 5000 cars – its highest-ever figure. As details of the all-new Esprit for 2007/08 have begun to emerge, there has been great debate about production being either wholly or in part in Malaysia.

position (the driver's seat moved but was not for the fuller figure and was set nearer the car's centre line). Spanning the gap between the rear rollbar/bulkhead and the windscreen was a simple (some said flimsy) hood which could be unclipped and rolled up to stow behind the seats.

With little time and few resources available, there was no question of an all-Lotus engine but the relationship with Rover yielded a contract for it to supply the all-alloy K-series. Dating from 1989 and used across the Rover range from the Metro to the 200 and the 1995 MGF, it was satisfyingly light and free-revving. Initially Lotus opted for the 118bhp 1796cc 16-valve engine of the MG but there was

potential to use the variable-valve-timing version and even for Rover's V6 derivative of the K-series. With a final 1996 kerb weight of only 723kg or 14.2cwt (the previous Elan weighed 22.3cwt), the Elise was set to outpace the MG and all its competitors, while at the same time offering supermini fuel economy. The naming was simple: Elise, after Artioli's new granddaughter.

The new Lotus had been scheduled to be revealed at the October 1995 London show but Artioli insisted it be brought forward to the much larger Frankfurt event that September. The revolutionary chassis was unveiled at the same time as the Elise and it was announced that deliveries would start

in mid-1996. Although at the time Artioli had said Lotus was not for sale, the Frankfurt showing was viewed as premature by some and a few days later Bugatti's Italian business was put into receivership, setting the clock running to find a new backer for Lotus.

With buyers clamouring to place deposits, the Elise clearly had a wider market than Lotus had thought and the emphatic positive reaction was followed by frantic durability and safety testing. During 1996 a crash programme was initiated to gear up for higher production, and at the same time Malaysia's Proton took a major share from Bugatti International. A pilot assembly line started in April and the first customer car was

delivered on 1 August, at long-serving Surrey dealership Bell & Colvill.

Road tests pronounced the new Lotus a masterpiece. 'No other car on earth extracts more magic from 118bhp than the standard Elise,' said Evo magazine. Former Autocar editor Ray Hutton sums up the emotional effect: "As a leap of faith it was quite a big thing. I wasn't at all sure it was going to work, and it wasn't even cheap either, but it obviously rang bells with people of my age who had wanted an Elan, and inspired the same sort of feelings in the next generation."

The 1996 Elise 1.8i was priced at £18,950, cheaper than the expected £20,000. Autocar performance figures established a top speed of 124mph and a 0–60mph time of 5.5secs with a hard-tested fuel consumption of 28.7mpg – the official combined figure was an impressive 39.4mpg. The first year's run of only 400 cars was soon snapped up, with more than three times as many buyers putting down deposits.

After the Elan disaster, dealers had a welcome return to form. "I'll never forget the day we first saw one," recalls Bobby Bell of Bell & Colvill. "We were having an open day at Goodwood and the factory turned up with this new Elise and I thought 'that

is absolutely fantastic'. It's been a fabulous little car."

The K-series took readily to tuning and merely changing the engine-management chip brought a small power increase. Bell & Colvill and others soon saw a market for owners who wanted a tailor-made Elise and produced its own power-upgrade options for 1997. "With the Series 1

Above: From the track to the road, the race-bred Exige looks aggressive but its bodywork additions further refine high-speed handling. The vent on the roof is for channelling cooling air into the engine compartment.

Below: Rear visibility in an Exige is minimal; the rear 'clamshell' is unique to the car. There is a removable rear window rather than a conventional bootlid.

In 2000, Lotus shocked the motoring world by presenting a fully restyled Elise; the removable body sections at the same time changed to an easier volume-manufacturing process. The project was made simpler by the aluminium tub being unchanged. Note the rear diffuser under the numberplate; hidden on the previous car, it is now a styling feature. Although less retro, some find the looks of the 'MkII' Elise too fussy.

people were crazy for any sort of enhancement, any tuning," says Bobby Bell. "It was ultra-desirable as it was, but people were happy to spend more on their car to personalise it. You know, the 'mine's got 140bhp or 160bhp' sort of talk. And of course, at the track it was nice to have an Elise that would blow the others away."

The factory joined in the power game and the Elise range quickly evolved by numbers rather than names. Cars were active in Lotus-supported racing from 1996 and Lotus launched the Sport 190 option for racing customers for 1997. Developed with RoverSport, the VHPD – Very High Performance Derivative – K-series engine option featured a modified cylinder head, and with a competition exhaust system and suspension upgrades 145mph was possible. In 1998 the more road-friendly Sport 135 matched a number of options including a sports exhaust, close-ratio gears and engine-management changes, for an extra 17bhp. In 1999 this was followed by the full production 111S which gained the

VVC (Variable Valve Control) engine from the MGF. Combined with other modifications, this boosted power to 143bhp by varying the sequence of valve opening and closing.

Team Lotus had bowed out of Formula 1 in 1994 but the Elise took Lotus roaring back into mainstream racing. The US racing Esprits inspired the short-lived 1997 GT1 cars, pumped up Elise look-alikes with the Lotus V8, only for these to be scuppered by engine rule confusion: seven GT1s were built for racing and just one for road use. Of more relevance was the 1998 formation of Lotus Motorsport, to build on the Elise's track prowess and filter this through to production versions. Its first product was the 1999 Sport Elise, a pumped up race-only Elise with an enclosed rear shell,

Track-day toys: Sprint, 340R and the Circuit Car

The Elise has ridden a wave of real commercial growth in amateur track days. Oppressed by congested roads and speed cameras, British sports car and superbike owners are increasingly paying for organised days where you turn up and cane your machine in controlled conditions with driving tuition on hand – more about letting off steam than racing.

Tuning options aside, Lotus's first attempt at a minimal track-day Elise was the Sprint concept for the 1996 Birmingham show. It had no windscreen, side windows or hood, with only a wind deflector for comfort, but although Lotus promised the Sprint would go on sale for around £20,000 and be supported by its own race championship, it progressed no further.

Two years later a far more outlandish concept car actually made it into production: the 340R. Emboldened by the success of the Elise, in 2000 Lotus produced 340 examples of this sensational track-day toy for £35,000 apiece, rendering it an instant classic. With no windows, roof or doors and a partially-exposed exhaust system, it demonstrated the rigidity of the Elise tub and was fully road-legal, yet the suspension could be adjusted to the driver's tastes on the track, while removing the catalytic converter could boost the power of the K-series engine from 177bhp to 195bhp.

The idea returned in 2005 as the prototype Circuit Car broke cover at the famous Shelsley Walsh hillclimb. For 2006, Lotus announced it as a 100-cars-a-year dedicated special that could be tailored for a number of racing combinations. With no windscreen and one seat (a second was optional), weight was down to a claimed 600kg (11.8cwt). Once more derived from the Elise platform and using the supercharged Toyota engine of the 240R, it was claimed to have a 0–60mph time of around 3.5 seconds;

the 190 option used the normally-aspirated Elise engine. The bodywork was striking and a study in aerodynamic function, with panels bolted on for easy access and repair. A myriad of racing options included wet, dry, and hillclimb tyres.

Above: The astonishing 340R of 1998 was a mark of new-found confidence at Lotus. With only 340 produced, some were snapped up by collectors but others were used to the full at track days.

Left: Shown under construction at Lotus, the 340R possessed neither doors nor a roof but was still a strong structure. Note the front box of the Elise body tub.

Taking weight-saving to extreme levels, the 2001 Exposé had a polycarbonate shell which revealed its inner workings. It made 0–60mph in 3.5sec.

The Vauxhall VX220

The Vauxhall VX220/Opel Speedster (left) is based on the Elise tub and ushered in the brand's square-edged look. Faster at top speed but less frenetic than the Elise (right), its assembly has been an important source of revenue for Group Lotus.

Despite Proton ownership, General Motors has remained a key Lotus client and a deal was struck in 1998 to build a dedicated Opel/Vauxhall sports car, not least to launch the VX performance brand in the UK. It was a move Lotus was keen to encourage, having developed the extruded aluminium chassis concept and wanting to find buyers for it, and at the same time seeking to expand Elise production: both cars were to be built on the same line.

The Opel Speedster and Vauxhall VX220 were, like the Lotus Omega/Carlton, twins in all but badging, with annual production set at 2000/1000 respectively. Built round an Elise tub, the GM car was longer, wider and heavier, as much as anything because it carried GM's own

engine; a 2198cc 145bhp four-cylinder unit, this gave the car a 0–60mph time of around 6 seconds but a more flexible delivery from lower revs. While raw for a Vauxhall or Opel, handling was tuned on the safer side, tending to understeer more than the Elise.

The first concept car was seen at the 1999 Geneva show and production cars went on sale the following year. Having expected a softer Elise clone, enthusiasts were surprise to see just how minimal the new Vauxhall had dared to be. There was still plenty of exposed aluminium in the cabin, manual windows, and no air conditioning, but there had to be a servo and anti-lock brakes, while the hood was better-designed.

Sales were disappointing, though, with a number of special editions being necessary. Thus the 2003 VX220 Turbo saw power boosted to 200bhp, giving more urge than the Elise but delivered in a different way. The 2004 VXR220 special edition added an extra 10 per cent power

hike but production ended in July 2005 at 7000 units overall. GM has not repeated the experiment for the car's successor, which is a conventional US-built car available from 2006, only as an Opel in Europe. But the Vauxhall turbo engine has become the power unit for the new Europa S, which aims to take up lost production and broaden the Lotus range.

Although commentators expected the VX220 (above) to be more luxurious than the Elise, there is little to choose between the cars in terms of interior equipment. However, some aspects of its design, such as the roof, are better executed.

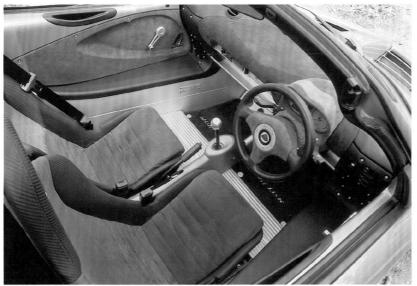

Above: Wheels are larger and the tyres specially developed by Bridgestone, working with Lotus. The new-generation Elise also benefits from advances in damper technology.

Left: The second generation cabin is not plush, but buyers can choose colourful trim combinations and floor mats. Seats and instruments are redesigned, and stowage space improved.

unique Kamm-tail styling, a central driving position and 203bhp. Within the cost of the £55,000-plus car, wealthy owners could expect total track support for one season of the Autobytel Lotus Championship. The championship ended after a couple of years but the Sport Elise and to some

extent the short-lived GT1 put Lotus in mind of a more hardcore Elise road car, the Exige.

Based around the standard Elise structure, with a Sport Elise shell, the 2000 Exige gained a unique rear clamshell like Darth Vader's helmet and with an equal amount of visibility.

With extra cooling vents and no separate boot, there was just a clear cover for the engine and a box behind it for melting any luggage. Built to order for £29,995, the standard engine was the 177bhp K-series of the 340R (see panel) or the 190bhp VHPD, and the Exige offered no further

The M120 and the M250

The path to the 2006 Europa S coupé has clocked up a number of blind alleys. Lotus teased early Elise buyers with brochure images of the Sprint – a standard car and a little coupé with cutaway doors in its roof. The latter was the 1997 M120 coupé, intended to fit in the chasm that separated Elise and Esprit and to take the Rover KV6 engine. It would have been a luxury model with more luggage space, better trim, and options such as air conditioning, and could have taken the Elise into the US market. A full-sized clay model was built, but Lotus bosses got cold feet when it looked as if it might have a price tag of over £30,000.

The dramatic M250 of 1999 was a much greater source of frustration, being promised for production only to be withdrawn two years later. Designed by Russell Carr, the concept car was unveiled at the 1999 Frankfurt show, and pitched, like the M120, as a mid-engined car to fit between Elise and Esprit. By the London show it had gained an interior and striking scissor-action doors, and Lotus was already talking in terms of a production car.

The M250 was said to have a Lotus-developed 3-litre V6 of 250bhp from an outside supplier (the concept engine was a Renault V6), along with a six-speed gearbox, power steering, anti-lock brakes and – clearly a pointer to its biggest market – seats to cater for larger occupants and room for two golf bags behind the front seats. Nonetheless, it was said to have a weight of less than 1000kg (19.6cwt), thanks to the 'next generation' bonded extruded-aluminium chassis, and the new composite materials used throughout its construction.

With its dramatic looks and gullwing doors, when the M250 was announced buyers raced to place deposits, but their expectation of it entering production was dashed.

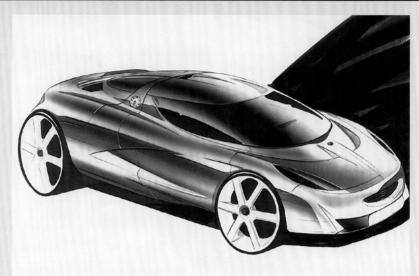

Taking the hint, 1000 people had already placed orders by January 2000, when enthusiasts were thrilled to hear that it was set for production two years later at around £40,000 – firmly in Porsche Boxster territory. Target production was set at 4000 cars a year but there was still some vagueness about the specification, while Lotus was once more suffering financial troubles. A team was set up to develop the car, but in May 2001 the M250 was canned. A study of

An early rendering of the M250 concept car from 1999. Lotus was riding high on the success of the Elise and ready to extend the range upwards into Porsche territory.

world markets had shown the need to redesign it for US buyers, said new chief executive Terry Playle. In a humiliating U-turn, the would-be buyers had to have their deposits returned or were offered discounts on an existing Lotus model.

concessions to comfort for the extra money. There was still no radio (not that you'd hear it) and a full racing harness was an option. The Sport Elise rear, front splitter spoiler and stand-alone rear wing added 80kg (176lbs) of downforce at 100mph and although fully road legal, the Exige was better on the track than off, being a real licence-loser on the road.

There was another faster Elise for 2000, the Sport 160, but by the latter half of the year it had become yesterday's car, as to everyone's surprise Lotus unveiled a completely restyled Elise at the October 2000 Birmingham show. This was a real Lotus breakthrough: a full restyle a mere four years after the original Elise, which was still selling like hot cakes – and also the first Lotus to be computer-designed. After the Vauxhall VX220, there had been a feeling that the Elise could be a little more aggressive, a little less retro, and a little more mass-market, so work started on a new shape in late 1998. Styled by in-house designer Steve Crijns, the new look owed a lot to the extrovert 340R in its frontal and headlamp treatment and the rear lights were similar to those of the ill-fated M250. The new Elise sat lower on the ground and with wheels placed to fill the arches, and the rear diffuser was brought out on show as a styling feature. A revised hood design was claimed to be easier to use.

The aluminium tub was still a groundbreaking design and stayed largely the same although the sills were cut down to (slightly) help entry and the extruded aluminum suspension uprights were replaced by steel components. To optimise handling, Lotus worked with tyre manufacturer Bridgestone to tailor-make a grippier compound, while wheel diameters grew an inch, and there were new Bilstein dampers, springs and bushes.

Now sure of a higher sales volume, Lotus contracted manufacture of the body panels to French firm Sotira, ending the use of the VARI process but producing a higher-quality finish through the Resin Transfer Moulding

The Exige reappeared for 2004 with a new engine from Toyota, boasting 189bhp. Critics observed that it was no faster than the Elise 111R which shared the same unit.

(RTM) process of stamping pre-impregnated glassfibre matting at high pressure into steel moulds, resulting in panels that were both thinner and lighter.

The second-generation Elise majored on quality – not that the first car had any real build weakness – with the interior styled to give less of a component-car feel, with more bespoke switchgear and redesigned seats and instruments. Storage was boosted by an optional shelf under the dash with movable dividers to hold small objects. Staying true to the basic ethos, carpets were not standard but came with the £3195 Sports Touring pack, which included leather seats.

The Rover powerpacks were carried over, with revised gear ratios to cope with the marginal weight increase and with the engines tuned to meet current emissions standards. Starting at £22,995, the first Series 2 cars were delivered in spring 2001 and over the next couple of years the range mirrored the first series, comprising the Sport 135, the Sport 190 and the (now 156bhp) 111S. The Series 2 included a range of limited editions based on the Lotus racing Type numbers and in 'Heritage' colours.

Early 2004 saw a new engine option for UK buyers and a long-awaited version for the American market. Despite booming European Elise sales, Lotus had only the Esprit to

offer US buyers up to this point. It was thought that the Series 1 was not of sufficient quality, while the K-series engine would not satisfy US emissions requirements. But after careful market research, restructuring of its US operations, and informal showings at car shows, the December 2004 Los Angeles Motor Show saw the launch of a federal version of the Series 2, the M260. Project manager Roger Becker had revived the Toyota connection and a deal was done for the use of the four-cylinder 1796cc unit used in the Celica. The Toyota engine, tagged VVTL-i (Variable Valve Timing and Lift-intelligent in Toyota-speak) unit produced 189bhp and was coupled to a six-speed gearbox. Maximum power was developed at a heady 7800rpm, compared to the original Rover's 5500rpm.

UK buyers were now offered a wider range, with both Rover and Toyota engines (111R with Toyota while the 111S retained the K-series), but it seemed the choice was more a question of bhp and price than ability. Writing in 2004, *Autocar* observed that 'the Toyota engine is peaky (not very happy below 5500rpm), the gear ratios are way too

The 2006 Europa S

After a decade of successfully spinning off minor variations of the Elise and Exige, Lotus finally announced an all-new model, reviving an old Lotus name, at the 2006 Geneva show. Although new enough to merit Lotus Type number 121, The Europa S still owes a lot to the versatile construction method of the Elise, being built upon a largely unaltered tub – and also to the departing Vauxhall VX220. After some debate over making the entire car abroad, just body panels are sourced from Proton in Malaysia

After the stillborn M120 and the M250 failure, here at last is the GT car pitched at Porsche and Audi buyers. The Europa S has been launched with the VX220's 200bhp turbo engine, and although extra equipment has increased weight to a still-light 995kg (19.5cwt), a 140mph maximum speed and sub-six-second 0–60mph time are being claimed.

Thanks to its extra length, the two-seat Europa S has a bigger fully-trimmed boot under a hatch which also reveals the engine bay, and the cabin architecture will be familiar to Elise buyers, although the sills are cut down and the doors longer, to improve access.

Offered for sale in summer 2006 at a base price of £33,895, there are very few options, a full-leather interior, driver and passenger airbags, carpets and satellite

With the failure of the M250 project, Lotus played safe in extending the Elise family during 2006. The Europa has taken over the space vacated at Hethel by the VX220 and is again designed round the Elise chassis, but with Vauxhall power. (Lotus)

navigation all being standard for UK buyers. However, while it may seem a natural fit, the Europa S has not initially been launched in the US or Canadian markets, where the engine is not emissions-certified, and Lotus has limited itself to a build of 500 Europas a year. Unimpressed road testers have made noises that the Europa S is more a way of prolonging VX220 production than a valid luxury Elise...

Lotus became adept at spinning the Elise off into limited editions but the surprising 2005 Exige Espionage was an unlikely pairing with London tailor Gieves & Hawkes. It featured an interior trimmed in pinstripes, with silk on the rear of the seats. (Lotus)

long and the noise isn't especially pleasing. Overall, it out-drives the old Rover engine, but not by much.'

An airbag was a legal requirement for the US and – another first on an Elise – Lotus-developed anti-lock brakes were fitted, with servo assistance. This would have seemed a heresy to some, but testers agreed that the system just made the Elise that little bit more usable on a daily basis without interfering with track-day fun.

After a three-year gap, the Exige made a reappearance in 2004 with the Toyota engine. Although the rear wing had been slimmed down, the detachable hardtop with its mesh rear windows and the blacked-out wheels and Yokohama tyres clearly marked out the Exige from the Elise, especially if you chose the bright-orange paint option. The Exige was still extreme by most people's standards and with its stiffer springing was still more track-day than road-car, but you could add the Touring Pack of carpets, electric windows, stereo and air conditioning for a further £1295 on top of the listed £29,995. Despite the aerodynamic and suspension changes *Autocar* found performance near-identical to that of the Elise 111R, at 4.9secs to 60mph as opposed to 5.1secs, with the car being 15kg (33lbs) heavier.

There was yet more power to come, without adding extra engine capacity. In late 2005 Lotus turned to supercharging for the 243bhp Exige 240R. Produced in a batch of 50, it was aimed at wealthy track-day enthusiasts, with the option to change suspension and damper settings included in the £43,995 price. With its Eaton M62 supercharger, the Toyota engine was designed to have the output of a 3-litre power unit from its 1800cc capacity.

In 2005 the final collapse of Rover called time on the K-series cars, which gave way entirely to Toyota versions for 2006, with the lower-powered 134bhp engine providing power for that summer's 'entry level' Elise S, priced at £23,995. Other 2006 model-year changes for the Elise and Exige included an optional limited-slip differential and traction control and Lotus-developed lightweight air conditioning. There was a new pedal box for improved travel, and ProBax seats, claimed to offer medically-correct spine support and do away with the need for lumbar adjustment. The Exige 240R spawned a nominally slower (218bhp and 0–60mph in 4.1secs) production-line car, the Exige S, and this formed the basis of the Lotus Sport Exige GT3 for the FIA GT3 sportscar championship.

Ultimately, though, for 2006 greater efforts were expended on the second significant derivative of the Elise tub, the new Europa S. For the immediate future, attention will be focused less on the Elise than on a five-year plan announced by reinstalled CEO Mike Kimberley. This promises a new V6 2+2 for 2008, a Lotus-Proton hot hatch, and the long-awaited new Esprit. Lotus could still have its most exciting years ahead of it.

Driving an Elise Series 1

Are you Elise-shaped? It's a valid question. Swing open the tiny door and the deep sills widen as they go further into the cabin, making for quite a mound to clamber over (just as well Lotus provides some padding). Hood-up, access is just about possible.

Once you're in, the cabin is a great place to be. From the driver's seat, even the view around your feet delights. The designers really took seriously the Lotus maxim of making an object serve two purposes – take the metal spar dividing the floor that also has a clutch footrest attached to it. You can then go on to marvel at the engineering of the drilled crossmembers at your feet. Best not be too worried about scratches inside and out – you can hear stones from the road pinging off the underbody as you zoom down country lanes.

Again there's borrowed switchgear but used sparingly and imaginatively, blended into the single-piece dashboard. Why waste weight with gloveboxes? There's a net behind the front seats, small ledges either side of the dash on the S1 and a few more cubbyholes on the S2. Those very thin moulded weight-saving seats look slightly painful but are well shaped and hold you in place across the shoulders in corners.

It's quite hard not to want to scream off into the sunset every time you get into an Elise. It just wants you to take it by the scruff of the neck and hurl it at some bends. There is no power steering in this featherweight and none is needed as you point-and-go exactly where you want. Meanwhile, small movements on the unassisted brake pedal shave off speed without fuss. The suspension is taut but insulates you well from all but the biggest potholes.

This is not a quiet car. From the moment you start it up you know exactly that the engine is right behind your ears, even down to the fuel pump whirring away. On the move the Rover K-series can perhaps seem a little whiney but it revs freely and is flexible, with a good spread of torque. You'll find yourself changing gear for the sake of it: the metal-topped gearlever moves in precise, short throws with a well-engineered mechanical 'clack-clack' action like that of a Ferrari, although fifth sometimes needs a determined shove.

The two bumps of the front wheelarches help you place the delicate Elise precisely on the road and although to the rear it has some of the finned look of the first Europa, it is far easier to see out of, with a well-sized glass rear window framing the 'bee sting' aerial.

In summer 2006, Lotus launched an entry-level Elise to replace the previous K-series car. The Elise 111S uses a 134bhp version of the 1.8-litre Toyota engine with variable valve timing. (Lotus)

Buying Hints

1. The Elise is a well-built car although many suffer hard wear and tear. Because of the amount of aftermarket tuning options and accessories, it can be quite difficult to narrow down the choice, but even a standard Elise is not slow by most people's standards. Think hard before paying over the odds for a tuned car or one with suspension modifications which are only suited to track use. Standard cars are also more insurance-friendly, but all Elise variants are Group 19 or 20.

2. Some early Elises suffer from overheating and head-gasket failure. The signs are a smell of anti-freeze in the cabin and steam coming from the front of the engine, but head-gasket replacement is not a hugely costly job. The K-series is otherwise durable but servicing intervals are shorter for the Exige and Sport 160 which – along with the VHPD cars – require

more attention. The cambelt on a standard Elise should be replaced at 54,000 miles. A difficult gearchange may only require cable adjustment.

3. At 50,000–60,000 miles most cars need a set of suspension bushes and these should be replaced, in one set, by a dealer or specialist who can then restore the suspension settings. The onset of a collection of knocking noises can happen even at a low mileage. Cars generally wear their mileages well but despite this there is no particular problem of odometer readings being falsified. A good indication of use is the amount of scuffing the sills and floor panels have suffered.

4. A visual inspection on a ramp is a must. The underside of the chassis tub should be smooth and ripple-free and without anything but minor damage from road debris. The entire tub should be

replaced rather than repaired after a serious accident.

5. Stone-chipping and paint damage to an Elise is quite probable. While localised repairs can be made to the glassfibre panels, it is easier to replace the entire clamshell as it simply bolts on and is not as frighteningly expensive as it sounds; a new front can also disguise a crashed car, on the other hand.

6. The MMC brake discs are unique to early cars and expensive to replace. They should be carefully inspected for scoring and have regular replacement of their pads. Cast-iron discs were fitted to later cars. Being on such a light car, though, Elise brakes are generally long-lasting.

7. Windows can come off their runners and the winding mechanisms can give trouble. Boot-release catches can seize on early cars.

appendix I
Lotus Type Numbers

Although many people know Lotus cars by their names, enthusiasts are just as conversant with the Lotus 'Type' numbers, which have evolved in a sometimes haphazard way since the 1950s. The first 'Lotus' was Colin Chapman's second car and naming it Lotus has been in retrospect. Even by the mid-'50s Chapman saw that the 'Mark' cars were becoming too confusing and named the Seven and Eleven in letters. Unlucky thirteen has always been left out.

Type numbers have primarily been used to distinguish one rapidly-evolving racing car from another, but as Lotus road cars often have racing derivatives they too fall into the sequence. It has (on the whole) been the practice that if a radical enough change is made, such as a 'federal' bodyshell or a new engine, then a new Type number can be used. Within each Type number there have also been numbered 'Series' and some derivatives have had an 'a' or 'b' applied to them. Some Types have never been allocated and sometimes two cars have shared the same number: the Type 89 is both a Formula 1 car and the Eclat Excel.

Further confusion was added in the 1970s when the new generation of wedge-shaped road cars was also referred to by internal project names such as M50 and M70 (Elite and Esprit). Each decade has its oddities: in the 1980s project M90 became the X100 then the M100 (front-wheel-drive Elan) and in the 1990s Lotus Type numbers 108 and 110 were for high-tech racing pushbikes. Type numbers 116 and 117 were not allocated to the VX220 and Elise S2, to avoid having to re-crash test and re-homologate. For a bit of fun, the Lotus Type 119 is a series of high-tech soap-box racers built for the 2002 Goodwood Festival of Speed!

The list below is for guidance on the Lotus road cars, with thanks to those who had the foresight to start keeping records.

Number	Year(s) produced	Identity
MkI	1948	Austin Seven Special
MkII	1949	Ford/Austin trials car, first Lotus
MkIII	1951	750MC Austin trials/race car
MkVI	1953–55	Six – first spaceframe component car, produced for road and track use with various engines
Seven	1957–72	Produced in four series with variety of engines; became the Caterham (see also Type 60)
MkVIII	1954	Aerodynamic sports-racer
MkIX	1955	Derivative of MkVIII
MkX	1955	Derivative of MkVIII
Eleven	1956–58	Sports-racer equipped for road and track use. Series 2 should have been Thirteen
Type 14	1957–63	Elite
Type 26	1962–66	Elan convertible S1 and S2
Type 26R	1964–66	Race-ready version of the Elan
Type 28	1963–66	Lotus-Cortina MkI
Type 36	1965–73	Elan coupé S3, S4 and Sprint
Type 45	1966–73	Elan convertible S3 and S4
Type 46	1966–68	Europa S1
Type 47	1966–68	Racing version of Europa; twin-cam engine

Number	Year(s) produced	Identity
Type 47D	1968	One-off V8-engined Europa
Type 50	1967–74	Elan +2 range
Type 52	1968	One-off Europa twin-cam
Type 54	1969–71	Europa Series 2 for UK sale
Type 60	1969–72	Glassfibre-bodied Seven S4
Type 65	1969–71	Federal-bodied Europa
Type 74	1971–75	Europa Twin Cam and Special
Type 75	1974–80	'New Elite' S1
Type 76	1975–80	Eclat S1
Type 79	1976–81	Esprit S1 and S2
Type 81	1979–81	Talbot Sunbeam Lotus
Type 82	1980–87	Esprit Turbo
Type 83	1980–82	Elite S2
Type 84	1980–82	Eclat S2
Type 85	1981–87	Esprit Series 3
Type 89	1982–92	Eclat Excel, later Excel
Type 90		M90 sports car (never built)
Type 100	1989–92	M100 front-wheel-drive Elan
Type 104	1990–92	Lotus Carlton/Omega
Type 105/6	1992	X180 racing Esprit (US only)
Type 111	1996-on	Elise and derivatives
Type 114	1996-2003	Esprit V8
Type 118	1999	Project M250 concept
Type 121	2006-on	Elise-based Europa

appendix II
The DeLorean Saga

In January 2006 Fred Bushell, the accountant who had done so much to pull Lotus out of trouble, died after a long illness. His passing followed that of John Zachary DeLorean the previous year, perhaps finally drawing a line under a tale of intrigue that still haunts Lotus history. Only Fred Bushell was jailed for his part in a massive fraud, perpetrated by DeLorean and Colin Chapman and unbeknown to the engineers at Lotus who worked tirelessly to turn the gull-winged DMC12 into a passable car, only to see it flop in the marketplace.

John DeLorean trained as an engineer and in the 1960s rose rapidly through the ranks of General Motors, where he also developed a talent for creating his own mythology and a liking for the finer things in life. It was there that he started to dream about creating a new sports car and produced a proposal for Pontiac which was promptly turned down. On leaving GM in 1973 as the oil crisis was in full swing, he announced he would go his own way with an ethical economy car, then a luxury saloon and then a gull-winged sports car. Once he had sufficient backing, the John Z DeLorean Corporation was formed and by 1975 he had signed up Italian stylist Giugiaro.

Before the concept was seen, DeLorean boasted that the production car would have a plastic chassis, moulded by a process called Elastic Reservoir Moulding (ERM), and be clad with unpainted stainless-steel panels. He claimed it would be ready by 1978, have fantastic economy, and safety features such as twin airbags.

The engine-less mock-up was paraded in front of investors and the press while DeLorean started to throw money at setting up the DeLorean Motor Company and poaching staff. The car's potential price, volume and specification fluctuated wildly, and behind his own team's back DeLorean started talking to Colin Chapman, seen as offering a potent image to attach to the car.

Ultimately, DeLorean secured a generous grant to locate production in Belfast, Northern Ireland, in an area of high unemployment. In summer 1978 he breezed into Hethel and talked about buying the whole company, which Chapman instantly rejected, but he did come round to the idea of carrying out development work to productionalise the car, especially when he knew the sums involved – money that would keep him on top in Formula 1.

Key to the deal – and the scandal – was a firm that Chapman set up via Swiss contacts, called GDP Services Inc, and which was registered in Panama. DeLorean was on the board and it was understood that Chapman had only created the company to avoid paying large sums of tax on the deal. It was also set up to avoid any product liability for failures of the finished product.

As soon as he saw the first designs, Chapman fought hard to start again. DeLorean gave in to most of his demands but would not budge on the gull-wing doors or the rear-engined layout dictated by his requirement to fit the wealthy bachelor's golf clubs behind the back seat. Journalist Ray Hutton recalls meeting Chapman at the time the deal was done. "They took the project on knowing it was hopeless," he remembers. "The engine was in the wrong place, it had a plastic structure and metal cladding – it was a ridiculous car. John DeLorean was an impossible bloke but Chapman was determined to get some of that

money, so they took this thing on. It was in no way a Lotus design, not the way Chapman would have done it."

Mike Kimberley took one look at the unproven ERM chassis concept and, after crash projections showed the structure to be lethal, he scrapped it. To meet the proposed deadline, Lotus was paid $5.5m just for rights to use the VARI process for a shell which would then be dropped onto an Esprit-like steel backbone chassis and then clothed in steel. "We had to use the VARI process for the body to meet all the legislation, including crash and crush," says Kimberley. "So therefore it finished up with almost two bodies, which is a redundancy to our way of thinking." From summer 1978 until the end of 1980, on ploughed Lotus, bringing more and more engineers on board while a parallel team was working on the new Belfast factory and the production process.

Through 1979 the DeLorean DMC-12 continued to change, creating a nightmare for the production engineers – while Chapman became more distant. The most striking change was a decision to have Giugiaro 'freshen' the styling. This meant every drawing had to be re-done and many chassis details altered. The hopeless airbag design was ditched and the target weight went up. Lotus also had to do a thorough job re-engineering the DMC-12's chosen engine, a federalised version of the Peugeot/Renault 2849cc V6, lest its performance be completely strangled.

Mike Kimberley remains proud of the struggle. "We had at one stage 365 engineers working on that project and we worked seven days a week, 24 hours a day, and so did all the engineers from DeLorean – they lived it 22–23 months from a clean sheet of paper, and meeting every single

The DMC-12's gullwing doors looked impressive in brochures but Chapman hated them and they could never be made to work satisfactorily. Lotus tried hard to make a decent car from an unpromising design promoted by a maverick would-be manufacturer.

American legislative requirement was a terrific achievement."

Meanwhile, from his plush New York offices DeLorean was happily spending money on other schemes, such as a school bus project, branded clothing and an attempt to take over a manufacturer of snow-grooming equipment. He even started talking about a saloon car, as a way of begging for more handouts.

Government unhappiness was growing even before the first cars were sold but there was a great will for the project to work. The Labour government of the time saw it made sense to create employment in Northern Ireland and thus lessen the impact of the IRA's campaigns of violence.

The timetable was so stretched that the first production cars had to be driven round the clock to complete development testing and, once in the States (the car was never sold in the UK), early examples had to be rebuilt before going to customers.

Nonetheless, in summer 1981 buyers were excited enough to be paying a premium for the first examples. DeLorean then started to increase his workforce up to 2400 and boost production to make the company look confident in the face of a proposed share issue which would make him further millions. But the unsold cars simply piled up in Belfast.

It was Marian Gibson, DeLorean's English-born personal assistant, who first blew the whistle on her boss's swindling ways. Prime Minister Margaret Thatcher was alerted, but an initial investigation foundered. Then the DMC-12's compromised design started to bite back: gull-wing doors jammed shut, front suspensions collapsed and there were numerous electrical problems. The US economy was in recession yet the factory was still producing as if for a market of 20,000 cars, when a more realistic figure would have been 8000 sales annually. In the end only around 9000 DeLoreans were to be made.

Hard economics and a less credible batch of politicians finally snapped shut the taxpayers' purse and eventually sent the factory into receivership in 1982. For a time the receivers and DeLorean talked of saving the DMC-12 project and even of building a 'TR7-like' sports car, but in reality the venture was doomed. DeLorean then put an end to all hopes when he was taped by the FBI trying to broker a drug deal to save his company – although he escaped jail because a US court determined he had been the victim of entrapment.

In all, the British government put £77m into the project and even over 25 years later it was still unclear where the money had gone. In 2004 the

Northern Ireland Audit Office reported that GDP was to have received just under £9m for the Lotus research and development. DMCL then paid GDP a further £11.5m of taxpayers' money for Lotus services but none of this money actually reached Lotus Engineering, Lotus being paid directly by the Northern Ireland Development Agency.

In 1982, receiver Sir Kenneth Cork was quoted as saying the money 'went walkabout'. Further millions were spent trying to recover the money but somehow DeLorean managed to escape civil and criminal prosecution. Not so Fred Bushell who, in 1992, pleaded guilty to his part in the fraud, was jailed for three years, and fined £2.25m. Sentencing him, Lord Justice Murray told Belfast Crown Court that if John DeLorean could have been brought to Britain, and if Chapman had still been alive, they would each have received ten years in prison for the 'bare-faced, outrageous and massive' conspiracy.

"The sad thing about the whole DeLorean business was the fact that Chapman made a complete sham of a car into a working vehicle in about two years," say former Lotus colleague Roger Putnam. "He was never recognised for this. Everyone just remembered the fact that he and DeLorean were in league to defraud."

appendix III
A Beginner's Guide to Lotus Racing Cars

For Colin Chapman, Lotus road cars always came second to the racers. Innovative though the road cars were, Lotus racers were pure engineering statements, limited only by their budgets, the technology of the time and the latest regulations (which Chapman often played a role in drawing up). And they were enormously successful.

As Lotus Engineering took its first steps, road cars and racers were the same thing, but with the formation in 1954 of Team Lotus and the arrival of the aerodynamic MkVIII, notice was given of serious intent. Nonetheless, the late '50s saw both Le Mans racers and road racers sharing the workshops at Hornsey. Although primarily a club racer, the highly successful Lotus Eleven was available with just enough equipment to qualify as a road car (a soft-top and a windscreen wiper).

This period saw an important crossover from front-engined two-seaters to the pure-bred Formula cars, starting with the single-seat Twelve – technically advanced but not regarded as an auspicious start. Racing lessons were quickly learned: for 1958 there followed the more successful 16 (called the 'baby-Vanwall' because of its good looks), which was the last front-engined grand prix Lotus.

The rear-engined 18, introduced for 1960, was a versatile racer designed to compete in several classes: Formula 1, F2 and Formula Junior with engine sizes of up to 2.5 litres. Meanwhile, the sports-racing cars also adopted mid-mounted engines, starting with the 19 of 1960. The Elan 26R and the Lotus 47 were the last competition-built cars

with any resemblance to a Lotus road car until the racing Esprits of the 1990s.

Race-car development was undertaken by burgeoning offshoots run alongside manufacture of the road cars, often with a handful of staff. In 1964 Team Lotus Ltd split into divisions for Formula 1, Formula 2 and saloon car racing (with Cortinas). Lotus Components and its successors made customer racing cars into the 1970s. Until wholesale sponsorship arrived, racing was funded by prize money and increasing sales of cars like the Elan. To remain competitive there had to be a new car for every season and the list can seem bewildering: the decade started with the Lotus Type 18 and ended with the 61 (with a few road car type numbers in between).

The 1960s saw a period of Lotus domination in international motor racing. In 1963 the revolutionary 25, the first racing car with a full monocoque chassis in place of the trusted spaceframe, took Jim Clark to the first of his two World

Small but significant, the rapidly-designed 1960 Lotus Type 18 marked a decisive move to rear-engined racers. It was sold in various versions to compete in different formulae.

Championships and also won the Constructors' title for Lotus. That same year the Lotus 29, the first car to result from the tie-up with Ford of America, had a profound effect on the design of cars raced at the Indianapolis 500. Driving the 29's successor, the 38, Clark was victorious at 'The Brickyard' in 1965 – and that year he was also World Champion again. Into 1967, another Formula 1 milestone was the Type 49, powered by the Cosworth-Ford DFV V8 engine, the grand prix unit of choice for years to come.

By the late 1960s the massive costs of running Team Lotus could not be bankrolled by road-car sales alone. Lotus had received some support from Esso but the fuel company withdrew at the end of the 1967 season. Rules were changed to allow advertising on European race cars and for 1968 the green and yellow of Team Lotus cars

The sleek lines of the 1962 Type 25 concealed a revolution in racing-car design. In place of a tubular chassis frame, it was essentially built round its fuel tanks. The idea had been tried before, but Chapman became famous for creating the first racing monocoque – and his driver Jim Clark was unbeatable in the 25.

was replaced by the red, gold and white of Gold Leaf cigarettes.

Developments in aerodynamics were continual and often the subject of controversy; Graham Hill walked away from a crash caused by a collapsed rear wing on his Lotus 49 at the 1969 Spanish Grand Prix. A temporary ban on wings shaped the thinking of the subsequent Lotus 72, a car that was to be the F1 blueprint for the 1970s. It was the first full development of the wedge shape started by the 56, with a magnesium alloy monocoque, a new design of rear wing, inboard front brakes, torsion bar suspension and mid-mounted radiators. After a slow start, the 72 won frequently and Jochen Rindt became the 1970 World Champion, although he was awarded the title posthumously following his tragic death at Monza.

The 72 was the basis of John Player Team Lotus, formed for 1972. This was commercial sponsorship on a grand scale, with support vehicles and team clothing in the black and gold style of the new John Player Special cigarette pack (the Europa and Esprit also appeared as JPS editions). Subsequent sponsors included Essex Petroleum and Camel cigarettes. Lotus continued to be successful in F1 during the 1970s, with Constructors' Cups in 1970, '72, '73 and '78, and Drivers' titles for Emerson Fittipaldi in '72 and Mario Andretti in '78.

Chapman's genius for innovation continued to thrive, although not always with good results. With the

Type 76, Chapman achieved his wish to rid racing drivers of the need to use a clutch pedal so they could use their feet for only the throttle and brake. An electro-hydraulic mechanism allowed the clutch of the 76 to be moved by a switch on the gear lever; it proved unreliable but the thinking pre-dated steering-wheel gear buttons by decades. The Type 77 was an attempt to produce an F1 car with suspension that could be easily adjusted to the demands of each race circuit, but it was only occasionally successful.

The car that brought Lotus back to real glory was the 78, which

introduced 'ground effect', a revolutionary means of generating downforce from airflow under the car. The 79 soon followed the 78 to become one of the most dominant Lotus designs ever, and during the 1978 season Lotus team-mates Andretti and Ronnie Peterson beat all rivals to finish 1–2 in the World Championship. Ground effect increased cornering speeds

Seen here in the Gold Leaf team colours, the 72 was the blueprint for 1970s F1 cars; it would soon change to the famous John Player Special livery.

The first to use wide side pods to gain 'ground effect', the Type 78 started a revolution in motor racing but ran into controversy in the 1980s.

dramatically and transformed F1, but, in what were to be Chapman's final years, it caused bitter political wrangling between teams and regulators and eventually ground-effect cars were banned.

One more innovation from Chapman's fertile mind was the 'twin-chassis' Type 88 of 1981. This immediately created a storm with rivals claiming that its unique design infringed the regulations, and they threatened to withdraw from races if the new Lotus ran. Chapman took his case to court, issuing a bitter press release warning that Formula 1 could end up 'a quagmire of plagiarism, chicanery and petty rule interpretation.' All this stress was set against the continuing financial troubles of Lotus Cars – and Chapman's sudden death was soon to follow, in December 1982.

Post-Chapman, the Type 92 was the first car to run with prototype active suspension (using hydraulic jacks in place of springs), and gained a victory in the hands of Nigel Mansell at the 1983 Brazilian Grand Prix (although due to weight penalties it soon reverted to conventional suspension). Mansell was replaced by the legendary Ayrton Senna and the long-serving Cosworth DFV V8 gave way to turbocharged Renault then Honda power. In 1987 Senna won at Monaco and Detroit in the Type 99T, fitted with further developed active suspension.

Unlike the passenger car division, Team Lotus remained family-owned but the 1990s saw a continued struggle for sponsorship and good results. Although the Lotus GT racing Esprit programme marked a successful return to sports car racing, Team Lotus was disbanded at the end of 1994. However, the grand prix heritage is not forgotten today, with Clive Chapman running Classic Team Lotus.

bibliography

Jensen (Foulis, 1989), Keith Anderson

Lotus Elan and Europa: A Collector's Guide (Motor Racing Publications, 1992), John Bolster

Complete Catalogue of Ford Cars in Britain (Bay View Books, 1991), David Burgess-Wise

Elise, Rebirth of the True Lotus (Haynes, 2003), Alastair Clements

Colin Chapman: The Man and his Cars, the authorised biography (Haynes, 2001), Gerard 'Jabby' Crombac

Dream Maker: The Rise and Fall of John Z. DeLorean (Crain Automotive, 1983), Ivan Fallon and James Srodes

Lotus: The Elite, Elan, Europa (Oxford Illustrated Press, reprinted 1987), Chris Harvey

Colin Chapman – Lotus Engineering (Osprey, 1993), Hugh Haskell

Lotus Elan (Osprey, 1992), Mark Hughes

Colin Chapman: Wayward Genius (Breedon Books, 2002), Mike Lawrence

The story of Lotus 1961 – 1971: The Growth of a Legend (Motor Racing Publications, 1972), Doug Nye

Legend of the Lotus Seven (Newport Press, 1981), Dennis E. Ortenburger

Lotus Elite: racing car for the road (Coterie Press, 2002), Dennis E. Ortenburger

The Lotus Eleven (Patrick Stephens Ltd, 1988), Dennis E. Ortenburger

Lotus: the sports racing cars (Patrick Stephens Ltd, 1987), Anthony Pritchard

Colin Chapman's Lotus, the early years, the Elite and the origins of the Elan (Haynes, 1989), Robin Read

The Magnificent 7 (Haynes, 2002), Chris Rees

Lotus since the '70s Volumes 1 & 2: A Collector's Guide (Motor Racing Publications, 1993), Graham Robson

The Sporting Fords Volume 1: A Collector's Guide (Motor Racing Publications, 1982), Graham Robson

Lotus: the early years (Coterie Press, 2004), Peter Ross

The Story of Lotus – 1947-1960: Birth of a Legend (Motor Racing Publications, 1970), Ian H Smith

Ford Capri – 'The Car You Always Promised Yourself' (Crowood, 1995), Mike Taylor

Lotus Racing Cars: Club Racers to World Champions, 1948-1968 (Sutton, 2000), John Tipler

Lotus Elan (Osprey, 1984), Ian Ward

Ford Cortina Mk1 (Osprey, 1984), Jonathan Wood

index